On Screen Rival

D1424609

Also by Jane Stokes:

The Media in Britain (co-edited with Anna Reading) Macmillan, 1999.

On Screen Rivals

Cinema and Television in the United States and Britain

Jane Stokes

First published 1999 by
MACMILLAN PRESS LTD
Houndmills, Basingstoke, Hampshire RG21 6XS
and London
Companies and representatives
throughout the world

ISBN 0–333–66515–5 hardcover
ISBN 0–333–66516–3 paperback

A catalogue record for this book is available
from the British Library.

This book is printed on paper suitable for recycling and made from fully managed and sustained forest sources.

10 9 8 7 6 5 4 3 2 1
08 07 06 05 04 03 02 01 00 99

Editing and origination by
Aardvark Editorial, Mendham, Suffolk

Typeset by T & A Typesetting Services, Rochdale

Printed in Hong Kong

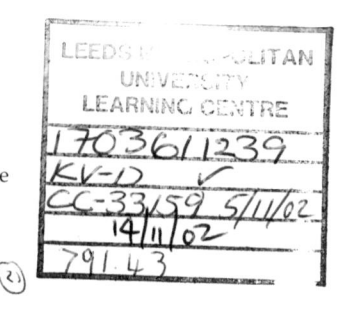

For
George and Ann Stokes
and
Russell Schechter

CONTENTS

LIST OF TABLES

List of Figures

PREFACE

On Screen Rivals offers a new approach to the study of technology, providing an *historical culturalist* analysis of responses to television by its rival, the cinema. This book proposes that some part of the meaning of a cultural technology can be understood and studied through analysis of its construction in related technologies. It takes films as its object of analysis but is about the idea of television contained within the films. *On Screen Rivals* examines how the relationship between two cultural technologies affects the kinds of cultural products each generates. To write about film *and* television in one study challenges the prevailing trend towards increased academic specialism by which the two media are typically written about in different journals and come under the rubric of separate methodological approaches. In *On Screen Rivals* I maintain that the interconnectedness of culture should be reflected in more interdisciplinary approaches to media and culture. I hope this unorthodox approach to television studies will ripple the ponds that have been still for too long and promote some new ways of thinking about the meaning of the media and cultural technologies.

The research for this book was conducted using a wide range of methods, including semiotics, narrative analysis and historical research. This promiscuity of approach is correct, I think, when attempting to break new ground. For, in making the subject of films my focus, rather than the more accepted categories such as genre, director or period, I am challenging some prevailing notions about what constitutes appropriate academic writing about film. One finds books about the content of films more typically in the 'popular' film section than in the 'academic'. *On Screen Rivals* aims to show that the subject of a film is as valuable an area of study as any other. This may seem iconoclastic but in order to understand the meanings of culture it is essential to study the content of its cultural artifacts.

A note on spelling: I have used American spelling throughout for the sake of consistency except in the case of quotations where English spelling is used in the original. Some British readers may be offended by mention of their *favorite programs* in such a manner, for which I *apologize*. I am aware of writing *between* two dialects of English which is at once stimulating and sobering. It encourages one to make new connections, but also gives one pause about the inevitability of transcultural misunderstanding. I have tried to avoid exclusively American or British expressions, and also made every effort not to allow such concerns to produce stilted prose. Often this book is as much concerned with the relationship between the British and American cultures as it is about the relationship between film and television. I have lived and worked in both countries and have learned that the differences can generate some exciting insights: I hope the implicit and explicit comparative cultural history in this book inspires people to look more closely at the relationship between the two cultures that have made me.

Author's Acknowledgements

I would have liked to have included many more illustrations in the book, but, alas, film distributors guard their property rights carefully and permissions to use images have proved very difficult to obtain. All the more reason, then, to thank the kind folks at Canal+Image UK Limited, Carlton International Media Limited and the Ronald Grant Archive for their generous permission to reproduce images for this book. A special thank you to the staff of The Ronald Grant Archive for their courteous and professional help and kind interest in this project. Thanks also to the film archives of the University of Southern California, the University of California at Los Angeles and the British Film Institute for allowing me to view films on their premises and to the BBC's Written Archives Centre. Most of the research for this book was conducted in Britain, where scholars are seriously hindered by the problem of *access to films*. There are too few viewing copies around and there were many films that I simply could not get to see and consequently could not analyze for this study (despite prints existing in some cases). However, thanks to improvements in information science, I have been helped by the relative ease of *access to information* about films provided by databases such as the British Film Institute's Film Index International and SIFT. I would like to thank the staff of the British Film Institute Library for their friendly and knowledgeable support during the writing of this book. I hope that the BFI will soon make more of their films and other materials more freely available to the scholar.

I would not have been able to complete this book without the generous support of South Bank University and my Dean, Jeffrey Weeks: Thanks, Boss. Other people at South Bank who have helped me carry off the difficult balancing act of teaching, administration and research that academics have to perform deserve acknowledgment. To my colleagues Rolando Gaete, Pat Ladly, Stina Lyon, Heidi Mirza, Anna Reading and Hillegonda Reitveld – many thanks for your support and encouragement during the gestation of this book. When I began this project, I was working at the University of Kent and many colleagues and students there were generous with their support. I would like to thank in particular Michael Grant, Steve Neale, Murray Smith and Miri Song for their friendship.

I am fortunate to have wonderfully indulgent friends and family. For always being on my side special thanks to Ruth and Fred Walton, and Keith Baxter. My parents, Ann and George Stokes, sister Susan Gilbert, and brothers Terence, Lawrence and George all helped make me this way – and that's the way I like it – Thank You, One and All. Finally, and most importantly, thanks to my partner, Russell, to whom I solemnly swear I will never make you watch another 'tv movie' again.

ACKNOWLEDGEMENTS

The author and publisher wish to thank the following for permission to use copyright material:

Canal+Image UK Limited for Figures 5.1 and 6.1
Carlton International Media Limited for Figures 5.2 and 6.2
The Ronald Grant Archive for Figures 5.3, 6.3, 7.1, 8.1, 8.2, 8.3, 9.1 and 9.2.

Every effort has been made to trace all the copyright holders but if any have been inadvertently overlooked the publishers will be pleased to make the necessary arrangements at the first opportunity.

INTRODUCTION:
ON SCREEN RIVALS AND THE
MEANING OF TELEVISION

This is a book about television. It is also about representation. Unlike many previous books on these subjects, however, *On Screen Rivals* is not about how television represents (or misrepresents) the world, but looks instead at how television itself is represented. The primary goal of this book is to begin to answer the question: *'what does television mean?'* If we are to understand the meaning of television we must look at images of, and ideas about, television and study how these enter the popular imagination.

The word 'television' refers to many different aspects of a complex cultural technology: it is an entertainment medium; a scientific phenomenon; a multifaceted industry. Television is a feature of modern *public* life which has a place in nearly every *private* home. 'Television' carries many different meanings, each resonant with concomitantly complex connotations. Using the dictionary we learn that the word 'television' has its roots in the Greek word 'tele' ('afar' or 'far off') and the Latin 'vision' ('sight' or 'seeing') and literally means 'far-seeing'. But where do we go to find out why television is also sometimes called 'the idiot box'? To which root can we trace the origin of the belief that children should not watch too much television? How can we find out why some commentators express alarm at the fact that television is now most people's source of news? It is the origins of some of these underlying, connotative, meanings of television which this book seeks to unearth.

1

One of the most powerful contributors to the idea of television is its erstwhile rival and latter-day ally, the cinema. *On
Screen Rivals* examines how the meaning of television has been
constructed by the film industry. The cinema industry makes
manifest its attitudes towards television in its films. Television
has been a topic addressed by many film-makers and there is
a large, fairly consistent and currently growing, body of movies
on the subject, from *Murder by Television* (Clifford Sanforth,
1935) to *Network* (Sidney Lumet, 1976) with more recent work
including *Quiz Show* (Robert Redford, 1994), *Up Close and
Personal* (Jon Avnet, 1996) and *The Truman Show* (Peter Weir,
1998). These texts provide the object of analysis for *On Screen
Rivals'* study of the relationship between television and film in
general and of cinema's construction of television in particular.
The cinema is a partial contributor to our idea of television:
partial in the sense of 'incomplete' – there are many other
factors that contribute to the concept of television; partial also
in the sense of 'prejudicial' – the cinema industry has an interest
in portraying television in a particular way. A complete and
unbiased appraisal of what television means could never be
achieved: our understanding of television is necessarily subjec-
tive and changing. This is the case with all cultural technologies, not least film and television, because they are centrally
concerned with creating meaning. Strictly speaking, of course,
all technologies create meaning: some excellent studies on the
social role of artifacts as different from one another as the pencil
(Petroski, 1990) and the bicycle (Pinch and Bijker, 1987) illus-
trate this point. But there is a small subset of technologies that
generate artifacts that have value only because they generate
meanings; these become conduits of cultural ideas. All of the
mass media can be accommodated into this category (cinema,
broadcasting, the press and so on); each produces artifacts
(films, television programs, newspapers) that are marketed for
the meanings they create. Media that are less obviously 'mass',
such as music, theater, painting or photography, also produce
commodities, artifacts and events that contribute to the
economy of meaning in our society. All of these media,
including television and the cinema, we will call *cultural technologies* defined as:

Those technologies that produce artifacts that have economic value by virtue of the *meanings* they generate.

The meanings might be contained in images or stories, they could be poetic or prosaic, material or ephemeral in form. The key feature of a cultural technology is that the end product comprises artifacts or events whose market prices are a function of their symbolic value rather than the sum of the labor, commodities and capital costs which normally comprise the economic value of ordinary goods and services. This criterion challenges divisions of 'high' and 'low' and enables the comparison of poetry, situation comedy, installation art and Hollywood cinema. The significance of understanding these cultural technologies as in some respects similar, and therefore also comparable, is that we can thereby better appreciate the cultural world as intertwined and mutually defining.

On Screen Rivals begins from the premise that each cultural technology defines itself through its relationship with other cultural technologies. Film and television are two cultural technologies that are closely related and that are fecund sources of information about one another. This is not the same as being *reflexive* which would imply that the texts refer to the medium in which they are created. A reflexive film is one that is about its own medium of production. Some films foreground their technology for radical effects, as Brecht (1964) prescribed, in for example, *Man with a Movie Camera* (Dziga Vertov, 1929), or for the more popular pleasures identified by Feuer (1982) in films such as *Singin' in the Rain* (Gene Kelly and Stanley Donen, 1952) or in Woody Allen's *Purple Rose of Cairo* (1984). There is a pleasure in watching *films about films* and a thrill in seeing the means of production of a medium revealed. It is the same pleasure that abstract paintings or modernist novels can give us. Whenever attention is drawn to the processes of production, the viewer is invited to admire his or her own ability, first to recognize the conventions, and second to apprehend that they are being subverted. Reflexive texts flatter the readers, who can recognize themselves as among the cognoscenti able to understand the form. But reflexive films are relatively rare and the convention in most cinematic genres is to elide the production process.

Mainstream British and American cinema does not draw attention to its processes of production.

Although they are not often self-reflexive, films frequently comment on other media. This mutually defining characteristic is a feature of all cultural technologies. For the multiple meanings of cultural technologies are formed in what Bourdieu (1984) calls a *field*, something like an electrical field, where the products of each cultural technology exercise forces of attraction and repulsion to one another. The strength and direction of these forces vary paradigmatically (according to how close the technologies are to one another at a given time) and syntagmatically (depending on their historical trajectory *vis-à-vis* one another). Television and film comprise two of the many technologies in this complex constellation of cultural technologies struggling to define one another. At times their attraction to one another has been strong; at other times the pull towards different cultural technologies has been more powerful; and throughout their history external agencies have intervened to push them together or pull them apart.

On Screen Rivals explores the shifting relationship between two of the most popular cultural technologies of the century focusing especially on how television has been culturally constructed by the cinema. This book proposes a new object of analysis in the study of technology: the process by which one cultural technology contributes to the construction of another. I call this process *technogenesis*, and my objective in the following is to elaborate on this phenomenon through an extended case study.

In his essay, 'The Cultural Biography of Things', Igor Kopytoff (1986) maintains that commodities cannot be conceived of as exclusively economic phenomena. Kopytoff states:

> From a cultural perspective, the production of commodities is also a cultural and cognitive process: commodities must be not only produced materially as things, but also culturally marked as being a certain kind of thing (Kopytoff, 1986: 64).

Television is a commodity that is heavily marked as 'a certain kind of thing', but the exact nature of television has been under constant flux for most of its history. Part I of *On Screen Rivals* chronicles the processes by which television has come to be characterized in our culture. Kopytoff compares the transformations of a commodity to those of the human life cycle, maintaining that commodities have 'cultural biographies'. Chapters 1 and 2 of *On Screen Rivals* present a cultural biography of television. All good biographies focus on key relationships of their subject grounded in a broader history: here I concentrate on the formative relationship between cinema and television in Britain and America. Chapter 1 examines the early history of television and its relationship to film until the end of World War II; Chapter 2 brings the history up to date, looking at the rises and falls in the fortunes of television relative to film in the latter half of the twentieth century.

The historical groundwork of Part I sets the scene for 'The Technogenesis of Television: Cinema's On Screen Representation of its Rival'. Part II analyzes the representation of television in British and American films in some detail, concentrating each chapter on one major genre and situating the changing representation of television within its historical framework. For reasons of access, I have restricted my analysis to films made in Britain or the United States. The appendix provides an Annotated Filmography of relevant films in alphabetic order: included here are American and British theatrically released films that have television as their central theme or as a strong setting. The filmography is not intended to include all the films that have been made about television in the relevant countries, but provides a good survey of the hundred or so films that have informed this study.

The earliest films to be included in this book were made at the very beginning of television, in the 1920s. Between-the-wars films about television fall into two broad categories: they either show television as a new, potentially dangerous technology (as in *Murder By Television*) or as an extension of the music hall or variety tradition (for example in *Elstree Calling*, (Adrian Brunel, 1930)). The first of our chapters in Part II, Chapter 3, focuses on musicals that have used television as a narrative device to justify on-screen singing and dancing. Films such as the W.C. Fields' vehicle of 1933, *International House* (A. Edward Sutherland), which brings an array of stars to the screen as performers on television or as witnesses to the invention of television.

Comparing British and American musicals that address television in the 1930s, *Elstree Calling*, *Band Waggon* and *International House* we find the identity of television is differently constructed in the cinemas of each country. The Hollywood musical has most to gain from collaborating with television and when Bob Crosby announces 'We're about to have a ball in your hall!' in *Two Tickets to Broadway* (James V. Kern, 1951), he expresses the positive hope of many entertainers that television will provide a vibrant new outlet for their work. The mutually beneficial relationship many hoped for did not materialize and by the mid-1950s the dream had soured. We look at *It's Always Fair Weather* as a pivotal film in the representation of television in the musical. The musical exploited television as a narrative device to extend the possibilities of the genre, but by the 1960s the genre could not survive the restructuring of the music industry and all but expired. Chapter 3 examines how the changing relationships among film, television and musical entertainment contributed to the collapse of the musical film.

The relationship between the nascent television industry and the well-established Hollywood majors was equivocal in the inter-war years. Following the war, however, the American cinema industry was systematically refused ownership and control of the television industry. Most Hollywood studios were relegated to the role of provider of product only, as we will see in Chapter 2. In Chapter 4, *On Screen Rivals* examines films that were part of the response of the Hollywood film industry to their exclusion from television. It is from this period that we find some of the most virulently anti-television tracts. Anti-television films from the 1950s discussed here include *The Glass Web* (Jack Arnold, 1953) and Elia Kazan's *A Face in the Crowd* (1957). The latter was made, according to the director: 'To warn the public: look out for television' (Ciment, 1974: 115). One characteristic of television that made film-makers most wary was the influence of women, both as audience and as television workers. Many of the Hollywood films of the 1950s equate television with femininity and damn it as a consequence. Here we look at how the challenge of television was constructed as a specifically feminine danger.

When we look at British films made during the same approximate period, as we do in Chapter 5, we find a completely different construction of television. British films of the 1950s and early 1960s vary enormously from their American counterparts in their representation of television. These differences are no doubt a function of the fact that television and film both occupy unique positions as cultural technologies in Britain and America. One crucial difference results from the varying role of advertising in the two countries. The fact that commercial television arrived so late in Britain, after public service television was established as the norm, created a unique identity for advertising-supported television in Britain. Many films made during this period treat television and the BBC as coterminous, so powerful was the influence of the Corporation on broadcasting. Films such as *The Body Said No* and *Simon and Laura* depict the BBC as the only television provider. After 1955, however, Independent Television (ITV) brought new program genres and sought to cater to specifically working-class audiences for the first time. Advertisements on television were markers of commercialism, of course, but commercialism itself signaled popularity, and advertisements were interpreted as symbols of television's social inclusiveness. British films of the 1950s and early 1960s display a delight in advertising, in refreshing contrast to the baneful ill-boding of American film portrayals of commercialization. Films like *Make Mine a Million* (Lance Comfort, 1959) and *Dentist on the Job* (C.M. Pennington-Richards, 1961) link popular entertainers (Arthur Askey and Bob Monkhouse respectively) to television advertising, implying that commercial television is fun.

In the 1960s, television consolidated its hold as the dominant system of image-making in Britain and the United States at the same time as the Hollywood studio system declined. In the cultural revolution which these changes betokened, a key phenomenon, Pop, emerged. In Chapter 6, representations of television are explored in relation to the nascent pop music industry. Movies such as the British *Expresso Bongo* (Val Guest, 1959) and *A Hard Day's Night* (Richard Lester, 1964), and the American *Bye Bye Birdie* (George Sidney, 1963) are discussed for their construction of television as part of the mobilization of a new youth culture. The demise of the musical is linked to the ascendance of pop music. The new music was better suited to television than cinema – in this chapter we examine how pop

movies became cynical, as the relationships among youth, television, music and movies was reconfigured in the 1960s.

The most serious films about television attack the medium for
its misrepresentation of the real world, especially through the
manipulation of news. When Howard Beale declares on national
television in *Network*: 'I'm as mad as hell and I'm not going to
take it any more!' his words resonate with his audience. Beale
becomes 'an angry prophet denouncing the hypocrisies of our
time'. *Network* is a self-conscious, self-important work, which
appears to set out to unravel the convoluted power struggles
that torture the television industry and that push the workers
over the brink into insanity. Chapter 7 explores how television
news workers have been represented in this and other more
recent films. It shows that news workers are often shown in a
more benign light.

Some of the earliest depictions of television can be found in
fantasy films such as *High Treason* (Maurice Elvey, 1929). The
horror and science fiction genres have frequently exploited television as a vehicle for exploring the unknown and in Chapter
8 we chart how the function of television has changed in the
fantastic film. Included in this discussion is a cluster of films
from the 1980s, including *Videodrome* (David Cronenberg, 1983),
Poltergeist (Tobe Hooper, 1982) and *The Running Man* (Paul
Michael Glaser, 1987). Uncertainty about the future of television
and cinema and anxiety about nascent media technologies are
responsible for many of these frightening images of television.
However, we also observe that the representations of television
as frightening are frequently underpinned by a growing sense
of reflexivity in the horror and science fiction genres. The representation of television in these films has become increasingly
camp as the cinema has acquired an increasingly sophisticated
and knowing audience.

Television has not always been taken seriously, and even
when the threat it posed to the cinema seemed most dire, the
Hollywood film industry was capable of turning out a comedy
to condemn the new medium with callous mockery. Chapter 9
discusses the construction of television in comedy films such as
The Thrill of it All (Norman Jewison, 1963), *The Groove Tube* (Ken
Shapiro, 1974) and *Kentucky Fried Movie* (John Landis, 1977). The
comedy film is a good barometer of the changing identity of

television from the perspective of the cinema industry. In this chapter we consider whether the contemporary comedy film expresses the cinema industry's reconciliation with television. We can identify a sophisticated and urbane image of television workers in contemporary Hollywood comedies such as *Groundhog Day* (Harold Ramis, 1993) and *Mrs Doubtfire* (Chris Columbus, 1993). Other comedies, such as *The Cable Guy*, show a residual anxiety about television as a deleterious mass medium.

In summing up the themes of the book, Chapter 10 cuts across genre classifications to examine a range of films. The image of television as menacing abides. Oliver Stone's pretentious *Natural Born Killers* takes potshots at the whole panoply of visual media. Perhaps the most virulently anti-television film of recent times is not a serious piece, but a popular film, starring Jim Carrey as the darkly antipathetic eponymous anti-hero in *The Cable Guy* (Ben Stiller, 1996). Most contemporary depictions of television are fairly benign, though, showing television as part of the rhythm of everyday life and as not particularly exceptional. In Robert Altman's *Short Cuts* (1993) television provides a structuring icon linking the various Los Angeles locations of the characters. *William Shakespeare's Romeo & Juliet* (Baz Luhrmann, 1996) replaces the play's chorus with a television news crew as it updates the iconography of the Shakespearean stage for a modern sensibility. The image of television affords a film contemporaneity and the familiar conventions of broadcasting can provide a narrative cohesion to current films. The close relationship between film and television is evident in the number of films made that use television programs as their subjects. This trend became more common recently, as old television properties are acquired by film studios through buy-outs and conglomerations. *The Flintstones* (Brian Levant, 1994) and *The Brady Bunch Movie* (Betty Thomas, 1995) are examples of these nostalgic retro-films.

Finally, I offer some generalizations about the construction of television in films from Britain and America. Reflecting on the task undertaken in *On Screen Rivals*, in Chapter 10 I ask whether unraveling the processes of technogenesis is a valuable way to study the media. I consider how the specific example of television's construction in film contributes to our broader understanding of how technologies construct one another.

The category 'films about television' cuts across many genres: I will discuss horror, comedy, high drama and low camp in this book. The films studied are worth exploring as a body of texts because of the way they collectively construct television and because they show shifts in the *idea of television*. *On Screen Rivals* makes connections between fields of study usually considered discrete. Film and television; Britain and the United States; history and representation: in the rationalization of academe these are, unfortunately, more commonly studied separately than in relation to one another. *On Screen Rivals* makes the subject of films its object of study linking cinema studies to representation. This book proposes that the cultural construction of technology should be studied through the analysis of technogenetic texts. Each cultural technology is entwined in a system of mutual interpretation and definition which the analyst can unpack. *On Screen Rivals* presents a new method of thinking about the social and cultural construction of technology, one that acknowledges and relishes in the interrelated and interpenetrative discourses of culture.

Part I

A Cultural Biography of Television in Britain and the United States

INTRODUCTION

It is a commonplace in historical accounts of the media to refer to the 'advent' of a new technology, and television seems especially prone to being the subject of this metaphor. 'Advent' is, of course, a Christian term, referring to the birth of Jesus Christ and the period in the Christian calendar when that event is celebrated. To talk about the 'advent of television' is to imply that the technology arrived, like the baby Jesus, with little human intervention and predestined to a life of great significance. Whether one believes the story of Christ is a matter of faith, but television's arrival can only be explained in rational terms: television was developed piecemeal by various scientists and inventors, in a number of different countries. The history of television's arrival, and of its increasing importance in the gamut of media, is a tale of material forces. There is nothing mystical about television's invention, introduction and adoption: its trajectory has been shaped by multiple economic, social and scientific determinants.

Television's Antecedent Technologies

The main industrial precursors of television are the film and radio industries, both of which developed as popular entertainment media in the early part of the twentieth century. The Lumière Brothers patented their Cinématographe in 1895 and were the first to exhibit films to a paying audience in December of that year. Inventors in Germany, England and the US rapidly followed suit and before long the cinema had become an entertainment phenomenon across Europe and the United States of

America (Sklar, 1993). Synchronous sound was not viable until the late 1920s, although films were rarely shown without accompaniment of some kind (Robinson, 1996). One advantage of silent film was that, being unfettered by constraints of language, the medium developed a visual vocabulary and grammar that could be understood by a global community of spectators regardless of ethnicity, education or linguistic competence (Salt, 1992; Bordwell and Thompson, 1997). An international film business burgeoned, exploiting this largely extra-verbal medium. In countries such as France and Britain, which retained the vestiges of expansive empires, film distributors were able to exploit an advanced international transport infrastructure and develop global markets for their product. Kristin Thompson (1985) describes how World War I decimated established trading patterns and created a shift in the hub of world commerce from London to New York. Thompson shows how, as a consequence of this upheaval, the international film industry was restructured and US producers acquired world dominance. American film has retained its hegemony in the West since the end of World War I and continues to exert a powerful influence on the film cultures of the rest of the world. During the inter-war period, the production of films shifted from the East coast to California, and Hollywood has since remained the epicenter of the western cinema industry.

Throughout its history, the British cinema, like that of most European countries, has been secondary to the American even on its own turf. The number of films produced in Britain has always been small compared with American output.

Moreover, many films produced in Britain have been financed by American companies taking advantage of the relatively low cost of UK facilities and workers. Britain has also provided an important secondary market for American films: as early as 1925, US films captured 95% of the British market while one-third of American overseas revenue from film was earned in the UK (Guback, 1976). For most of its existence, then, film has been an international medium with Hollywood as home to the most powerful producers. The British cinema, like that of comparable European countries, has always been small relative to its American counterpart. The cinema originated in the peep show and the fairground, but by the 1920s it was an established industry with its own patterns of production, distribution and exhibition. It provided a ready audience for audiovisual entertainment on which television was subsequently to build.

The other major precursor to television, radio, developed out of telegraphy as a means of point-to-point communication. Its origin as a communication tool, rather than an entertainment medium, differentiates it from cinema. In Britain and the US, radio was given a technological impetus during World War I and was marketed commercially for the first time in the inter-war period. The first regularly scheduled programs were made in the 1920s, when radio became something of a popular craze (Briggs, 1961; Barnouw, 1966). At first, radio was seen as a rival to the cinema by industry observers, many of whom feared that the popularity of radio might keep audiences at home. In an early commentary, Harold B. Franklin explains why this did not happen:

> As the novelty of wireless wore off and it became part of everyday life, it helped the motion picture by cultivating a taste for entertainment in many who had not been entertainment minded before (Franklin, 1929: 342).

Consequently, both radio and cinema became complementary media both relying on a public that was 'entertainment minded'. The enormous popularity of radio established it as a necessity in every household. Early broadcasting helped develop a domestic audience for entertainment and prepared the ground in which television would later thrive.

Television has characteristics in common with the cinema and radio: it is an audiovisual medium, like film; and, like radio, it is a broadcast medium. Television was marketed to its first audiences as a combination of two media already very familiar and was advertised variously as 'radio with pictures', or as 'a theater of the home'. The new technology was produced and sold within a sophisticated and expanding industrial entertainments complex. The scope of *On Screen Rivals* prohibits a comprehensive account of all the relationships, rivalries and alliances that have contributed to the development of television. There are many excellent accounts of this history including Erik Barnouw's study of American broadcasting (Barnouw, 1966,

1968, 1970, 1982) and Asa Briggs' comprehensive account of the British scene (Briggs, 1961, 1965, 1970, 1979, 1995). In this section of *On Screen Rivals*, comprising Chapters 1 and 2, we will focus on the relationship between the film and television industries in Britain and America. These relationships are obviously not equal. It is quite evident that the American economy is considerably larger and more dynamic than the British, while the American entertainment and media industries are massive in comparison with most of their British counterparts. This disequilibrium between the two national systems does not disqualify us from studying their relationship, however, as such inequities are mirrored all around the world. The American film and television industries swamp those of most European countries, as the Indian 'Bollywood' dominates the film industry of smaller Asian countries.

The following historical survey will help us understand how the cultural identities of both 'television' and 'cinema' have been formed in relation to one another. The discussion in Chapters 1 and 2 will provide us with what Kopytoff (1986) refers to as a *cultural biography,* and provides a grounding for subsequent discussion of the images of television in British and American films.

1

THE AGE OF EXPERIMENT 1880–1945

The Birth of a Medium

The cultural biography of television, like all biographies, should address the question of its subject's provenance. Television had a truly multicultural origin, being developed in several different countries, at approximately the same time, in the 1880s (Abramson, 1987). Demonstrations of a range of technologies that would eventually lead to the development of modern television were made to the public during the 1920s, when television displays were made in Germany, Japan, America and Britain. Experimental television services operated in these, and other, countries during the 1930s. It was not until after World War II, however, that television began to develop an independent cultural identity. This chapter explores the formative years of television's biography, up to the end of World War II, when the idea of television was first being shaped. The following chapter analyzes how television matured into a major entertainment and information medium in the post-war period and brings the story up to date.

When the first, primitive television systems were demonstrated, in the 1920s, the radio and film industries were among those most involved. Radio manufacturers anticipated that sales of radio sets would soon reach saturation point; they regarded television as a new product from which they could profit with some minor retooling of their existing factories. Companies such as Marconi in Britain and RCA in the USA were responsible for funding much early television research. It was not only manufacturers, but also radio performers, producers and advertisers who saw television as a new outlet for their work. In the cinema industry, too, many were quick to identify the possible benefits of television. In Britain, Gaumont-British backed early television experiments while Paramount was one of the Hollywood studios most heavily investing in television during the 1920s and 30s. In addition to those from the broadcasting and cinema industries, other companies were also involved in television's early development, such as America Telephone and Telegraph (AT&T), General Electric and Westinghouse.

Radio Days

Radio was the communication technology that most clearly anticipated television, and provided the most direct economic model on which television would be based. Starting life as a means of one-to-one communication, there were some 1000 amateur ham radio operators in the US prior to World War I (Engelman, 1996). Wartime imperatives ensured that radio technology was made the purview of the state with little controversy on both sides of the Atlantic. All individuals were required to cease transmitting and radio came under the exclusive control of the military in both the US and the UK. The history of radio followed different paths in the two countries after World War I.

In Britain, broadcasting had been the remit of the State since the 1904 Wireless Telegraphy Act gave the Postmaster General responsibility for allocating frequencies. From the earliest days, broadcasting in Britain was mistrusted by the government. In 1920, Marconi's experimental station in Chelmsford was closed down, just as it was gaining popularity (Wood, 1992). When broadcasting was subsequently permitted to resume, in 1922, the Post Office received nearly 100 further applications to broadcast. Fearing a 'chaos of the airwaves' similar to that perceived to have occurred in the US, the Postmaster General reached an accommodation with the radio manufacturers: The British Broadcasting Company was formed by a cartel of electronics companies in 1922 to be the sole provider of programming. The responsibility for being Britain's only official broadcaster was passed on to the BBC when it was national-ized in 1926. Although theoretically separate from the govern-ment, funded by license fee, and operated under a Royal Charter, in practice the BBC's relationship to the state has always been problematic. Radio broadcasting remained the exclusive domain of the BBC in British law until October 1973, when the first 'Independent' stations – LBC and Capital Radio – both began broadcasting to London within a couple of weeks of each other. Unofficially, of course, there have been many illegal commercial stations operating from the waters around the British Isles, from the European mainland or, since the miniaturization of transmission equipment, from secret loca-tions within Britain. Among the most renowned are Radio Normandie, which began broadcasting to England in 1931, and Radio Luxembourg which first broadcast to the British main-land in 1933. So popular were these 'pirates' that an estimated four million listeners regularly tuned into Radio Luxembourg before World War II (Thomas, 1977). Roger Eckersley, while working for the BBC in Wales during the 1930s, found that on Sundays, when the BBC broadcast mainly religious programs, '70–80% of the population listened to dance music and light entertainment from Luxembourg' (Eckersley, 1946: 164). Despite the popularity of the pirates, public service broadcasting was early established as the state-sanctioned norm, and the BBC was given a monopoly in the form of a Royal Charter. The idea of the BBC as a public service provider was founded on the high moral principles of its first Director General, John Reith. After Reith resigned in 1938, the public service image was further developed and consolidated, especially during the wartime years when BBC radio acquired the identity of loyal public servant and morale booster to the nation (Scannell and Cardiff, 1982, 1991). By the end of World War II, the terms 'radio' and 'BBC' had become virtually coterminous in Britain.

In the United States, radio came to occupy a very different cultural location. The Radio Corporation of America (RCA) was formed as a state monopoly during World War I to consolidate all knowledge about radio and to ensure that the allies had the superior communication technology. After World War I, RCA was privatized and henceforth American entrepreneurialism was to shape the future of radio. In 1922, AT&T's WEAF station

became the first to sell air time and established the model of
commercial radio under which RCA, General Electric, AT&T
and Western Electric were to broadcast during the early 1920s.
Public service radio is not unknown in the US – schools,
colleges and church groups are among those who have broadcast alongside commercial enterprises (Engleman, 1996) – but it
has a considerably lower profile and reaches smaller audiences
than its commercial counterparts. American radio rapidly developed as a complex pattern of interrelated networks: it became
a highly commercial and extremely competitive system with
multiple stations, especially in the more lucrative big city
markets. Radio in the US has been identified with big business,
large networks and commercial sponsorship since the 1930s
(Barnouw, 1968).

Vision On: The Introduction of Television

In Britain, credit for the invention of television is usually given
to John Logie Baird, who claimed to be the first person to
publicly demonstrate 'practical' television in Britain at Selfridges
department store in London in April 1925. Baird's early system,
in keeping with similar ones being developed in the United
States at the time, was *mechanical*, with rotating scanners that
recorded light on a selenium cell. Ian Anderson describes the
scene the first time he visited Baird's laboratory:

> The whole of his equipment was a most Heath Robinson
> affair, tied together with bits of string, bits of wire, old bicycle
> lamps and so on (Moseley, 1952: 87).

In spite of his amateurism in the laboratory, Baird was an
active publicist of his own work, and was jealous of other people
working in the field. When HMV Gramophone Ltd demonstrated their television system at the Annual exhibition of the
Physical and Optical Society at the Imperial College of Science
in 1931, Baird was so furious that he threatened to sue
(Abramson, 1987). Baird's hagiographer and erstwhile partner,
Sydney Moseley, lauds him as a romantic hero; a genius who
was often misunderstood in his own time (Moseley, 1952). Other

commentators are less eager to give the Scot so much credit. The historian Asa Briggs calls Baird:

> An eccentric who lived in a world of his own rather than dreamed of a new world of television opening up for millions of viewers (Briggs, 1965: 547).

While Baird rushed to be the first to show television, his American counterparts, better businessmen one and all, delayed launching television to the public until they had a marketable system.

Researchers at AT&T's Bell Labs were advancing with television experiments during the 1920s, but they 'kept their work shrouded in mystery' (Abramson, 1987: 86–7). American experiments in television were largely conducted by professional scientists, funded by an expanding electronics and communications industry, with the aim of exploiting the commercial possibilities of the technology. As early as 1919, Vladimir K. Zworykin had been investigating the possibilities of television at Westinghouse's laboratories, in spite of some reticence, 'because the possibilities seemed so remote' (Barnouw, 1966: 66). At General Electric, Ernst F.W. Alexanderson transmitted daily test signals throughout 1928 and the station, W2XAD, transmitted the first American television drama production, *The Queen's Messenger*, on 11 September of that year. David Sarnoff, head of RCA, pronounced that television would become: 'as much a part of our life' as radio within five years (Barnouw, 1966: 231). 'Radio, which made the world a whispering gallery, will turn it into a world of mirrors through television', Sarnoff said (Bilby, 1986: 5).

By the end of 1928, 21 experimental television licenses had been issued and television stations were operating in all of the major American cities, including New York, Los Angeles, Boston and Chicago (Udelson, 1982). There was significantly more experimental and commercial exploitation of television in the United States than in the United Kingdom in these very early days. Early television experiments often included film broadcasts, for example, in January 1929 WCFL – a station run by the Chicago Federation of Labor – broadcast motion pictures, and in February of that year General Electric engineers broadcast

D. W. Griffiths' address from WGY in New York to Los Angeles
(Franklin, 1929).

The Institutional Control of Television

Television entered the public consciousness at a time of intense
cultural, economic and social change. The 1920s were a period
of great optimism when the idealism of the modernist dream
seemed to have largely survived the ravages of the Great War.
Television was greeted by adherents of the modernist project as
a wonderful scientific development, and is described as the
latest addition in a modernist rostra of advances in the extension of human knowledge and power, each more wonderful
than the last. In 1929, two American writers, H. Horton Sheldon
and Edgar Norman Grisewood, declared:

> Television is not like collecting postage stamps, an avocation
> which may appeal to a few or be in vogue for a few years
> and then subside. It is not like police dogs or short skirts
> which are for the moment fashionable. It is the realization of
> a desire that has existed in man from his earliest beginnings.
> The automobile, giving man the speed he has always desired,
> has stayed. The airplane, giving him the wings he has always
> sought, has stayed. Television, giving him the distant sight he
> has longed for ever since, in his ape-like form, he climbed to
> the topmost, swaying branches of the tallest tree to look afar
> is here to stay (Sheldon and Grisewood, 1929: 1).

In the UK experimental television broadcasts were only
possible using the BBC's transmitters and permission to use
them was not readily forthcoming. Baird Television Limited and
Marconi-EMI were locked in furious competition to develop
television and both companies maintained that they should have
exclusive access to the BBC facilities. BBC Director General John
Reith settled the argument with Solomonic justice when he
permitted experiments by both Baird Television Limited and
Marconi-EMI using the BBC transmitter at Alexandra Palace.
The London Television Service began broadcasting on 2
November 1936 with Baird and Marconi providing the program-

ming on alternate weeks (British Broadcasting Company, 1937). The dual service arrangement ended when it became evident that the Marconi-EMI system was superior, and Baird's outfit was obliged to leave the site. According to Abramson:

> The end of 1935 found Marconi-EMI with the most advanced television system in the world. By this time, they had passed up every other company including RCA (Abramson, 1987: 225).

By 1937, the London Television Service had acquired an international reputation and was much admired by scientists and broadcasters from around the world. Many Americans visited it:

> Arriving in a constant stream, visitors from the United States were astounded by (1) the uniform high quality of the pictures, (2) the regularly scheduled programs and (3) the coverage of outside events (Abramson, 1987: 239).

Despite the technical success of the London Television Service, sales of television sets remained disappointingly low, and the audiences were concomitantly negligible. When on 1 September 1939 the BBC's London Television Service was closed down, 23,000 television sets had been sold since the station opened (Abramson, 1987).

In the US, the economic application of television was unclear, as was its likely effect on audio broadcasting. In 1935, David Sarnoff put a halt to plans for a television broadcasting station, for fear it might be too premature and could have an adverse impact upon his radio interests (Abramson, 1987). That grandiose celebration of the modern, the New York World's Fair of 1939, was the location for the inauguration of NBC's television service. President Franklin D. Roosevelt opened the fair on television, and the broadcast was transmitted to 200 receivers. By May 1940 there were some 23 television stations broadcasting in the United States. Pre-war television may have been piecemeal in Britain and the United States, but in the US it was already a much larger and more diverse concern than in the UK.

The close relationship between radio and television, technologically and institutionally, characterized the early development of the nascent medium. Radio, in the shape of the public service BBC in the UK and the growing networks in the US, was a formative influence on early television. However, radio was by no means the only influence, and the film industry's role is often by-passed in traditional histories of television.

The Film Industry and Early Television

Throughout this experimental period of television, the film industry on both sides of the Atlantic invested sporadically in the neophyte industry. In the US, the Hollywood studio system had matured during the 1920s so that by the 1930s most studios owned diverse portfolios of companies. The Big Five studios (Warner Brothers, Loew's, Paramount, RKO and Twentieth Century Fox) were fully integrated – that is, they held interests in all aspects of the industry from production through to distribution and exhibition. Film production companies also owned significant investments in musical theater, publishing, radio and other areas of the entertainment and leisure business (Jewell, 1984). Paramount, in particular, had strong interests in television; as early as 1929 they acquired 49% of the stock of Columbia Phonograph Broadcasting System (later CBS) (Barnouw, 1966). In 1938, Paramount allied with DuMont, a company that manufactured television sets. Moreover, Paramount owned interests in television broadcasting stations such as W9XBK, the first television station in Chicago, which they acquired through their exhibition chain, Balaban and Katz (White, 1990). Even before World War II, then, some American film studios were including television among their holdings.

In Britain, we can identify a similar pattern, albeit on a smaller scale, of film companies showing an interest in television. Gaumont-British films took over Baird Television Limited in 1932 and continued to fund it through the war. In 1939, Isidore Ostrer, chairman of the company, announced that although Baird Television Limited was costing Gaumont-British substantial sums of money, there had been significant advances in both domestic and theater television which justified continued support (*The Times*, 11 August 1939). In 1940, Gaumont-British was taken over by Rank, a fully integrated film conglomerate, which had grown rapidly to control two-thirds of the British Industry. First Gaumont-British, then the Rank Organization, repeatedly sought permission to make regular television broadcasts to their cinemas, but permission was continually denied. Nonetheless, the theater was a frequent venue for television displays, as, for example, when Baird demonstrated 'big screen' television on 28 July 1930, at the Coliseum Theatre in London. Large-screen television displays could be seen in theaters throughout the south of England during the 1930s, and in 1937 Gaumont-British announced their plan to install large-screen televisions in fifteen London theaters (Abramson, 1987). The London theater, the Dominion, Tottenham Court Road, was the venue for Baird's color television experiment on 4 February 1938 (Abramson, 1987). In 1938, Sydney Moseley and H. J. Barton Chapple described the situation thus:

> The television screen is making its appearance in the cinemas, so that the audiences can see, as a regular feature, news items at the instant they occur. It has also been prophesied that the television screen will ultimately supercede the cinema screen, and it may be that we shall see our cinemas replaced by 'Tele-oramas' in which audiences will view plays, films, topical events and all other scenes being relayed from central studios (Moseley and Barton Chapple, 1938: 5–6).

The British film industry lobbied for the right to broadcast television in the cinemas during the 1930s, arguing that it was wrong to deprive 20–30 million cinema-goers of the opportunity to see television. But theater television did not survive, largely because of BBC objections to applications from theater owners, on the grounds that these posed a threat to the BBC's broadcast monopoly.

On the eve of World War II, television was beginning to take on a clearer identity in Britain and the US. British television had become the exclusive purview of the BBC and acquired the mantle of public service from its parent institution. Television was not only controlled by the BBC, but also rather stifled by a corporation that saw radio as its primary concern. In the US, television was also founded on a model inherited from the dominant radio interests, but in this instance radio itself was a quite different phenomenon. During the formative years of American television, the commercial networks, NBC, ABC, DuMont and CBS, provided the most influential antecedent. Television was the invention of many minds; the product of many inventors and the progeny of workers in diverse industries. Entering the public arena during the 'wonderful age' (Tiltman, 1927) of modernity's heyday, television's birth was hailed as a miracle of the modern. The western world went to war before it could forge an identity independent of its antecedents. Television was still 'radio with pictures' or 'cinema in the home' until after World War II.

2

THE MATURE MEDIUM: 1945–PRESENT DAY

At the end of World War II, the relationships between the western world's nation states were reconfigured. America had become the dominant global economy while the European powers had been decimated. US recovery from the war was rapid as Americans reaped the benefits of victory in increased standards of living, improved housing and a burgeoning economy. The UK emerged at the end of the war impoverished and depleted: the guts had been blown out of the cities and every economic resource was spent. For British people, a time of economic austerity loomed and it was not until the end of the 1950s that there would be any recognizable 'post-war boom'. The economies of the two countries under consideration provided very different locales for the adoption of television.

The Film Industry Greets Television

On the eve of television's expansion, the cinema industry had every reason to look forward to the post-war period with optimism. A solid audience base had been built up during the war and, in 1946, attendances on both sides of the Atlantic were higher than ever before. The American film industry dominated the British as it did that of almost every other European country in the post-war period. In the newly liberated countries of Europe the US Office of War Information supported the distribution of American films. The government department was active in France, Italy, Belgium and the Netherlands, keeping the film industry alive until American companies could resume normal trading (Guback, 1976). Hollywood prepared for a boom time in domestic and international cinema box office (Balio, 1976).

The indigenous British film industry had been significantly reduced, and the Americans had been permitted to take up the slack during the war. After 1945, though, British film companies underwent something of a renaissance. Two key figures rose to prominence in the British film industry, with aspirations to becoming international players: Alexander Korda and J. Arthur Rank. In the 1930s, Alexander Korda established a reputation as the only British producer able to sell films in the US (Balio, 1993). It was Korda who pioneered the sale of British films to American television, pre-selling Richard III to NBC Television for $500,000 and selling twenty-four films to WPIX in New York in 1948 (Threadgall, 1994).

According to Geoffrey Macnab, J. Arthur Rank was: 'the single most influential figure in British film history' (Macnab, 1993: x). Rank had entered the film business in the 1930s to promote the message of evangelism through a 'Cinema for Christ' and rapidly expanded his mission (Macnab, 1993). By the end of World War II, Rank was Britain's leading film producer, owning cinemas, studios and a distribution network. Rank built up a company that could compete on almost equal terms with the American studios to become arguably the most important player in British cinema during the 1940s and 50s.

The Rank Organization made some attempt at gaining a toe-hold in television. In 1940, Rank acquired Gaumont-British, and with it Baird Television Limited; Rank also owned Cinema-Television Limited (Chappell, undated). Despite repeated attempts to break into television, many experimental screenings of television in their theaters, and several overtures to the BBC, Rank was never granted a license to broadcast (Macnab, 1993). British governments saw broadcasting as beyond the purview of cinema companies and protected the BBC monopoly.

The collective response of the British film industry to television was to adopt 'a stance which derived ultimately from King Canute' (Buscombe, 1991: 206). The Film Industry Defence Organization (FIDO) attempted to stymie television growth by buying up television rights to British films and preventing them from being shown on British television until they had earned out their box-office take. FIDO collapsed when the funds raised from the cinema industry proved insufficient to pay off the producers (Buscombe, 1991).

The American cinema industry emerged from the war a strengthened international force, but with several menaces looming on the domestic front. An anti-trust suit, which had been filed against the Hollywood majors before the war, was finally decided in 1947, charging Paramount and other studios with a restraint of trade. The *Paramount et al.* decree demanded the dissolution of the vertically integrated studio: in effect, the Hollywood majors were required to divest themselves of the lucrative exhibition arm of the business by selling off their theater chains. At a time when new leisure attractions were entering the cultural domain, the biggest player was obliged to restructure its holding in the field (White, 1992). The Hollywood majors were struck a further blow by the actions of the House Un-American Activities Committee (HUAC) which held hearings to identify and prosecute present or former Communist Party members or sympathizers within the industry. These hearings, held in 1947 and again in 1951, created a witch hunt and resulted in blacklisting which hounded many Hollywood workers out of their jobs.

The Hollywood Reporter, in 1948, presented a positive gloss on a very uncertain situation when it published a 'fact booklet', *Television... and What the Motion Picture Industry Is Thinking and Doing About It*. The editors confidently predicted that:

> With its abundant talent and proven techniques, Hollywood obviously will be the center of television film production (*The Hollywood Reporter*, 1948: 1).

Such brashness masks the fears expressed by some of the contributors that television formed a potential threat to the industry's position. One response of American film producers to television was to make films more *cinematic*, enhancing the specificity of their medium. To this end the 1950s saw the rejuvenation and development of all manner of cinematic wizardry including 3-D, Cinerama, and CinemaScope. A second approach was to turn over film production facilities to the manufacture of short features and series for television. Some Hollywood studios were more ready to adopt this option than others: Paramount established Television Productions Incorporated in 1941 expressly to make short films for television, and other studios followed suit.

Experiments in theater television, begun in the 1930s, continued in the post-war period. In April 1948, broadcasts were first made at Paramount's Times Square Theater in New York (Gomery, 1984; White, 1990). Perhaps the most successful use of theater television was for the simultaneous broadcast of major sporting events: in 1952 the telecast fight between Jersey Joe Walcott and Rocky Marciano attracted record audiences and grossed over $400,000. This was to be the zenith for theater television; the Federal Communications Commission (FCC) refused to allocate the industry the required UHF spectrum – the so-called 'movie band' – on which to carry its broadcasts. As television was available at home to more and more people, the appeal of theater television dwindled. By 1953 theater television had become unprofitable and was abandoned.

Pay television offered another opportunity for Hollywood to exploit the possibilities of broadcasting (Hilmes, 1985). Paramount was at the forefront of an experimental subscriber service, Telemeter, by which scrambled signals were broadcast to the subscriber's home. When the viewer inserted the appropriate coins in the slot, the signals would be unscrambled and recorded on a tape. A representative of Telemeter would call once a month to collect the money and the tape. The first commercial program was of a 1939 USC v. Notre Dame football game and cost the viewer one dollar. Other companies also developed subscription services: Zenith launched Phonevision and Skiatron joined forces with IBM to create Subscribervision. This intervention into television was stymied by the judiciary when the courts ruled that the Telemeter constituted exhibition and was therefore a breach in the conditions of divestiture laid down in the *Paramount et al.* decrees (White, 1990). According to Michele Hilmes, 'Hollywood came closer to the cable industry in the 1950s than ever again until the 1980s', with its experiments in pay television (Hilmes 1990: 125).

When it came to acquiring licenses to broadcast television signals after the war, Hollywood companies were halted by the

FCC. The majority of successful bids for the first tranches of television stations came from radio and newspaper companies. Paul Porter, FCC chairman, warned Hollywood industry executives that they 'should not count on extensive ownership and control of the post-war television industry' (Gomery, 1984: 225). The FCC was true to its word, as for example when it blocked a merger between United Paramount, Paramount's former exhibition chain, and the broadcasters ABC (White, 1992). The consequences of the FCC's decisions shaped the relationship between the American film and television companies for many years to come.

The Networks Take Control

Despite the efforts of film and other interests, it was the radio companies that dominated television in the United States (Boddy, 1990). The two major radio networks, NBC and CBS, and two lesser ones, ABC and DuMont, competed head on for control over the limited number of television stations (Boddy, 1995). In terms of ownership and exhibition, as franchise holders or as owners of theater and subscription television, the film industry was excluded from having any controlling stake in television. Hollywood was left largely to be a supplier of films, a fairly subservient position for an industry that had enjoyed the benefits of absolute vertical integration in its heyday. Timothy White argues against the received wisdom of historians who accuse the cinema industry of doing 'too little too late', and states plainly that:

> The failure of the studios to establish themselves as forces in television broadcasting was a result of FCC policy, not Hollywood impotence (White, 1990: 146).

By about 1954 it was clear that the Hollywood majors were to have no significant ownership interests in television and would be relegated to a position of suppliers of material at best. Concomitant with their exclusion from television, the Hollywood studios faced a decline in box office so precipitous and so unrelenting that it could not be explained away by reference to the traditional fall guy, the economic cycle. It may not have been rational, but it was perhaps understandable that cinema workers should vent their anger on television: the movies turned on television with the fury of one spurned. Firing the only weapon left in its arsenal, the cinema set about representing television as a wicked, corrupt, and ruthlessly commercial industry. Films such as *The Glass Web* and *A Face in the Crowd* were produced in an era when Hollywood homed in on television as its nemesis (these films are among those discussed in Chapter 4).

The Adoption of Television in Britain

Television broadcasting services resumed in Britain and the United States in the same year: 1946, but there are few other similarities to be found in the post-war history of television. In Britain, the BBC was the sole provider of television and not a very enthusiastic one at that (Goldie, 1977). Maurice Gorham observed the differences between British and American television in the 1940s and noted: 'Television is expanding fast in the United States, whereas in Britain it is hardly moving at all' (Gorham, 1949: 10).

The assumption that the BBC should dominate television, as it had radio, went virtually unquestioned in Britain in the 1940s. As Denis Forman put it many years later:

> The War Office ran the army, the Admiralty ruled the waves and the BBC the airwaves. Radio had emerged from the war covered in battle honours and was credited, along with Monty and Churchill, as one of the reasons why we won it (Forman, 1997: 34).

The BBC's control over television was reaffirmed by the Television Committee, established during the war under Lord Hankey, and the BBC's monopoly position was strengthened. Television expansion was constrained due to the dire economic circumstances of post-war austerity. The manufacture of non-essential items was limited, with the production of television sets restricted to 100,000 in any one year (Hulbert, 1949: 208). The transmitter at Alexandra Palace in North London had a range of only 40 kilometers. The use of steel was also strictly regulated and requests for materials to build the transmitters necessary to broaden the reach of the BBC's television signals were refused. The growth of television to areas outside of London was slow: it was 1949 before a second transmitter was put into commission, serving the Midlands from Birmingham. The north of England had to wait until 1951 for a transmitter to be built in Manchester; while Scotland, Wales and the West Country were not within reach of a television signal until 1952. It is hardly surprising that sales of television sets grew only slowly. Only 14,560 television licenses were issued in 1947, and it would be five years before they exceeded the million mark (MacDonald, 1993: 80). The breakthrough event for English television was the Coronation of Queen Elizabeth II in 1953 (Smith, 1995b). An estimated 20 million people watched the Coronation ceremony on television, compared with 12 million who tuned in to their radios: this was the first time that more people in the country had witnessed a state occasion on television than on radio (Briggs, 1979).

Pressure grew during the 1950s for a commercial television service to challenge the BBC's monopoly. Eventually, the British television scene was completely revolutionized by the introduction of Independent Television (ITV) in 1955 (Sendall, 1982, 1983). Britain's first commercial service comprised a single network of regional stations, funded through advertising and controlled by a central authority, the Independent Television Authority (ITA). Commercial television promised greater choice of viewing, an expansion of the market, and a new optimism about popular broadcasting.

The BBC had found it difficult to reach agreements with the film industry on the appropriate remuneration for showing films on television. For many years, British films were not shown on the BBC and the BBC relied on in-house production for its topical and dramatic programming. The attitude of the ITV companies towards the film industry was entirely different from that of the BBC, and the relationship between the two sectors was transformed by commercial television. From its inception, commercial television in Britain had the backing of cinema interests. The film production and exhibition chain

Granada, owned by Cecil and Sidney Bernstein, was among the first tranche of those granted television broadcast licenses. Sidney Bernstein had previously submitted to the Beveridge Committee that the BBC should maintain its monopoly over broadcasting to the home:

> The right of access to the *domestic* sound and television receivers of millions of people carries with it such great propaganda power that it cannot be entrusted to any persons or bodies other than a public corporation or a number of public corporations (Buscombe, 1981).

At the same time, however, Sidney Bernstein had frequently petitioned the Postmaster General for the right to broadcast television to his theaters. After being effectively excluded from exhibiting television, the film industry grew more committed to acquiring a piece of the domestic broadcasting pie, and strove to break the BBC monopoly on television. Of the first six licenses granted, the two major cinema companies – Granada and ABC – held three; Lew Grade's entertainment company supported Associated Television and was a major shareholder of the other three. Rediffusion, a company specializing in the hire of TV and radio sets was also a major backer (Seymour-Ure, 1991). Independent Television provided a lively counter to the stuffiness of the BBC and proved vastly more popular than the established service.

The introduction of commercial television radicalized the public perception of television and made it a popular medium for the first time in Britain (Corner, 1991). However, the first commercial stations were anxious to distance themselves from the connotations of materialism that seemed to adhere to any commercial enterprise in Britain in the post-war period. Granada television went so far as to warn its viewers against excessive consumption the first night it went on the air, on 22 September 1955:

> For most of you, Independent Television has been a new experience. We have brought advertisements to your television screens at home... You can use Granada advertisements as a trustworthy guide to wise spending. Wise spending eventually saves money. And savings can help deal with one aspect

of our country's economic problems. So before we shop let us say to ourselves 'is it essential?' If it is not essential can we save? Save not only for a rainy day but also to make sure that tomorrow and the day after will be sunny (Buscombe, 1981: 30–1).

Denis Forman, a Director of Granada, explains how this extraordinary announcement was planned by his boss, Sidney Bernstein, 'to mollify his Labour Party critics who accused ITV of encouraging people to spend money they could not afford' (Forman, 1997: 61). The fear was justified, it seems, and Howard Thomas affirms that people did change their consumption patterns:

The first commercial began at 8.12 pm for a branded toothpaste. Some six years later the total usage of all toothpaste had doubled and the potential audience had soared to eleven million ITV homes (Thomas, 1962: 211).

The significance of television advertising in improving the nation's dental hygiene is not known, but the impact of commercial television on audiences is well documented. Television viewership expanded dramatically following the introduction of commercial television and the BBC was put on the defensive when the majority of British people would tune into 'the other side' if given the option. Commercial television was *popular*, in both the quantitative and the political senses of the word. The decline in the BBC audience made the license fee paid by all owners of television sets difficult to justify and the BBC came under attack as a consequence. The BBC built up its response to ITV slowly, eventually rising to the challenge by developing more popular programs. The period of 'duopoly', which was to dominate British television for the next fifty years, had begun.

Television and the Mass Media

The single biggest difference between British and American television since World War II has been that there is simply more television in the US than in the UK. In terms of hours of programming; sales of sets; numbers of viewers and stations – the growth of US television was considerably more rapid than that in the UK. The size and scale of the industry in the US, added to its predominantly commercial character, ensured that television came under virulent attack from critics of 'mass society' (Rosenberg and White, 1957).

Television was sold to a burgeoning American middle class (Spigel, 1990; Tischi, 1991) and the new medium was both a contributor to 1950s rejuvenation and a product of it (Marling, 1994). In the US, the television set came to symbolize a new domestic order centered around the 'electronic hearth' (Tischi, 1991) as the focal point of the home. According to Laura Mulvey, television 'represents the triumph... of the home as point of consumption of capitalist circulation of commodities' (1986: 98). The films and television programs produced during the 1950s reflect a social concern with the family: the family reformulated for post-war needs. Television was rapidly established as a popular entertainment medium during the 1950s, and the combined strength of the US networks could attract audience shares of 95% for prime time.

The identity of television in the 1950s was tainted by cold war hysteria. The McCarthy/HUAC witch hunts, which persecuted Hollywood talent, turned their attention to the 'Red Menace' in television in the 1950s. Paranoia about communists taking over the American media was fuelled by the publication of *Counterattack* – a newsletter listing the names of communist sympathizers in broadcasting. To their shame, the networks cooperated with the anti-communists, and either refused to hire or dismissed people black-listed by the anti-communists. A 'grey list' continued up to the 1960s, supported by fear of advertiser response (Hilliard and Keith, 1997). Other scandals dogged the industry even while it was producing some of its best work. Game shows became a highly successful and lucrative television genre, when the 'quiz show scandal' broke in 1958 revealing contestant fixing on the popular show *Twenty One*. American television was tainted with connotations of rabid anti-liberalism and overt commercialism. Anti-mass media rhetoric helped McCarthy's sympathizers to fuel a deep mistrust about television which in turn provided a focus for anti-television feeling in Hollywood.

In the immediate post-war period the British film industry was able to diversify into television and survived as independent television production companies like Granada were formed by the film industry. By the end of the 1950s, the fortunes of the Hollywood film industry were on the wane while those of the British film industry looked more positive. British television, dominated so long by the BBC, was emerging from beneath the cloud of monopolistic control by the late 1950s and looked set to flourish. In the US, television crawled into a dominant position relative to cinema and was set to become the leading purveyor of images to the public. In the 1960s, television was to reach a new equilibrium in relation to other cultural technologies. The film industry, however, was to enter the deepest depression in its history.

Television: The Nation's Witness

The 1960s were a time of cultural revolution in all the arts, including popular entertainment (Moore-Gilbert and Seed, 1992). Television became a potent cultural force exceeding the reach of every previous mass medium, and establishing itself as the central cultural technology. By 1962, 90% of American homes had television sets and 75% of British households owned a television license. During the course of the decade television would be present at most key historic events. The televised debate between Richard M. Nixon and Senator John F. Kennedy in September, 1960, was watched by some 75 million people, the largest ever audience for a television program. When elected President, Kennedy opened up government to television, even allowing his press conferences to be televised. Harold Wilson, who became Prime Minister in 1964, was the first British leader to court the attention of television cameras. Television became another means by which governments and politicians could communicate with their electorate.

Events such as the televising of the 1960 Olympic Games and the launch of the first transatlantic communications satellite, TELSTAR, in 1962, helped confirm television's status as instrumental in creating 'the global village' (McLuhan, 1964). When the first landing on the moon was telecast live in 1969, television seemed to unite the world in wonder at the miracle of modern technology. But the assassination of President Kennedy on 22 November 1963 and the television coverage of this event showed how the electronic media's instant reportage could unite a world in shock. The Kennedy assassination signalled the first 'media event' in the modern style (Dayan and Katz, 1992).

In the 1960s, television demonstrated its unprecedented ability to cover news and current affairs, but struggled to reflect the social revolution that was brewing in the US. Challenges to the Establishment in the shape of the Civil Rights Movement, the welling antagonism to the US war in Vietnam and campaigns for greater gender equality were real world phenomena which television was obliged to chronicle. The bloody brutality of the American war in Vietnam, the first 'television war', appalled many Americans. The networks were at first uncritical of the government but gradually gave way to anti-war sentiment and presented oppositional programs. The role of television in increasing the numbers of people opposed to US involvement remains controversial. The year 1968 brought the assassinations of Dr Martin Luther King and Senator Robert Kennedy; politics was a violent business in the US to which television had become the nation's witness.

The Film Industry Since the 1960s

The significance of the movies as chroniclers of real events had been declining since the introduction of television; the 1960s saw the final demise of the newsreel (see Chapter 7). Television had the edge in news and current affairs by virtue of its immediacy and almost universal audience reach. Hollywood looked increasingly out of step in the rapidly changing social world. The dwindling appeal of Hollywood films and a growing counter culture helped spawn a 'new cinema' to chronicle the souring of the American dream. In 1967 a group of students organized to make films opposed to mainstream values, they dubbed themselves the New York Newsreel (Bordwell and Thompson, 1994). Radical film-makers challenged the Hollywood mainstream and a new generation of film-makers, all highly cine-literate, began to emerge. Film-makers such as Francis Ford Coppola, Arthur Penn and Sam Peckinpah shattered the conventions of Hollywood with iconoclastic movies such as *Bonnie and Clyde* (Arthur Penn, 1967), *The Graduate* (Mike Nichols, 1967), *Easy Rider* (Denis Hopper, 1969), and *The Wild Bunch* (Sam Peckinpah, 1969). As recession hit the film industry, American producers turned to alternative, rebellious, subjects in an effort to woo the youth audience. The counter culture provided the most exciting films of the 1960s.

The declining symbolic power of Hollywood's product went hand in hand with the economic slump in the industry. The major studios became the target of a number of successful takeover bids in the 1960s: MCA took over Universal in 1962; Paramount was acquired by Gulf and Western in 1966; Warner Brothers was acquired by Seven Arts Productions in 1967 and in 1969 they were bought out by Kinney National Service which later became Warner Communications. The industry emerged from its slump better financed and managed, but it was not until the 1970s and 80s that the release of several blockbusters began to reap profits. Table 2.1 shows the 1960s as the nadir of American film production.

In Britain, the film industry has never approached the level of output seen in the US (see Table 2.1). The peak year for film production in Britain was 1936 with 192 films produced. British cinema struggled along in the 1960s making films that largely achieved little critical or box-office success. Since the 1960s, less than 100 films have been produced in Britain each year. In the 1970s, film production declined drastically and in the 1980s the removal of the NFFC and the Eady Fund further impoverished the industry. By 1981, film production in Britain had reached an all time low, with just 24 films produced (BFI, 1996). In more recent years, new money from co-productions and from television has stimulated the British film industry. Film production is currently undergoing a minor renaissance, but remains low relative to that of the United States. Table 2.2 gives the number of films released in selected countries from 1970 to 1995; it shows the dominant position of Hollywood relative to the cinema industries of most other countries except India.

Table 2.1   Number of films produced in the UK and released in the US, selected years, 1929–97

Year	UK	US
1929	81	562
1934	145	480
1939	84	483
1944	35	401
1949	101	356
1954	150	253
1959	122	187
1964	95	141
1969	92	*
1974	88	155
1979	61	214
1984	53	410
1989	30	472
1994	84	462
1995	78	419
1996	128	421
1997	116	425

* = figures unavailable

Sources: BFI, 1997; *The Film Daily*, 1968; *International Motion Picture Almanac*, various years. BFI, 1998.

Table 2.2   Number of feature films released in selected countries, in selected years, 1970–95

	1970	*1980*	*1990*	*1995*
India	396	742	948	*
USA	236	264	385	420
Japan	423	320	239	251
France	138	189	146	141
Italy	240	160	115	96
UK	85	57	53	78

* = figures unavailable

Source: UNESCO, 1997.

New Technologies

Some of the most important determinants in the shifting relationship between the film and television industries in recent
years have been technology led. Advances in satellite, video and
cable during the 1970s and 80s promised to enhance the delivery
of all manner of audiovisual services to the home, while they
also threatened to undermine the film industry's roles at the
level of distribution and exhibition. In 1975, Sony introduced
the home VCR, Betamax, enabling off-air domestic recording for
the first time. Throughout the late 1970s and early 1980s, video
penetration grew rapidly as a new television technology (Levy
and Gunter, 1988). The potential for cable television delivery
was expanding exponentially in the US as AT&T were installing
optical fibre. In 1979 COMSAT announced plans to introduce
satellite programming direct to the home. The late 1970s and
early 1980s saw a boom in the launch of new satellite stations:
Showtime in 1978; Cable Satellite Public Affairs Network (C-
SPAN), Nickelodeon and Spanish International Network in
1979; and in 1980 Black Entertainment Network, the Movie
Channel and Cable News Network (CNN). The networks, for
so long the dominant providers of television, were losing market
share and the importance of terrestrial broadcasting diminished.
New technologies heralded greater control over program choice
for the viewer but, more importantly for the present discussion,
increased access to television exhibition for other players,
including the cinema industry.

British Terrestrial Television

British television services are significantly more limited, and
more closely controlled, than their American counterparts. The
cautiously regulated economy of British television ensured that
the industry remained relatively static during the 1960s and
70s. British television was run as a mature duopoly, a virtual
cartel, with ITV and the BBC in open competition with one
another from 1955 to 1982. Throughout the 1960s and 70s there
were demands for an expansion of television and an end to the
restrictive practices that had developed in the duopoly. BBC2

was launched in 1964, but it was nearly two decades before a fourth channel, Channel 4, began broadcasting. A number of social groups claimed to be ill-served by the mainstream and demanded that a broader range of images and voices be seen and heard. Black and Asian Britons, gays and lesbians, women and trades unionists organized to change the structure of television. At the same time, a second group, led by advertisers and producers, was claiming that the monopoly the ITV stations enjoyed over television advertising revenues gave them an unfair market advantage. The Annan Committee was established in 1974 to investigate the allocation of a new channel. Annan's report submitted in 1979, laid the way for the fourth national broadcasting channel in Britain. Initiated by a liberal Labour government, and implemented by a right-wing Conservative one: Channel 4 was the product of liberal inclusiveness mixed with market-driven profiteering. Cross-subsidies from the ITV stations seemed the only insurance of economic viability for the new channel. Against all the odds, Channel 4 has not only survived but has become a great success and now provides a vital complement to the ITV and BBC services. The latest addition to the UK broadcast television scene is Channel 5, launched in March 1997. But the channel has failed to make much of an impact on the overall television scene, achieving an audience share of less than 2.6% in its first ten weeks, rising to 3.4% in the last quarter of 1997. Channel 5 is constrained by technical limitations that ensure that it reaches less than 70% of homes, and nearly half of these receive signals that are too weak to watch.

British television remains small in comparison to American. Table 2.3 shows that the number of television sets in the US is larger than that in the UK by several factors, indicating the much larger market American stations have to serve. When we take into account the population, and look at the number of sets per head of population, we see that approximately twice as many people have televisions in the US than in the UK (Table 2.4). In both countries the differences between television and film have been eroding in recent years. In the following section we will consider two television stations which have done much to merge the boundaries between our rival media: Channel 4 in the UK and HBO in the US.

Table 2.3   Estimated number of television receivers in use in the US and the UK (in 000s), 1970–94

	1970	1980	1985	1990	1994
US	84,600	155,800	190,000	203,000	213,000
UK	18,000	22,600	24,500	24,900	25,500

Source: UNESCO, 1997.

Table 2.4   Estimated number of television receivers per 1000 head of population, in the US and UK, 1970–94

	1970	1980	1985	1990	1994
US	413	684	797	812	817
UK	324	401	433	434	439

Source: UNESCO, 1997.

New Styles of Television: Home Box Office and Channel 4

During the 1970s and 80s, several key developments resulted in the reconfiguration of the relationship between film and television companies. Two new television companies were crucial forces in this reconfiguration: Home Box Office (HBO) in the US and Channel 4 in the UK. The name 'Home Box Office' announces the channel's intention to challenge the divide between television and cinema. Established in 1972, the company used satellite technology to deliver subscriber services direct to households across the US and gradually built up a strong base. In 1981, HBO produced its first made-for-cable movie, *The Terry Fox Story*, and in that same year began twenty-four hour a day broadcasting. HBO shook up existing patterns of funding films by offering independent film-makers financial support for their projects in exchange for pay-TV rights and a share of the profit. The studios grew anxious when HBO formed Tri-Star Pictures in 1983, with CBS and Columbia Pictures (owned by Coca-Cola), to produce films. In the 1980s, HBO negotiated with the major studios to acquire exclusive pay-TV rights to films made by Columbia, Orion, Warner Brothers and Paramount Pictures (*New York Times* 5 June 1986; 15 July 1987). The movie industry was shocked at how quickly HBO made its presence felt as a major player in its territory. Frank Biondi, President and CEO of HBO told Jack Egan of the *New York Times* what he thought of the studios' response:

> They do get a bit emotional about the fact that pay television was built on movie features. And for some reason, up until this point they didn't carve out a significant ownership role for themselves in cable distribution (Egan, 1983).

In the UK, too, a television company took the initiative in shifting the relationship between film and television. Channel 4 has revolutionized the way films are funded, made and exhibited in Britain. Channel 4's commissioning editors dispensed with the hackneyed television format of the single drama and opted instead for a series of films, *Film on Four*, which produced features with a theatrical and television release (Pym, 1992). This initiative has been a great spur to the British film industry, and Channel 4 has been involved in the funding of many of Britain's most successful films in recent years, including *Four Weddings and a Funeral* (Mike Newell, 1994) and *Trainspotting* (Danny Boyle, 1996). The relationship between the film and television industries in Britain is considerably more complex and lively since the introduction of Channel 4 and the station is now established as a major player in British film production.

Conglomeration and Convergence

During the 1980s the *Paramount et al.* decrees lapsed. At the same time the Hollywood studios were better financed and able to take advantage of the new opportunities for exhibition and distribution offered by new technologies. A number of major corporate takeovers saw the Hollywood studios fall into the hands of massive international conglomerates: Twentieth Century Fox was acquired by Rupert Murdoch's News Corporation and Warner Brothers was merged with Time Inc. The

Japanese giants Sony and Matsushita Electric Industrial entered the film business in strength; Sony bought Columbia and Tristar, and Matsushita Electric Industrial took over MCA-Universal. The massive scale of these multi-interest corporations meant that television and film companies found themselves bedded down in the same stables. The technological and economic histories of the television and film industries have subsequently developed along converging rather than diverging paths (Balio, 1990).

The television industry in the US and Europe has been deregulated to such an extent that multinational corporations are able to buy their way into most broadcasting markets unhindered by government intervention. The Hollywood giant Time-Warner now finds the European market of deregulated, free television, one of its most lucrative. Table 2.5 shows that Time-Warner is currently the most wealthy television company in the world, despite the fact that television makes up only 42% of its business. It is clear from this table that American media conglomerates dominate the world's television industry.

Table 2.5   The world's largest grossing television companies, 1997

Company	Country	TV Revenues in $m	TV as % of business
Time-Warner	USA	8816	42
Disney/ABC	USA	7282	34
TCI	USA	7038	100
NHK	Japan	5290	90
GE/NBC	USA	5232	6
ARD	Germany	4265	100
Comcast	USA	3612	97
Viacom	USA	3598	30
Westinghouse/CBS	USA	3400	93
News Corporation	Australia	3248	32
BBC	UK	3043	96

Source: Morgan and Westcott, 1997: 30.

Today, the three major American networks, ABC, NBC and CBS, remain significant forces in television, but their strength is considerably depleted, with combined shares in US prime time down to 57%. ABC was bought by Disney in 1995, making the combined company the second biggest fish in the pool after Time Warner (see Table 2.5). The other major networks are also part of huge conglomerates: NBC is part of the giant General Electric (for which television is just 6% of its business) and Westinghouse owns CBS (see Table 2.5). Along with the big three, Fox Network is now a keen player in the American broadcast and cable television business, and is owned by the Australian company, News Corporation. The BBC ranks eleventh in the world for television revenues, but this is a little misleading, since these 'revenues' come primarily in the form of a compulsary license fee. British television companies are minute in comparison with their American competitors in the global market. Clearly, American companies dominate the global television markets just as they do the film market.

The Contemporary Relationship Between the Film and Television Industries

What, then, is the present relationship between the film and television industries in Britain and the US? How much power do they have relative to one another and how important are they in the overall media industry?

As we have seen, film interests hold increasingly large stakes in the television industry (Hill and McLoone, 1996). Hollywood's interest in its erstwhile rival medium have expanded globally, especially since the deregulation of European terrestrial broadcasting. Warner Brothers reported to *Variety* in 1997 that:

> There's not a place in the world where we're not in active negotiations with free TV outlets for our product. Our bread-and-butter business has simply never been better (Guider and Williams, 1997: 37).

The film business has diversified into video, too, such that, 'video revenues dwarf film' (Carver, 1996: 9). The revenues from home video sales as a percentage of total global film industry income have risen from an estimated 38.3% in 1986 to 50.3% in 1996 (Carver, 1996). Video sales and rental are now more lucrative than theatrical releases: for example, Disney made more money from the video sales of *Beauty and the Beast* (1991) than from the net profits of any theatrical box-office release (Sklar, 1993). Sales to television are also becoming big business, with American networks paying tens of millions of dollars for broadcast rights. Fox paid Universal $80 million to screen *The Lost World* twelve times and NBC paid a record $50 million for five screenings of *Titanic* over five years (Dempsey, 1998). It is in the area of television sales that synergy can benefit a broadcaster: ABC, now owned by Disney, will automatically receive the rights to broadcast the studio's major releases such as *Con Air*, *Hercules* and *Flubber*. Table 2.6 shows the Japanese giant, Sony, to be the leading American film producer in 1997, followed by Disney's Buena Vista.

Table 2.6   The leading US film producers in 1997 (by gross income)

Company	No. of releases	Gross ($m)	Market share (%)
Sony	38	1271.1	20.4
Buena Vista	34	890.7	14.3
Paramount	27	734.9	11.8
Warner Bros	27	680.3	10.9
Fox	20	651.4	10.4
Universal	13	613.3	9.9
Miramax	33	421	6.7
New Line	31	389.6	6.2
MGM	13	158.5	2.5
Dreamworks	3	89.4	1.4

Source: Variety, 5–11 January, 1998: 98.

The back catalogues of films, deemed worthless in the 1940s, are now some of the most lucrative properties the film companies own. The ever-expanding appetite of the growing numbers of cable, satellite and digital television stations around the world has created a sellers' market with programmers scrambling for material. When British television company Carlton bought Rank in 1997, a major reason was the acquisition of their library of films. Although terrestrial television is declining in importance, the world television business is experiencing a boom with new channels, expanding systems of delivery and greater interactivity opening up the field for new players.

Table 2.7   The leading investors in British film in 1997 by investment

$m	No. of films	Company
86.9	14	Polygram
44	4	Miramax
35.1	20	Arts Council of England
23.7	12	Channel 4
19.4	17	BBC
19.4	6	Granada
13.1	4	J & M Entertainment
10	4	Capital Films

Source: Variety, 15–21 December, 1997: 18.

The exhibition arm of the cinema industry is growing ever more healthy. Attendances are increasing in Britain and the United States as the trend in multi- and mega-plexes grows, boosted by heavy investment from giant integrated entertainment corporations. The first multiplex was opened in Britain in 1985, and now there are 98 with 875 screens accounting for 40% of total number of screens in the UK (Moser *et al.*, 1998). In the US, a similar trend has helped boost takings at the box-office, which were up 8.3% on the previous year in 1997, making the number of admissions, at 1.31 billion, higher than they have been for over thirty years (Klady, 1998: 1). The British box-office improvement was even greater, up 18.4% in 1997 compared to

1996 (Groves, 1998: 11). In large part this was due to the phenomenal success of *The Full Monty*, which took a total of $74.5 million in the UK, exceeding the second most popular film, *Men in Black*, by nearly $15 million.

The trend in film production in Britain and the US is also on the increase: in the US, 425 films were released in 1997 (see Table 2.1). The engorgement of budgets to make ever bigger blockbusters continues: *Titanic* was the most expensive film ever made, costing an estimated $200 million. There is a concomitant increase in box-office returns with a dozen films grossing more than $100 million in the US market in 1997 and 17 exceeded that total internationally (Klady, 1998: 1). *Men in Black* was the most lucrative film of 1997, grossing over $250 million but *Titanic* exceeded that: at the time of writing it has made an estimated $600 million in the US and $1.5 billion internationally.

The relationship between the US and the UK film and television industries remains dominated by the considerably greater size of the American market and American companies. It is difficult to compare film production statistics directly, but Tables 2.6 and 2.7 allow for some comparison of the relative strengths and weaknesses of the British and American film industries. We can see that fewer British films are made by the leading funders and the sums of money are significantly less.

In the global television market, American and British companies are both important players, but the US has a better track record on sales. American television sells better globally than British in part because the production values are much higher. Fox are willing to pay out $550 million *per annum* for 8 years to keep National Football League as a cornerstone of their programming, and NBC currently pay Warner Brothers $13 million an episode for *ER* (*Variety*, 19–25 January 1998). Few British films cost this much, never mind television programs. However, some commentators fear that such spiraling costs are unsustainable given the decline of audiences for terrestrial television.

In terms of production costs, salaries, and international business, television is becoming increasingly similar to cinema. Salaries paid to some stars are certainly approaching film industry proportions: Jerry Seinfeld turned down an offer of $5 million per episode from NBC for his top rated situation comedy (*Variety*, 19–25 January 1998). Some in the industry believe that television is now beginning to exploit the star potential of its performers along similar lines to Hollywood (Vogel, 1998). The recent expansion in television costs and profits can be explained by the enormous power of television advertising, which is exploited by all other areas of the entertainments complex, including the film industry. As Greg Mediel, Chairman of Universal Television Group says:

> There's still no more efficient way to reach a mass audience [than television]... If I have a big movie debuting this weekend, I have to buy NBC on Thursday night and I'll pay whatever they want (Katz and Dempsey, 1998: 103).

The complex patterns of the entertainment industry have made the film and television industries increasingly intertwined. The cultural biography of their relationship in this section of *On Screen Rivals* shows that the two media industries have had their ups and downs both relative to one another and in absolute terms. Film and television, which became rivals in the early part of the history of television, have now become part of larger multinational concerns in which they often have more in common than they do differences.

So, What's the Idea of Television?

In chronicling the history of television in Britain and the United States one cannot fail to acknowledge that the American industry is considerably more developed than the British. The market is much larger in the US and, despite being closely controlled by the FCC, television is generally freer from government regulation than in the UK. The slow growth of British television is testament to this: five terrestrial channels in fifty years is slow going by any measure. American television is considerably more competitive and dynamic. Despite the massive differences, there have always been close alliances between British and American television companies, and these have grown stronger recently.

How do the historical facts influence the idea of television that British and American people have? What are the cultural implications of the economic relations between the two countries and their culture industries? We could begin by thinking about the image people of each nation have of the television produced by the other country.

British and American people like to compare their television services with one another. American commentators like to pay homage to the BBC as the finest broadcaster in the world, although one often feels this is founded more on old-fashioned American courtesy than any dispassionate evaluation of the facts. British television has acquired an image based on the kinds of British programs that are typically shown in the United States. Although these are not necessarily BBC products they have become coterminous with the Corporation for many Americans. Costume drama series, such as *Brideshead Revisited*, *Emma* or *Middlemarch*, often nostalgic in tone, complement the middle-brow fare of American public service broadcasting. Americans see the whole of British television much as they do their own public service television: boring, and worthy – the kind of thing that one perhaps *should* like, although one would not choose to watch such programs.

In Britain, by contrast, an equally unfounded image of American television prevails. In all areas of life, from crime to dining habits, the United States is often conjured as representing a dystopian future. The spectre of a dreaded *Americanization* haunts the British vision of the future. As in the rest of Europe, fears of cultural imperialism, of 'wall-to-wall Dallas', fuel English anxieties. The popular image of American television in Britain is based on more direct knowledge: American situation comedies, like *Friends*, and dramatic series, such as *ER*, have acquired deserved reputations as quality programs. The *idea* of American television is not informed by apprehension of these excellent shows, but by a deep-rooted prejudice. All too often, American television represents blatant commercialism, vulgarity and violence.

The image of television in films, British and American, has been shaped by the history of television, discussed above, and also by more irrational ideas. The cultural construction of television in the movies is the product of economic and cultural phenomena. We have discussed the changing fortunes in the relationship between film and television in Britain and the US above. Television has been, at various times, cinema's rival and its ally, a competitor and a colleague. It is no wonder, then, that television has been portrayed in many different lights by the cinema. In the chapters that follow I investigate some of the transformations in the idea of television put forward by films from Britain and America.

Part II

The Technogenesis
of Television: Cinema's
On Screen Representation
of its Rival

INTRODUCTION

The first part of *On Screen Rivals* examined the historical relationship between the film and television industries. We have seen that the two media have a long and complex history, including times of fierce competition and occasional collaboration. Part II of this book explores how the changing relationship between the two visual media has influenced the depiction of television. The chapters that follow examine the symbolic rivalry between film and television, using the films produced during the last 80 or so years as evidence of the changing representation of television in the cinema.

At the beginning of this book, I defined the process by which one cultural technology represents another as *technogenesis*. There are many examples of 'technogenetic' films that contribute to the cultural construction of other technologies. Films frequently depict rival media, whether snootily as in *The Great Man* (1956), José Ferrer's attack on broadcasting, or respectfully as in Vincente Minnelli's treatment of painting in *An American in Paris* (1951). *Films about television,* which will be discussed in the following chapters, show cinema's rival in a myriad of different ways. Some films depict television as an evil, corrupting force; films such as *Network* or *The Truman Show* represent television workers as megalomaniacs. Treatises against television allow film-makers to be critical of contemporary image-making while denying any responsibility themselves. Many Hollywood films about television offer a pleasure less liberating than it is sadistic, for this is the pleasure of watching something very like us, but different – our 'Other' – being humiliated and ridiculed. Indeed, many movies about television propagate an image of television as a despised Other, degraded for sadistic scopophilia. Several of the films to be discussed in the following chapters are highly critical, pulling apart the broadcasting medium and ridiculing workers and viewers. In the long and varied history of the relationship between film and television, however, there have been moments when the two media have looked upon one another more affectionately. In the following chapters we find many films that show television in a benign or even positive light. We will find throughout the history of the representation of television in the cinema that the varied depictions are evidence of a complex relationship.

In the beginning of television, during the pre World War II period, the medium had a cultural identity that, like its images, was crude and unstable and the public perception of television remained vague (Walker, 1991; Jowett, 1994). Television experiments were reported in the press during the 1920s and 30s and television was displayed in successive Radio Exhibitions and at Expositions and World's Fairs. Still, most people had not yet seen television, and it was representations in other media – magazines, radio and, of course, films – that provided the public with their understanding of the new technology. During the period before television was generally available, news and magazine reports formed the basis of most people's understanding of television. These depictions both chronicled the development of the new medium and also anticipated its application, serving to contribute to the very *idea* of television.

Television was greeted by its first commentators as a most modern invention. The first exhibitions of television occurred at a time when the dream of the modern still fired the popular imagination. The idea of a future world better than the past, informed by scientific advance and improved by invention, was a fertile one at the beginning of this century. Early commentators on television identify television as an important stage in human endeavor, and hail its inventors as heroes. Books and magazines purporting to explain television to 'every man' and to the 'amateur' flourished during the 1920s and 30s (see, for example, Dinsdale, 1928; Larner, 1928; Moseley and Barton Chapple, 1930; Moseley and McKay, 1936). In all of this writing, television is greeted as a wonderful scientific development. The positivist, and positive, spirit of the early twentieth century towards new technology is encapsulated in Ronald Tiltman's *Television for the Home*, published in 1927:

It is a wonderful age that we live in, for scientific achieve-
ments have crowded upon us in the past years at an ever-
increasing rate... Knowing that we can travel in the air and
under the water in comparative safety, and easily communicate with the most distant parts of the globe without any
delay, we should hardly be surprised at any further marvels
that scientists may pry from Nature's jealously-guarded store
(Tiltman, 1927: 1–2).

A significant dose of jingoism can be found in Tiltman's account
of John Logie Baird's role in the development of television:

So, television, one of the most difficult scientific problems of
recent years, was at last mastered by a young British scientist working unaided. We, and Mr. Baird, should be
immensely proud of this wonderful All-British achievement,
which adds further to the glory of our scientific history
(Tiltman, 1927: 52).

The idea of the scientist as romantic hero in a noble quest is
perpetuated in several early accounts of television.
    In the earliest extant British film that makes reference to tele-
vision, we find the inventor portrayed as romantic hero. One of
the last silent films, *The Vagabond Queen* (Geza von Bolvary,
1927) stars popular British actress Betty Balfour in the dual roles
of Sally (a humble domestic servant) and the aristocratic
Princess of Bolonia (Pedler, 1984). Balfour's star persona is that
of an active heroine (Macnab, 1996), and both her roles in *The
Vagabond Queen* subvert the stereotype of woman as passive
romantic interest in the cinema. In *The Vagabond Queen,* Sally is
enamored of Jimmy Carr (Glen Byam Shaw), a tenant in the
rooming house where she works, who is obsessively working
on the invention of television. His interest in television is so
great that Jimmy neglects more quotidian concerns like paying
for his food and lodging. The inventor bears some passing
resemblance to John Logie Baird: he is a Scot with a dreamy
attitude to life and a single-minded obsession with developing
television. Although the film remains neutral regarding the likelihood of Jimmy's success, his landlady is clearly sceptical: 'Calls
himself an inventor! All he invents are excuses!' she says as she

prepares to evict him for non-payment of rent. Jimmy relies on Sally to pursue traditionally masculine goals on his behalf; it is she who lands the job that will earn the couple the money they need to escape poverty. The public image of the inventor in the 1920s, especially one working on such a modern invention as television, is sufficient to identify Jimmy as the Romantic Hero. It can be no surprise that the representation of television is sketchy, this film was released in 1927, just a year after Baird made his first demonstrations of television. But to identify the male lead as an inventor of television was sufficient character-ization for Jimmy, who, like Baird, is heroic through his associ-ation with television.

The science fiction genre was the first to address television technology directly, with the release of *High Treason* (Maurice Elvey, 1929) which depicts how the world might look in 1940 (Barr, 1986: 209). During the 1930s, many film representations of television contained an element of anxiety about the nascent medium: *Murder by Television*, *Trapped by Television* (Del Lord, 1936) and *Television Spy* (Edward Dmytryk, 1939) are all Amer-ican films whose titles alone strongly connote anxiety about tele-vision. These fall within the category of horror and science fiction film which will be discussed further in Chapter 8. During the early period of television's history, many films were made that show no particular anxiety about the new technology; films such as the British *Television Talent* (Robert Edmunds, 1937) or Paramount Pictures' *International House* (A. Edward Sutherland, 1933). In these films, television provides a novel way of show-casing music hall and variety talent and is nothing more sinister than a new means of putting on a show. The following chapter explores how the cinema industry in Britain and America constructed television as simply one more way to extend the repertoire of the musical genre.

3

HAVING A BALL IN YOUR HALL: TELEVISION IN THE MUSICAL

The musical film was developed simultaneously with the sound picture when Warner Brothers released The Jazz Singer (Alan Crosland, 1927) starring Al Jolson. As the new technology of synchronized sound recording was introduced, studios in England and America rushed to enlist musical performers to exploit the potential of the novelty. Stars from vaudeville, music hall and radio were employed to make the cinema 'all singing, all dancing'. In order to motivate the displays of singing and dancing, musicals are very often about putting on a show: the worlds of vaudeville, theater and even the film studio, provide frequent settings (Feuer, 1982). The television program, too, provides an ideal narrative motivation for musical performance.

Two British musicals, one made at the beginning of the 1930s, one at the end, show how familiarity with the new medium grew rapidly during the pre-war period. Television provides a rather vague motivation for the string of musical numbers presented in Elstree Calling (Adrian Brunel, 1930), while a film released nine years later, Band Waggon (Marcel Varnel, 1939), gives British television a clear institutional and cultural location. In the 1930s Elstree aimed to be a studio every bit like its Hollywood counterparts (Banks, 1949; Warren, 1983). Renowned for its stable of popular stars, Elstree had an ambitious project to build a reputation for sound pictures as promptly as possible; Elstree Calling was one of the first offerings to exploit the new sound technology (Bioscope, 1930). Some twenty musical hall and theatrical acts are presented, linked by master of ceremonies Tommy Handley in what he announces to be:

> An all star vaudeville and revue entertainment televised from our studio at Elstree.

Handley, a popular radio presenter, stands before a microphone introducing the acts. Through the medium of television *Elstree Calling* presents a series of performers including Jack Hulbert, Donald Calthrop, Little Teddy Brown, The Balalaika Choral Orchestra and Anna May Wong. Some of the acts are extraordinarily old-fashioned, for example André Charlot's troupe, the Charlot Girls, who perform 'A Lady's Maid is Always in the Know', one of the few colorized sequences in the film. Young women dance in a curiously sedate awkwardness wearing voluminous yellow dresses before revealing their large lacy bloomers in a clumsy can-can. Cicely Courtneidge, star of the British musical stage, appears here in her first film, alongside her husband, Jack Hulbert (Braun, 1980). She performs an awfully hammy song which includes the refrain:

> Sing a cadenza
> It's not influenza
> Don't tell the censor
> I've fallen in love

With the terrible rhyme:

> Life is a failure,
> So be a dahlia!

This last number provides the finale piece to the Elstree 'broadcast' and is no doubt intended as the showcase for a major British talent.

The more deliberately funny numbers have not aged so badly, as in the comedy singing of Lily Morris. Morris gives a brilliant rendition of the music hall number 'Why am I Always a Bridesmaid', in which she dances energetically and raucously wearing utterly unglamorous heavy boots and a baggy dress. Will Fyffe sings a paean to Scottish whiskey, 'It's Twelve and a Tanner a Bottle', in which he poses the question:

How can a fella be happy,
When happiness costs such a lot?

As he sings Fyffe's speech becomes slurred and he reels around in an hilarious show of increasing inebriation.

Some narrative structure is provided by Handley's humorous linking commentary and by two running gags which weave through the series of performances. The first concerns the cultural register of television: Donald Calthrop repeatedly attempts to perform Shakespeare, in spite of the fact that Handley is dubious about the likelihood that the thespian's act will entertain. Calthrop is frequently introduced only to be interrupted or interceded by another performer. Finally, Tommy Handley leans on the television 'camera' and faces the audience; a look of resigned boredom on his face.

> Well, hello, everybody, at last we've found room for Mr Calthrop to do his Shakespearean item. Mr Calthrop, you know, is the greatest Shakespearean actor in captivity. He had a very large and extensive training at Stratford-on-Avon and his name is inscribed to this day on the slate of every public house in the town. He has chosen for his subject today *The Taming of the Shrew*. Why, I don't know. In which he will do his marvellous impersonation... mmm... of Douglas Fairbanks. He has really shown good taste in choosing for his leading lady Anna May Wong. Now for a little Shakespeare.

Closure to this narrative strand is afforded by Calthrop's long withheld performance of an anarchic satire of *The Taming of the Shrew* that degenerates into a riotous custard pie fight. Television is evidently not suited to anything so highbrow as Shakespeare played straight, and *Elstree Calling* makes a strong case for popular entertainment through satirizing the theatrical mainstream.

A second humorous theme concerns the audience for television, represented here by two battling neighbors. Joe, a younger man in the upstairs flat has bought a factory-produced television, while downstairs George (Gordon Harker) struggles to receive a picture on his home-made set. Joe pops his head round George's door periodically to tease him: 'Hear the last one?

Beautiful! Three Eddies next.' George twiddles some more with his device: 'It's coming!' he exclaims, but there follows an explosion before we cut away and the film's audience can see the entertainment that George and his wife are denied. It is only at the end of the film, by which time George is bandaged from the wounds inflicted trying to make his television work, that he finally tunes into an image. The picture clears and the sound squeaks through just in time to hear Tommy Handley's signature expression, 'Good night, everybody, good night'. The bantering of the two neighbors about the relative benefits of the two kinds of television sets establishes that the new medium is on the cusp of consumerism. Joe is the smart neighbor who buys a factory-made set; George is an old-fashioned amateur who self-builds and is the butt of the film's humor. The status of television as a consumer item would be more fully developed in the post-war period, but in *Elstree Calling* its identity is still in flux.

The main discursive construction of television in *Elstree Calling* is of a technology with the potential to distribute and exhibit performances by top theatrical and radio acts. *Elstree Calling* promises to bring live entertainment to the theater and thus constitutes a bid for 'theater television' and for Elstree to have a significant role in providing such television. There were many displays of television in cinemas during the 1920s and 30s, as we saw in Chapter 1. However, because of the BBC's monopoly over broadcasting, television broadcasts in the cinema were a short-lived phenomenon. By the late 1930s it was clear that television in Britain was to be defined principally through its association with the BBC and that there would be no place for theatrical exhibition of television. The BBC had acquired a somewhat elitist and establishment image, thanks in no small part to the work of its first Director General, John Reith. Within the BBC, television remained very much the poor relation of radio and no attempt was made to disguise this attitude (Goldie, 1977). The BBC's reputation for attempting to uplift its audience, and for neglecting popular music, alienated many radio listeners, and encouraged illegal 'pirate' stations. For British working-class people in the 1930s, television was seen as an extension of the BBC, an institution that was at best indifferent, but more likely hostile, to the tastes of ordinary people.

The elitist image of television in the pre-war period was reinforced by the fact that television sets remained well beyond the budget of most working class people. Furthermore, signals could only be received within approximately forty miles of the Alexandra Palace transmitter in North London reinforcing the popular conception that the BBC was exclusively concerned with the metropolitan South.

Band Waggon (Marcel Varnel, 1939) was made for Gainsborough/Gaumont-British with the permission of the BBC. The film is based on a BBC variety radio program of the same name which was introduced in imitation of American variety programs to enhance the BBC's provision of popular entertainment (Neale and Krutnik, 1990). *Band Waggon*, the radio variety show, featured Arthur Askey and his side-kick Richard ('Stinker') Murdoch as the comic leads. The show became highly popular and there were many lucrative spin-offs which cashed in on Askey's growing star persona (Everson, 1986). There was an Askey comic strip devoted to his antics as well as Askey dolls, glove puppets and buttons; *Band Waggon* even went on tour after Jack Hylton bought the stage rights (Logan, 1995). Shooting of the film began on Monday, 29 August, 1939; the following Sunday Chamberlain declared war on Germany. The film was hurriedly rewritten to include a topical war-time element: the ousting of German spies who are using a secret television station to relay plans of British airplanes back to Germany.

The film opens with a shot of the exterior of Broadcasting House in London and follows The Six Jitterbug Boys as they arrive for an audition with the Director General of the BBC, John Pilkington. The BBC's antipathy towards popular music is established when the band are asked to wait, and we learn from the desk clerks that the band are likely to be there for a long time as Pilkington hates music. Askey and Murdoch play a double act who arrived at the BBC some months previously for an audition, and have been waiting ever since, making their temporary abode on the roof of Broadcasting House. The film *Band Waggon* mines the same vein of humor as the radio show, making especially satirical swipes at the Director General, caricatured as 'the Pilk' in a cartoon on the wall of the room where Askey and Murdoch have erected their camp beds. When Pilkington discovers the two squatting on the roof of his building, a lively exchange ensues between the Little Man and the Director General. Pilkington fails to see the funny side and has the chums evicted, establishing himself as humorless and tarring the BBC with the same anti-popular brush by extension.

Band Waggon's subplot charts the efforts of bandleader Jack Hylton and singer Patricia Kirkwood, who were regulars on the radio show (Logan, 1995), to persuade the Director General to listen to their music. When fair means fail, Hylton's band resort to foul ones, bursting Pilkington's tyres as he drives past the Jack in the Box diner where Hylton and his orchestra perform nightly. When the band strike up Hylton's theme tune, 'Melody Maker', Pilkington reads his newspaper, indifferent to the music and Hylton's plot is foiled.

In a lucky twist of fate, Askey, Murdoch, Hylton and Kirkwood come upon the television station abandoned by the German spies in an old castle they are renting. Murdoch realizes the significance of the find:

Murdoch:	Arthur, this is the biggest break we've ever had! We don't need the BBC now!
Askey:	What?
Hylton:	That's right, we can broadcast without them!
Murdoch:	We can start in opposition!
Kirkwood:	What a swell idea! We can get the band and the girls and put on a terrific show!

The television technology is easily taken over by the playmates with the help of Freddy (Freddy Schweitzer), a member of Hylton's band. Freddy's facility with television transmitters is cryptically explained by the fact that 'he used to work in a radio shop'. The gang have no difficulty in being able to receive and transmit their own signals and are even able to intercept broadcast programs. Great hilarity erupts at Askey's fooling around when his rendition of 'A Busy Busy Bee' is transmitted, interrupting first a BBC radio program and then a speech by Hitler. When Pilkington addresses the BBC audience on the subject of the new medium, Askey offers his ripostes to the pompous man's statements for the benefit of his friends in the room.

> *Pilkington*: Many of us are asking, 'what is the future of tele-
> vision?'
> *Askey*: And I bet you don't know the answer.

Then Freddy superimposes Askey onto the BBC broadcast so that he shares a frame with the Director General. When Pilkington says:

> Very shortly we hope to conduct a ballot.

Askey, from his side of the frame, can't resist chipping in:

> Yes, vote for Pilkington for putrid programming!

Although the response of the chums in the studio is one of great mirth at Askey's subversion, the po-faced executives at the BBC promptly fade their own broadcast out. Askey is left addressing the television audience alone, and delivers a monologue on the state of the BBC and a declaration of independence for popular performers:

> Well, playmates, I've done you one good turn: I've got rid of
> him. And now I can tell you what really does happen. He says
> he spends his time searching around for fresh talent. Shall I
> tell you what happens when he finds it? He keeps it hanging
> about for three months and then gives it the sack. Him and
> his experts! Why I could do better than him with my hands
> tied behind my back and what's more I will! You tune in on
> this wavelength at 8 o'clock tonight and I'll show you – I'll
> show you some of the talent that he's missed: Jack Hylton and
> his band, Pat Kirkwood, Arthur Askey, Richard Murdoch!

The newspaper headlines proclaim the news of the pirates as the chums ready themselves for a show and a revolution of the airwaves.

The broadcast is a success and Pilkington is obliged to relent and grant the popular entertainers their own show. Finally, the BBC shifts from being prejudiced and patriarchal to a popular patrician. The revolutionaries are co-opted to the mainstream and BBC authority remains unquestioned. *Band Waggon* begins by challenging the hegemony of the BBC over broadcasting, but in the end the monopoly broadcaster is firmly identified as the exclusive force in British television.

Band Waggon shows that, from the perspective of popular entertainers, the BBC was frequently perceived as the bastion of the upper classes and defender of highbrow taste. The BBC is depicted as perpetuating the divisive British class system by repeatedly refusing popular performers access to broadcasting. The exclusion of working-class entertainment from the BBC by pompous executives recurs as a theme in *Make Mine a Million* (Lance Comfort, 1955), which also stars Arthur Askey (discussed further in Chapter 5). In both *Band Waggon* and *Make Mine a Million* the idea of popular television is something for which people have to fight and which television bureaucrats, with their limited, class-bound tastes, prefer to stifle.

Elstree Calling was made at the beginning of the 1930s and *Band Waggon* at the end: it was the decade in which television changed from being a practical machine demonstrable in the lab to being a fully operational broadcast medium. By 1939 the BBC was broadcasting a regular television service of some repute and was acquiring international renown for the professionalism of its service (Hanna, 1976). At the same time, the concept of television was gaining definition in the public imagination as reports in the press, on radio and in film continued. *Band Waggon* inevitably displays a more sophisticated familiarity with television technology than *Elstree Calling*, and plays with the conventions of visual broadcasting in a way that assumes some audience familiarity with the medium. *Elstree Calling* showed a succession of acts with little narrative linking them. Television is portrayed in the earlier film as a simple medium for the reception of variety acts and there is no sense of the existence of television institutions controlling access. *Band Waggon*, made when the radio variety show was more sophisticated and the public were more familiar with television, constructs a more complex narrative in which television has a clear identity; one inextricably bound to the BBC. British musicals of the 1930s use television as a vehicle for popular performers, but the influence of the state authorized broadcaster over popular television is shown to be progressively more restrictive. This reflects the increasing control that the BBC exercised over television to the detriment of cinemas, theaters and music hall producers and performers.

American Depictions

The American production, *International House* (A. Edward Sutherland, 1933), like the British films discussed above, shows television as an entertainment medium first and foremost. The Paramount Studios' comedy vehicle for W.C. Fields also features Edmund Breese as Dr Wong, the creator of the 'radioscope', or 'televisor'. Dr Wong is selling the rights to his new invention and has invited potential bidders to the International House Hotel in Wu-Hu, China, to see a demonstration. *International House* employs television as a narrative device to motivate the assembly of some, and to present the performances of some more, variety and radio stars. George Burns and Gracie Allen, for example, are enormously comical as the hotel doctor and nurse. As one contemporary reviewer put it:

> Through the televisor [*International House*] finds an opportunity for introducing logically into the irresponsible story such warm radio favourites as Rudy Vallee, Colonel Stoopnagle and Bud, Cab Calloway and his Orchestra, and Baby Rose Marie (*Kinetograph Weekly*, 1933: 11).

Although we see the machine that is responsible for exhibiting the images, the processes of image-gathering remain as mysterious and strange as Dr Wong himself. Our first sight of the 'radioscope' reveals a muddle of tubes, belts and valves producing a fuzzy, often broken and distorted image onto a screen somewhat smaller than a cinema screen and certainly larger than most contemporary television sets. For Dr Wong, the primary application of television is to transmit images of events instantaneously across great distances and his avowed aim is to present a six-day bicycle race, live, from New York. Much to the doctor's annoyance, and the delight of his audiences, each time Wong tries to demonstrate this feat, the radioscope delivers popular variety acts instead. The most exhilarating of these is Cab Calloway's joyous tribute to marijuana, `Reefer Man'. The number begins with Cab Calloway and his orchestra addressing the bass player, who is evidently stoned ('what d'yer mean, he's high?'). The chorus asks:

Have you ever seen that funny Reefer Man?
He smokes a reefer he gets high,
Then he flies to the sky,
That funny, funny, funny Reefer Man.

It is `Reefer Man' which finally sells television to Tommy Nash, the American Representative (Stuart Erwin) who finds the performance 'Wonderful!'

In later films representing television we will see that much is made of the differences between the broadcast and the celluloid images. From the 1950s onwards the television image is shown to be poorer in quality and the range of camera movements significantly more limited than those of film. In *International House*, the formal differences between television and film are evident if we compare the 'televised' number, `Reefer Man', and `She Was a China Tea Cup, and He Was a Coffee Mug'. The latter number is performed as part of the hotel cabaret and features Sterling Holloway and Lona André as the principal dancers. A cinematically busy scene, `She Was a China Tea Cup...' includes a variety of point-of-view shots, moving cameras, long shots and close ups. Holloway leaps out of a huge coffee cup prop and André emerges rather more demurely from a matching tea cup as the chorus sings of the coffee mug's love for the china tea cup. Holloway, dressed in American sailor suit, turns down the advances of the other pieces of crockery and cutlery. Spoons, sugar bowl and a saucy saucer ('she was a torso tosser with lots of sex appeal') all offer themselves up for the sailor before he finally makes the plunge and leaps into the china tea cup. The tea cup and coffee mug are then transformed into jigsaw pieces and the floor is given over to the dance troupe, Sing Lows Syncopators. These dancers hold the jigsaw pieces aloft and a bird's eye shot shows the props being transformed into umbrellas which the dancers swirl as the music takes on a syncopated rhythm. We are shown shots of the audience watching the spectacle a number of times, and the dancers defy any suggestion of proscenium by gathering pieces of a jigsaw from the floor and walls of the hotel lounge. The number uses various camera angles typical of Busby Berkeley choreography: at one point the camera lunges between the legs of a female dancer standing astride with three smiling women's faces filling the triangular space between her legs. The camera dollies in between the woman's legs to reveal an apparently endless stream of women standing in line with their legs apart, each filled with three faces pulling away as the camera is propelled through the tunnel shape the women's limbs create. The diegetic space of the cabaret room is barely maintained and the camera is permitted to select angles and positions which would not be available to anyone viewing from the lounge of the International House Hotel. `She was a China Tea Cup...' uses a full array of camera angles and special effects photography to create a dance number approaching the best of the genre in terms of sophistication of technique.

By contrast, the filming of the performances transmitted via the 'radioscope' is considerably more constrained. All of the 'televised' performances are shot head on, using a limited variety of camera angles and movements, reflecting what was known of the television form at the time (Barker, 1991). Before the Cab Calloway number begins, we see the radioscope screen from Tommy's point of view, in an over the shoulder shot. The television image fills the central area of the cinema frame and at first appears blurry. The screen clears to reveal a medium-two-shot of Cab Calloway and the bass player, other orchestra members being visible in the background only, as the music begins. The song is filmed using three different kinds of shot: the group shot of the orchestra as a whole, with Calloway conducting; a two-shot of Calloway and the bass player; and a medium close up, either of Calloway waist-up singing or of his feet tap dancing. The whole scene is filmed front on, with some shots slightly to one side. The repertoire of the film form used for the 'television' act `Reefer Man', is significantly more limited than that used for the performance in the diegetic world of the hotel cabaret. Television is depicted as a visually less complex medium than cinema, and *International House* does not present the medium as a threat to cinema's scopic regime.

The construction of television in *International House* is of a potentially popular medium (Dr Wong always attracts an audi-

ence) which may be used by its inventors to quite boring effect
(few characters in the movie seem enamored of the prospect of
watching the advertised six-day bicycle race). To some extent
television is portrayed as cinema's oriental and sexual Other –
the technology itself is the brainchild of Chinese Dr Wong and
its main advocate is the powerful sex symbol Peggy Hopkins
Joyce. In explaining his radioscope device, Dr Wong claims that
through it: 'I can materialize anything, anywhere, anytime; the
radioscope needs no broadcast station.' By casting the radioscope's inventor as an oriental the script dispenses with the
practicalities of describing the broadcasting process while
relying on the stereotype of the cryptic Chinese. The only person
able to see a profitable future in television is Peggy Hopkins
Joyce, according to *Picturegoer*, she is: 'the woman who has
successfully married four millionaires' (*Picturegoer*, 1933: 30).
Here she plays up her public personae as a sassy gold-digger
and is one among many celebrities Dr Wong's demonstration
attracts. *En route* to Wu-Hu she tells her traveling companion:
'Dr Wong's invention is going to make millionaires and I intend
doing the same.' Peggy Hopkins Joyce's attitude to television
was no doubt shared by the many executives at Paramount who
were keen to exploit television's pecuniary potential. *International House* depicts television as a likely extension of Paramount's (and cinema's) reach by showing television as an
adjunct to the entertainment business.

The pre-World War II musical films that we have discussed,
Elstree Calling, *Band Waggon* and *International House*, present television as a cultural technology closely linked to radio. The stars
transmitted on the television screens are generally from the
world of broadcasting rather than cinema. In *Elstree Calling*
Tommy Handley, most renowned as a radio comic, is Master of
Ceremonies. Dr Wong in *International House* refers to television
as a 'radioscope' and the images, which are mysteriously gathered and transmitted by this device, are those of radio
performers. The cinema industry, keen to exploit the new technology of sound cinema, signed up many radio stars whose acts
would not have translated well to the screen in the early days.
The musicals discussed include singers and dancers, but also
comedians and other performers among their cast. The typical
depiction of television in musicals of the 1930s is of an exciting

new medium for the transmission of popular performances. Television does not present any challenge to cinema's hegemony, rather, it is represented as a welcome addition to the repertoire of entertainment media and a good subject for a film property.

The Dream Sours

Television services in Britain and the United States were suspended for the duration of World War II. Following the end of the war, television was relaunched with renewed vigor on both sides of the Atlantic. As the services grew, the identity of television in each country diverged along the lines established by radio broadcasting: the American system became firmly shaped along commercial lines; while in Britain television strengthened its public service identity. The primary depiction of television in American films of this period is of a useful means for putting on a show. Will Jason directed two musicals including television as themes: *Slightly Scandalous* (1946) and the country and western musical *Everybody's Dancin'* (1950). Television is a logical career move for popular radio stars Jack and Kitty Moran (Dan Dailey and Betty Grable) in *My Blue Heaven* (Henry Koster, 1950) while in *Sunny Side of the Street* (Richard Quine, 1951) Frankie Laine plays himself in a story about a young hopeful trying to break into television. A good example of the benign depiction of television in a post-war musical is *Two Tickets to Broadway* (James V. Kern, 1951). Tony Martin and Janet Leigh star in this reprise of backstage musicals of the 1930s such as *Footlight Parade* and *42nd Street*. Writing at the time, the *Motion Picture Herald* reviewer claimed:

> Not since the Fred Astaire classics has such a picture come from the RKO studios... The only difference is that, where at one time it was the theater or Hollywood which gave the youngsters a break, today talent-hungry television is the bene-factor (*Motion Picture Herald*, 13 October, 1951: 22).

Young Nancy Peterson (Janet Leigh) is the belle of small town Pelican Falls for whom the high school band play a rousing send-off number near the beginning of the film. On arriving in

New York she is the ingenue among a crowd of established performers who show her the ropes. In a variation on the 'Let's put on a show!' moment in the Andy Hardy series of musicals, one of the characters has an epiphany: 'I just got the greatest idea of my life – television!' His girlfriend is unimpressed and tells him: 'I think someone already thought of it.' His intention, though, is to put on a *television show*, and standard components of the 1930s musical – scenes of rehearsal and practice – follow. The preparations are not for a Broadway performance, however, but for an appearance on *The Bob Crosby Show*. (Bob Crosby, Bing Crosby's younger brother, hosted a daytime show on CBS from 1955 to 1957, but was not host of his own show until 1958 when *The Bob Crosby Show* ran for one season (Brooks, 1987).) The simple, old-fashioned, formula of the backstage musical is readily transplanted onto television. Any differences there might be between the modes of reception of stage musical and television variety numbers are neatly elided in Crosby's intro-duction to the musical performances: 'We're about to have a ball in your hall!' *Two Tickets to Broadway* depicts television as the next stage in the continuous development of popular musical entertainment. As Jane Feuer argues, writing about the Hollywood musical:

> In a sense the history of popular entertainment in America is rewritten as the show-within-a-film in musical entertainment. The materials change, but the process remains constant. The earlier form is recycled into the contemporary form (Feuer, 1982: 94).

Here the 'television show-within-a-film' is the vehicle for recy-cling singing and dancing.

The musicals discussed thus far depict television as a means of creating popular entertainment. It is not until the mid-1950s that we find more malevolent depictions of the electronic medium. *It's Always Fair Weather* (Gene Kelly and Stanley Donen, 1955) is one of the first Hollywood musicals to repre-sent television as a manipulative *arriviste* medium. *It's Always Fair Weather* is a musical from the genre's most accomplished and sophisticated production team, Arthur Freed's unit at MGM. The script is by Betty Comden and Adolph Green; Gene

Kelly and Stanley Donen direct and the stars include Gene Kelly, Dan Dailey and Cyd Charisse. The 'Freed Unit' musicals constitute a group of films that generate a whole constellation of cultural comparisons, drawing distinctions among opera, ballet, museums, vaudeville, magic shows and Shakespeare. *It's Always Fair Weather* opens and closes in Tim's Bar where, at the beginning of the film, three newly demobbed soldiers, Ted, Doug and Angie (Gene Kelly, Dan Dailey and Michael Kidd respectively) depart into the New York night vowing to reunite in the same place, on the same day, ten years later. The post-war euphoria and comradeship that was evident in an earlier Freed Unit film, *On the Town* (Stanley Donen and Gene Kelly, 1949), has dwindled in *It's Always Fair Weather*. When the soldiers are reunited as civilians, the former best pals have become ordinary Joes with little in common. Their reunion brings home to all three just how far reality has taken them from their dreams.

Further trouble comes in the form of a woman and a new technology. When Jackie Leighton (Cyd Charisse), a television program coordinator on *Midnight with Madeline*, finds out about the men's reunion, she decides their story would be perfect for the item 'The Heart Throb of Manhattan', in which Madeline showcases real life tales of New York folk. Without gaining their permission, Jackie and the show's presenter, Madeline (Dolores Gray), plot to ensure that the three 'boys' are kept occupied and brought to the studio at the appointed hour, to appear as surprise guests.

An early indication of the low regard in which television is held comes when Doug drops his guard after drinking too much at the pre-show party. When reminded that he must stay sober for the show, Doug refers to *Midnight with Madeline* as 'maudlin, disgusting junk'. He criticizes the slot on which, unbeknownst to him, he is about to appear, as one in which viewers 'see some poor helpless surprised guest make an idiot of himself'. By the time he launches into his solo number the chap is quite paralytically drunk and renders a damning pastiche of the stupidity of television genres and popular entertainment generally.

Madeline and Jackie succeed in tricking Doug, Ted and Angie to arrive at the appointed hour in the television studio – which is disguised to look like an ordinary club or cabaret room. 'The Heart Throb of Manhattan' item is introduced, 'the part of the

program that really means something', and the spotlight picks
out our reluctant heroes. They each look decidedly irritated as
they are pretty well frog-marched onto the stage by a chorus
line bearing banners aloft proclaiming their reunion. The
unhappy events of the day are twisted into a sentimental tale
as Madeline transforms their lives into consumable kitsch for
the viewers at home. Madeline introduces each man to the audience in turn, but they resist being categorized according to the
television script for their lives. Doug tells her, the studio audience and the viewers at home: 'Madeline, sincerely I deserve
every bit of it. Its truly a fitting climax to ten years of self-
degradation.' Angie tears up the vouchers for a washing
machine and new shoes for his kids, telling her he can look
after his own family, and repeats the words of her own song
back to her: 'Thanks a lot, but no thanks.' When Madeline asks
Ted what he does for a living, he will not play along with the
expectations of television; he turns to face the camera and
declares: 'I'm a bum. I feel terrible about showing my face in
decent homes all over the country.' When asked about the
men's 'glorious reunion', Ted is not about to lie:

> Look, Madeline, I'd like to help you out and give you all the
> phoney sentiment and corn you want, but – I'm afraid I'll
> have to disappoint you. When the three of us met today in
> Tim's bar for the big moment, it was horrible. The years had
> made us strangers. We hated one another.

His attack on corny television sentimentality changes gear as he
opens his heart and uses television as a vehicle for issuing a
confession:

> I know now why I hated them; it's because I hated myself.
> And I'm glad it happened. Cos I'd like the guys to know that,
> whatever they think of me, I don't blame them. And I'd give
> several arms and legs to win their friendship and respect
> again. I'll try and spend the next ten years winning it back.
> Goodnight, Madeline, it's been swell.

It's Always Fair Weather betrays the deep ambiguity about the
role of television. Television is ridiculed for being the vehicle of

false sentimentality, but the film's hero is able to use it as a means of self-realization and to express heartfelt emotion. There follows another televised confession, but this time the person is unaware that their words are being televised. The gangster, Charlie Culloran (Jay C. Flippen), has arrived in pursuit of Ted, and believes himself to be in a nightclub. Culloran is caught on the television cameras threatening Ted and dropping the names of a number of other big time operators. The television studio becomes the location for a grand finale punch up in which our three chums battle in choreographed unity. Finally, Madeline declares that Charlie Culloran is defeated and affirms television's role in ensuring his capture by the authorities. The television studio provides the location for a brawl which, finally, concludes with justice being done.

It's Always Fair Weather was released in the 1955, the time when, according to Jane Feuer, the Hollywood musical began to fade:

> What seemed to die out in the mid-1950s was the energy at the heart of the great MGM musicals, an energy based on faith in the power of singing and dancing connected with an almost religious belief in Hollywood itself as the great inheritor of the spirit of musical entertainer (Feuer, 1982: 87).

The burgeoning function of television as the predominant medium for musical entertainment was in some part responsible for the film genre's fading power. *It's Always Fair Weather* shows television muscling in on film's territory and conveying rather watered down versions of films' entertainment. The bitterness and misanthropy at the heart of this musical clashes with the genre's more typically upbeat and uplifting spirit. The Hollywood musical recognizes television as the harbinger of its demise in *It's Always Fair Weather*.

In this chapter we have seen how some musical films from the 1930s to the 1950s have represented television. Early depictions showed television as more of an ally than a rival, and a medium likely to provide new outlets for performance and entertainment. During the 1930s, 1940s and early 1950s the musical was a mainstay of the Hollywood studios. Although not often critically appreciated, the genre was highly lucrative and had consistently high production values (Altmann, 1981). However, by the mid-1950s the Hollywood musical had pretty well expired; television had replaced the movies as the predominant forum for popular musical performances. Variety programs such as *Saturday Night at the London Palladium* and *Your Show of Shows* became a prevalent feature of the television schedules in Britain and America respectively. Television was rapidly becoming the new means for music promoters to sell songs and market performers. By the time MGM released *It's Always Fair Weather* in 1955, the film industry was less willing to see television as an extension of itself and had even come to see the new medium as a successor technology. The musical genre was decimated by changes in the music industry which will be discussed further in Chapter 6. The Rock'n'Roll and pop movies of the 1960s and 70s were never to acquire the same status of the musicals of the 1930s and 40s. In the next chapter we look more closely at Hollywood's response to the ascendence of television in the 1950s. We return to the British scene in Chapter 5 to explore how the British film world responded to the BBC's first serious competition: commercial television.

4

ALL THE COMPANY YOU WANT: HOLLYWOOD AND THE FEMINIZING OF TELEVISION

American television became a mature medium and a serious challenge to the cinema during the 1950s (Boddy, 1985). Most importantly, television became a mass medium in several senses of the word: it was owned by large corporations; produced in factory-like studios; dependent on big business for commercial support, and reaching audiences of an unprecedented size. The ascent of television as a mass medium coincided with a period of vociferous anti-mass media discourse in the US. The modernist enchantment with the machine, which had welcomed television in its early years, had staled. Television began to be seen as instrumental in the development of an increasingly dehumanized and destructive mass society (Anderson, 1991, 1994).

Television and the Mass Media Debate

American critics of the mass media of the left and right united in condemning the lamentable impact of television on society. German émigrés Theodor Adorno and Max Horkheimer wrote of the deleterious effect of the industrialization of culture in general (Adorno and Horkheimer, 1977). Adorno further argued that television in particular was a totalitarian medium with deleterious effects on social mores and values (Adorno, 1991). The ideas of American critic Dwight Macdonald gained a great deal of cultural legitimation. Central to Macdonald's argument was the affirmation that:

> Since Mass Culture is not an art form but a manufactured commodity, it tends always downward, toward cheapness – and so standardization – of production (Macdonald, 1957: 72).

A 'Mass Culture thesis' developed which resonated with thinkers of diverse political persuasions in the 1950s (Rosenberg and White, 1957; Jacobs, 1964). Television was held in special disregard by subscribers to this view. Its status as a mass medium was further degraded by virtue of the taint of the anti-communist witch hunts and the high profile quiz show scandals (discussed in Chapter 2). The popular conception of television as fundamentally immoral and unscrupulous gelled with the mass media critics' assault on the medium.

Television: A Women's Medium?

The mass media have been associated with femininity since the nineteenth century, according to Andreas Huyssen (1986). Demands for class and gender equality in the last century threatened the hegemony of the ruling male elite, and spawned a defence of 'high culture' founded on condemnation of non-elite culture as inherently inferior while also attaching to it unpleasant connotations of 'femininity'. Huyssen argues that:

> In the age of nascent socialism *and* the first major women's movement in Europe, the masses knocking at the gate were also women, knocking at the gate of male dominated culture. It is indeed striking to observe how the political, psychological, and aesthetic discourse around the turn of the century consistently and obsessively genders mass culture and the masses as feminine, while high culture, whether traditional or modern, clearly remains the privileged realm of male activities (Huyssen, 1986: 47).

This construction of mass culture as a feminine 'other' to masculine high culture pervaded intellectual perceptions until the 1960s, argues Huyssen. During the 1950s, the period when television was the newest and most controversial mass medium, the association of mass culture with femininity was transferred by extension to television. Lynn Spigel applies Huyssen's insight to her discussion of depictions of television in magazines. She argues:

> Broadcasting quite literally was shown to disrupt the normative structures of patriarchal (high) culture and to turn 'real men' into passive homebodies (Spigel, 1991: 86).

Television acquired an image of femininity in the 1950s: women were recognized by industry as holders of the family purse strings and television was marketed to female consumers (Altman, 1989); women also made up the larger part of the audience for television and programmers acknowledged this, especially in daytime programming.

Television was thus targeting the traditional audience for cinema, which Hollywood had built up during World War II, namely the women of America. War work had put money in the purses of women but the war-time economy produced few items on which to spend it; the cinema was one of these and attendances soared as a consequence. Hollywood became geared up to produce a wide array of films specifically for female consumption and the 'women's picture', musicals and melodramas especially, reached the zenith of their popularity during the war. In the post-war reconstruction, and the baby boom that accompanied it, women were firmly relocated back into the home and now bought their solace at the household appliance store. Television flourished as a new form of entertainment located in the home and specifically targeted at women (Spigel, 1990). The female audience for cinema had found other interests and could no longer be relied upon as a solid consumer base for the movie moguls.

Film director Elia Kazan recognized in 1957 that television 'is fated to be much bigger than pictures ever were' (Kazan, 1957: xiii). During the 1950s, the cinema's attitude towards television grew increasingly hostile as film interests were excluded from any controlling stake in the new medium. Moreover, the depiction of television became increasingly one of hostility towards a dangerous feminized medium.

Television as a Female Domain in Hollywood Movies

Television is directly identified with femininity and the stage with masculinity in the 1952 comedy *Dreamboat* (Claude Binyon). Here the theater represents a stolid respectability exemplified by Professor of English Literature, Thornton Sayre (Clifton Webb). The students at Underhill College, where he teaches, name Sayre 'Old Ironheart', but his staunch façade is affected to prevent anyone learning about his earlier career as a star of the silent cinema. When the film opens, we find Sayre's adult daughter Carol (Anne Francis) earnestly working on her thesis and imitating her father in every regard, even to the extent of wearing a masculine two-piece suit of the same thick wool as him. Carol first learns about her father's former career when she is invited by a gaggle of sorority girls to the 'tri-U' house for: 'A night you'll never forget!' When she arrives, Carol finds her classmates sitting in the sorority lounge watching television, and the pompous young woman doesn't hide her indignation at being invited to view 'this idiot's delight'. Her attitude changes when she realizes that the program she has been invited to see features her own father, 'the original Dreamboat', playing the lead man in the swashbuckling romance *The Return of El Toro*. Carol's shock turns to embarrassment when she has to watch her Father 'make love' to the sex symbol Gloria Marlowe (Ginger Rogers) and she is confronted with her father's sexuality.

Gloria, Sayre's former co-star, is hell bent on making a killing out of the unexpected boost television offers to her washed-up career through reruns of their old movies. She tries to persuade her former lover and co-star of the sense of this: 'All of show business is open to us again', she tells him. Gloria attempts all manner of trickery to convince Sayre, but he refuses to agree to the television transmission of his old films. He has acquired a high culture status as Professor of English Literature which the exhibition of these films threatens to undermine. Sayre sues the television network with invading his privacy and the medium itself is literally put on trial, with a television set even placed in the dock during the court scene. In order to challenge the defense claim that television is the greatest educator, Sayre calls 'television' to the stand. An advertisement for Crazy Sam's used cars seems to confirm Sayre's case. Sayre directly contrasts television with cinema by showing one of his films first, 'as it was originally filmed', and then, 'the same picture deliberately distorted for television, thereby turning me into the world's foremost nincompoop'. The scene is presented to the court with the following soundtrack supplied as in the broadcast version:

Gloria: My loved one! Once more you have saved me!
Bruce: And I shall continue coming to your rescue as long as you use these glorious perfumes manufactured by Exotic!
Gloria: What you are smelling, my darling, is Double Passion – preferred by smart women everywhere
Bruce: I am helpless under the spell of its aroma, my sweet! Command me and I shall obey!

The courtroom breaks into uproarious laughter as the two kiss. A newspaper headline conveys the conclusion: '"Dreamboat" wins suit to keep film off TV.' Television is ridiculed for its crass commercialism and the 'high culture' position wins the day. But television is not universally damned in *Dreamboat*. The television world is to be applauded for the way Carol grows to sexual (feminine) maturity. Carol doffs her tweed suits for feminine dresses and a new hairstyle when she falls in love with the young television executive assigned to escort her during her father's trial. Carol is angry with her father for suppressing the truth about the real world and denying her sexual fulfilment: 'I've found out a little about living and I like it!' Despite his legal victory, Sayre finally relents and returns to the film business to become reconciled with popular culture. The punch line comes when Sayre is watching his first sound picture, *Sitting Pretty* (this is the title of Clifton Webb's first Mr Belvedere picture, released in 1948). Gloria delivers the final sting when she welcomes him back to the business, and says she is looking forward to working with him again: Gloria has bought the film company and now Sayre works for her.

For Thornton and Carol Sayre, television is at first equated with frivolity and silliness. Gloria is the embodiment of everything they hate about television: mercenary, materialistic and highly sexualized. *Dreamboat* charts the father and daughter's journey of self-discovery through their contact with television and Gloria. Carol is introduced to the world of adult sexuality, first by being forced to recognize her own father as a sexual being and then through a sexual relationship of her own. She and her father both cast off the constraints of the monastic academic life through their relationship with television. Thornton is reconciled with his own, youthful and romantic self as 'Dreamboat' and has a new career as a film star. Throughout *Dreamboat* Gloria embodies the paradox of the new medium: she is manipulative and powerful but also very beautiful and attractive. It is at her instigation that Thornton and Carol are transformed from asexual ascetics to sexual beings who are able to relax and enjoy popular culture.

Similarly strong, feminine characters who are identified with television can be found in *It's Always Fair Weather* (1955) discussed in Chapter 3. The executives who run the network may all be men, but it seems that Madeline (Dolores Gray), the presenter of *Midnight with Madeline* and her program coordinator, Jackie (Cyd Charisse), are both powerful women in the workplace. Jackie is very successful at her work and is well able to hold her own in a man's world. Even in the masculine stronghold of Stillman's Gym, she impresses the regulars by being able to recite the rostra of famous boxers who have trained there. She shocks Ted when she demonstrates how she deals with unwanted advances by 'taking the male initiative' – kissing men squarely and fully on the lips before they can decide what to do. *It's Always Fair Weather* and *Dreamboat* depict television as a highly feminized arena.

Television and a Crisis in Femininity

Television is strongly identified as a female preserve in *My Blue Heaven* (Henry Koster, 1950). Kitty and Jack Moran (Betty Grable and Dan Dailey) are well-established radio stars for whom television provides the next step in a successful career and an opportunity to advance. For Kitty, though, a move into television can only be undertaken at the expense of having a family. Kitty's femininity is at stake as she battles with the dilemma of wanting to have children and wanting to advance her career.

Cary Scott (Jane Wyman) undergoes a crisis in femininity of her own in Douglas Sirk's *All That Heaven Allows* (1955). For Cary, a middle-aged widow and mother of two adult children, ownership of a television set comes to symbolize the end of her hopes for personal, and especially sexual, fulfilment. The people of the small New England community in which Cary lives think it proper that, if she is to remarry, it should be to someone 'like Father', as her son says: someone like Harvey. Harvey is a kindly, although somewhat dull, man who looks much older than Cary's forty-something. Cary's daughter, Kay, who is training to be a social worker and so should know better, misquotes Freud when she declares: 'As Freud says, when you reach a certain age, sex becomes incongruous. I think Harvey understands that.' This is supposed to reassure her mother of Harvey's appropriateness as a suitor. Cary is horrified by Kay's refusal to acknowledge her mother's sexuality, especially as she is struggling to come to terms with the fact that she is powerfully attracted to the hulk who prunes her trees, Ron Kirby (played by Rock Hudson with his unique brand of stoic virility). Ron is a man in every respect different from Harvey, not least because he is such a vigorous, outdoor type while Harvey is so homely.

Cary is waiting for Ron to return from a trip away, in anticipation of their relationship developing, when her married friend Sarah (Agnes Morehead) calls at her home. Cary's disappointment is evident, and she hesitates to accept Sarah's dinner invitation before making an excuse not to go. Sarah rebukes Cary for not going out more often and tells her: 'Look, Cary, you can't sit around here with nothing to do. You should at least get a television set.' Cary's reply is plain enough: 'But I don't *want* a television set.' Unmindful of her friend's wishes, Sarah tells Cary that she has 'already spoken to the television man, that charming Mr Weeks'. Their conversation is interrupted by the sound of the doorbell. In a physically awkward scene at the threshold of her home – in which Cary's embarrassment is evident – Cary lets Ron into the house and Sarah out. Television is symbolically posited as the direct opposite of what Cary so obviously *does* want – Ron Kirby.

In a later scene the 'television man' takes it upon himself to call just as Cary is leaving the house to pay a visit on Ron. Again, this scene takes place on the threshold of the family home; Mr Weeks is quite insistent that Cary should consider buying a television: 'Most of my ladies tell me that television gives them something to do with their time,' he tells her, as she shoves him aside and fairly runs off to meet Ron. In the next scene she and Ron will have sex for the first time and Cary is clearly anxious to get Mr Weeks out of the way: 'I'm not interested in television', she tells the puny little man, pushing past him: 'I'm in a terrible hurry.' Ron is once again located within the film's narrative structure as the antithesis of television which the community is trying to foist upon Cary in place of a sexual relationship.

Under pressure from the community and from her terribly self-righteous children, Cary is compelled to break off the relationship with Ron and to suppress her own sexual desire. The following Christmas the children both announce that they are leaving home and the son proclaims that he wants to sell the house. Cary, feeling that she has forsaken her own fulfilment and Ron's love for these thankless children cries as she embraces her daughter: 'Don't you see, Kay, the whole thing's been so pointless.' Kay replies, 'Oh, Mom, I'm terribly sorry... it isn't too late, if he loves you.' At this heart-rending point in the melodrama, when the audience is sure to be sobbing with Cary and Kay, the 'television man' suddenly reappears. Mr Weeks enters the living room with Cary's pompous son, Ned, carrying a television set and wishing her 'Happy Christmas!' Mr Weeks explains how to use it:

> All you have to do is turn that dial and you have all the company you want, right there on the screen. Drama! Comedy! Life's parade at your fingertips.

The camera zooms in on the television set with a ribbon at the top-right corner. The television nearly fills the frame and we see Cary's washed-out reflection in dull monochrome staring at herself in the television glass. Cary is surrounded by all the trappings of a bourgeois home; she seems to be caged in by the television set as an ascetic alternative to Ron and, as her friend had laughingly said in the scene discussed above, 'the last refuge for lonely women'. Lynne Joyrich puts it neatly when she says Cary is:

Given a typical media solution to the problems inherent in her gender and class position – consumer compensation in exchange for an active pursuit of her desire (Joyrich, 1988: 129).

Reluctantly resigned to domesticity, it at first seems that Cary will learn to live without Ron. Her doctor, however, apparently a better Freudian than her daughter, recognizes the cause of Cary's persistent headaches and counsels her to go to Ron and marry him. In the final scene she is reunited with Ron, although by now he is damaged from a fall which leaves him prone on the sofa.

The closing shot of the movie has attracted some discussion because it is a little obtuse. Cary is left to nurse Ron who now seems to be emasculated by his accident. He is lying on the couch of his mill house home and she stands behind him. The background is provided by a massive window, the dimensions of a cinema screen, through which the idyllic New England countryside is revealed in brilliant shades of red. From the inside of Ron's country home the outside world is expansive and colorful; a deer walks nonchalantly in to view. Against such a panorama it seems possible to live a full life. But is this a happy ending? Cary has Ron, but their love is tainted by his incapacity. Will he be able to repeat the sexual performance of an earlier scene before a raging fire? The uncertainty of the ending makes the resolution timorous – does Cary get what she wants or just another needy dependant like her late husband and lately absent children? Perhaps it can be better understood if we think of the view offered by the window as an alternative to the dull, monochrome introspection offered by the television in the Christmas scene. Forsaking the false views of television and bourgeois conformity, Cary finally chooses life, and life looks a lot like Technicolor cinema. To find even the hope of happiness, Cary must turn away from the bourgeois home of her family; she must move in with Ron, with his real window on the world instead of the imitation view offered by television. Here, television not only represents the inverse of a fulfilled sex life, but it also serves as a convenient cipher for the sterility of post-war small town America and its stifling effects on single, older, women. While the townsfolk seem to welcome television as something to occupy the lonely, Sirk clearly takes the stance that at best it offers only desultory distraction.

All That Heaven Allows figures television as an icon for the dramatic changes in family and sexual relationships in post-war America. When Cary refuses to conform to the community norms imposed on her, she is almost brutalized by the presentation of the television set. The melodrama uses television as a symbol around which to organize gender relations. The set is powerfully associated with an oppressive and conformist femininity which threatens to confine Cary.

The Glass Web of Gender Relations in the Television Workplace

Films of the period representing television production, such as *The Glass Web* (1953) and *A Face in the Crowd* (1957), allow for some intricate investigations of sexual politics in the workplace. In both these films, part of the corrupting power of television is its capacity to undermine traditional gender roles: in the television world they depict, the gender identities and relationships between men and women become confused. In *The Glass Web*, Edward G. Robinson plays the anti-hero Henry Hayes, a lowly researcher on *Crime of the Week*. The show dramatizes topical crimes, with the added frisson provided by the fact that, as was the norm at the time, the program is broadcast live. *The Glass Web*, investigates just how far Henry will go in his quest for the perfect story to help him in his aspiration to become a writer. Henry infuriates his fellow workers early in the film both with his obsession for precise details and his unbridled ambition. Indeed, his insistence on accuracy is marked as approaching pathology by his colleagues. Such finicky behavior, in a 1950s Hollywood bewitched by Freudian psychoanalysis, no doubt signals a strongly 'anal retentive' tendency marking Henry as effeminate, if not homosexual. The effeteness of Henry's character is reinforced by his evident interest in the fine arts. Henry has 'tutored' Paula (Kathleen Hughes) in art appreciation, among other things. When Henry asks Paula for her opinion of a painting, she gives it and he is proud of what he has taught her: 'When I first met you you didn't know an impressionist from a surrealist', he tells her. That he should gloat at such an achievement marks him as perverse within the context of anti-intellectualism which runs through the film.

Paula is a whore without a heart; she uses Henry, and anyone else she can screw, to acquire acting parts in television plays. But when Henry outlives his usefulness to her, the two have a huge fight and Paula's accusations hint at Henry's impotence: 'you've got nothing I need', she blurts out. Henry protests that he will soon be a writer on the show earning lots of money, but Paula laughs in his face:

> You're just a glorified errand boy... a funny little character with a tiny little job... you small, disgusting old man... the big brain knows all about art and music and remembers everything you ever read. As far as I'm concerned you're disgusting and a nuisance and all you ever did for me was hand me one big laugh.

When Henry discovers that the apparently very well-balanced and masculine Don – who is, unlike Henry, married – is somewhat distracted of late, he detects a chink in the armor of an otherwise unbeatable rival and decides to investigate. Henry discovers that Paula is threatening to reveal details of a liaison with Don unless he pays up. When Paula is found murdered, Don and Henry both have motives, but it is another man, Paula's estranged husband, who is arrested and charged with the crime.

Arriving at the murder scene with the investigating police officers, Henry betrays his cruel and cold ambition when he declares: 'This would be a natural for *Crime of the Week*.' Paula's murder does indeed become the subject for the television program and Henry gets his much sought after debut as writer on the show. As the relevant episode is being shot and aired, Don realizes that the level of detail is such that Henry must have been in Paula's apartment on the night of her murder and could well have perpetrated the crime – he decides to confront him. Don and his wife chase Henry through the building before cornering him in an empty television studio. Henry turns a gun on the couple and admits to them that he killed Paula:

Why not? Why not me? After that little tramp said she was too good for me, of course I killed her.

This declaration of guilt, unbeknownst to Henry, is overheard by detectives in the control booth. The police surround him; a shot rings out and Henry falls to the floor. Dying from a police officer's bullet Henry tells Don: 'I took care of most of the details, didn't I? – almost all – was perfect up until – It would make a great script, Don.' A consummate television worker to the end, Henry is concerned only with the accuracy of his illusionism: the tragic flaw in Henry's personality is that he is the product of the television business. Television is an immoral world for men and women like Henry and Paula, who prostitute themselves, lie and even murder to advance their careers. Finally, Henry and Paula are martyred to television ambition. They are weak souls whose transgressions of their assigned gender roles make them ready prey for television's 'glass web' of intrigue and illusion.

A high point of 1950s anti-TV hysteria is reached in Elia Kazan's *A Face in the Crowd* (1957) which also presents some interesting comments on gender roles in a manipulative, modern business. Unlike the story of *The Glass Web*, the two leads don't end up literally dead; but they are so spiritually spent that they might as well be. *A Face in the Crowd* is the tale of the rise and fall of Lonesome Rhodes (Andy Griffith), a man of lowly birth, first seen lying in the dirt and mess of an Arkansas jail. The woman behind the man, Marcia Jeffries (Patricia Neal), transforms the hobo into a powerful media star. We first meet Marcia in Pickett, Arkansas, as she drives on the morning *after* the July 4th holiday to the jailhouse to see if any interesting characters are being held whom she can record for her radio program, *A Face in the Crowd*. We discover Larry Rhodes among the ne'er-do-wells, covered by some old boxes sleeping off a hangover. When stirred, Larry is a beast of a man, coarse and loud, grouchy from sleeping on the floor in his clothes on a hot summer night. Like all the other jail birds, Larry is reluctant to cooperate with Marcia, but when the Sheriff agrees that he will be released the next day if he sings for her, Lonesome picks up his guitar. He spontaneously composes what is to become his theme song, the raucous 'Free Man in the Morning'. Duping him into believing the tape recorder is turned off, Marcia holds her microphone hidden in the straw basket on her lap. Marcia gives Larry his stage name, calling him 'Lonesome Rhodes' when she introduces him on her tape recorder. She stares adoringly at him as she laps up the words and songs of the vulgar country boy. Her expression is ambiguous: it may well be lust, but it could also be the look of a television executive on the make who knows when she is in the presence of a star.

We know early in the film that Marcia refuses to conform to the traditional gender role ascribed by her class and background. Her refusal to contemplate marrying the nice Sheriff is incomprehensible to her uncle, to whom she explains her goal: 'Running the best radio program in North-east Arkansas.' 'Lonesome' at first shows no evidence of having any ambition and leaves Pickett as soon as he is released from jail. Marcia pursues him, though, reversing gender norms by picking him up in her uncle's car with the promise of a plane ticket out of Pickett if he will just take a chance and feature on her morning show. On his first radio broadcast Lonesome sings 'Free Man in the Morning'. At the allotted hour, Marcia, 'the boss lady of this program', indicates that it is time for Lonesome to wind up his act. He puts down his guitar, takes off his shoes, and pulls the microphone close to him and talks privately to his radio audience:

> Shucks, I's jus' getting ready to add on a verse about being a *free woman* in the morning. I bet a whole load of you dream about that sometimes. With all those breakfast dishes piling up in the sink and them cranky husbands to get off to work. Aint it a shame the way they get on at you about every little thing just 'cos they aint got the gumption to take it out on the boss. I hate to talk against my own kind, but I never have seen a man yet can appreciate how hard you women has to work. Now, they think running a little water over a dish is all there is to it. They aint never seen you cleaning the grease out of the sink, or wiping out of the oven the beef gravy or the apple juice that sizzles over the side of the dish onto the grill.

'How does he know that?' one listener asks herself as she scrubs the oven. Is it any wonder that letters flood into the radio station declaring that, 'they love his voice; they love his guitar; they love his ideas'. Lonesome has made a declaration of independence for women and becomes a great hit as a consequence.

When Marcia accompanies Lonesome to Memphis for his first television appearance, his feminization begins when he has to put on stage make-up:

Lonesome: If I'd known you were gonna put lipstick on me I'd never have come.
Marcia: Stop complaining. You look beautiful.

Television advances the narrative's reversal of the classical musical trope in which a young woman is transformed by an impresario; here Marcia makes over Lonesome *en route* to his becoming a temperamental star.

Marcia and Lonesome are both transformed by working in television. Lonesome's lust for women increases to bestial proportions and he tries to ascribe his infidelities to television, he tells Marcia:

It's dangerous – the power. You've got to be a Saint to stand up to the power that little box can give you.

Nonetheless, when Lonesome proposes to her Marcia deludes herself into thinking he will actually marry her. When Marcia goes to meet Lonesome at the airport, she fully expects him to declare that he has finalized his divorce from the first Mrs Rhodes and is free to fulfil his promise. She becomes distraught when Lonesome alights from the plane announcing his marriage to Betty-Lou (Lee Remick), a teenage cheerleader. Marcia understands why he has married the blonde bimbo instead of her:

Betty-Lou's your public. All wrapped up with young ribbons into one cute little package. She's the logical culmination of the great twentieth century love affair between Lonesome Rhodes and his mass audience.

By the end of the film Lonesome has become a power-infatuated demagogue and Marcia an embittered spinster. Ultimately, the responsibility falls upon Marcia to destroy the monster she has helped to create. Off air during a recording, Lonesome jokes about how he is duping the public and how:

> This whole country's just like my flock of sheep... they're more stupid than I am so I gotta think for them.

At the end of the broadcast the theme music is cued to drown out the studio sound, while the image continues to show Lonesome chatting with his cronies. Marcia rushes into the control room and turns on the studio microphones so that the audience at home can hear how Lonesome insults them for the entertainment of the stage hands.

> Morons... I can make them eat dog food... a cage full of guinea pigs... good night, you stupid idiots... they're a bunch of trained seals...

Marcia, deranged with anger and rejection, spreads herself across the mixing desk so that the engineers cannot prevent the audience from hearing Lonesome. Immediately, Lonesome is ruined. From everywhere around the country viewers are appalled. Nobody turns up to the party he was to host and Lonesome ends up reeling in drunkenness and hurling racial abuse at the waiters. Television and Marcia have revealed the true nature of the monster they have made.

Working in television is a dangerous pursuit for men and women because it threatens the security of clearly defined gender differences. The female lead characters in *The Glass Web* and *A Face in the Crowd*, Paula and Marcia respectively, are strong women working in the largely male environment of television. In order to succeed these women have to be aggressive and ambitious. They challenge the gender role they are expected to take and corrupt weak-willed men like Henry and Lonesome. Paula pays with her life; Marcia forgoes sexual fulfilment and becomes an embittered spinster. Television may offer women employment, but they risk losing their femininity if they do so. The men are also altered by television, becoming emasculated: Henry is effete; Lonesome narcissistic. Television is depicted as responsible for playing havoc with gender identities in 1950s America.

In the 1950s television was not only derided by the Hollywood cinema for being a form of mass culture, but, more significantly, because of its femininity. The identification of television
with 'feminine' occurred as the cinema struggled to claim the
terrain of masculine high art for itself, identifying television
with the low brow and the feminine in the process. Whether
portraying television audiences or television workers, the Hollywood movies discussed above show television as contributing
to a reconfiguration of gender in post-war America.

5

JOBS FOR THE BOYS: BRITISH CINEMA, THE BBC AND COMMERCIAL TELEVISION

.

In the last chapter we saw that television was maligned as a 'feminine' mass medium in the US in the 1950s. But while the expansion of television in America was seen to be detrimental to the cinema, in the UK the growth of television was welcomed by most film companies as a potential new outlet for their material. The BBC monopoly on television was effectively ended with the introduction of ITV in 1955, as we saw in Chapter 2. At the time that the American film industry was damning the medium that threatened to outstrip it, their British counterparts were successfully competing for contracts to operate the new regional commercial stations. In Britain, television offered the promise of new opportunities for work to an industry that had spent most of its history on the brink of collapse. The identity of television promulgated in British films of this era was consequently significantly different from the American portrayals discussed in the previous chapter. The technogensis of television in the UK focuses on television as a source of employment.

British Cinema and 'Television Consciousness'

The debates in the 1950s and early 1960s around the introduction of a second, commercial, television service were closely followed by the British film industry. For British cinema, as for society at large, the decade 1953–63 was a period of 'intense TV-consciousness' (Barr, 1986: 206), as is evident in the number of

British films made during this period that address television. In films as disparate as Anthony Asquith's psychological thriller *Libel* (1959), the Norman Wisdom comedy, *Man of the Moment* (John Paddy Carstairs, 1955) and Mario Zampi's *The Naked Truth*, television provides the narrative motivation for the presentation of performances of various kinds. For example, Mario Zampi casts Peter Sellers as Wee Sonny MacGregor, a television variety show host in *The Naked Truth* (1957). Television is used here as a means of establishing character and providing a narrative justification for Peter Sellers to impersonate a wide range of characters. In *Libel* (Anthony Asquith, 1959) Jeffrey Buckenham (Paul Massie) is drinking in a pub when he happens to see a BBC documentary in which Richard Dimbleby is being given a tour of a British stately home, by its owner Sir Mark Loddon (Dirk Bogarde) and his wife. Buckenham recognizes Loddon as one of the men with whom he was a prisoner-of-war but he grows more disturbed as he watches. The intensity of Buckenham's gaze as he watches Loddon on television draws us into the narrative.

Television initiates the plot of *Libel*, and provides the closure to the absurdly inane *Man of the Moment*. Here, Norman Wisdom plays a lowly clerk at the Foreign Office who becomes embroiled in an international diplomatic crisis over rights to the Polynesian island of Mahula inhabited by the Tawaki. Through a complicated trope of mistaken identity typical of Wisdom's characters, the clown endears himself to the Tawaki people, and is invited to appear on the television discussion programme *Town Topics*. True to the formula of the Wisdom *oeuvre*, the climactic scene is a chase; in this instance a romp through numerous BBC studios disrupting broadcasts and rehearsals before Norman finally ends up sitting in the television chef's soufflé bowl. The television studios provide a locale where chaos can reign, making it the ideal forum for Norman Wisdom's anarchic slapstick humor.

The films discussed above, and others, show the intense television consciousness of the period to which Barr referred. Barr also claims that television was represented as a threat in British films of the period. One film which is often cited as a vicious anti-television polemic is *Meet Mr Lucifer* (Anthony Pélissier, 1953). The film shows television as the agent of Satan, although, when the devil in question is Stanley Holloway dressed in a pantomime outfit, one would be foolish to take him too seriously. Stanley Holloway plays the roles of both Mr Lucifer and Mr Hollingsworth, an aging actor whose current stage role in a Christmas pantomime requires him to struggle with a fairy to determine the fate of the shipwrecked Robinson Crusoe. The old-fashioned repertory company is playing to empty houses in a decrepit theater; television provides a convenient scapegoat to explain their lack of success. Hollingsworth espouses his anti-television beliefs to the gathered ensemble in the pub:

Hallucination! That's what I call it, mass hallucination!

he declares as he gets increasingly drunk. Arriving back at the theater, stumbling with inebriation, he continues to mumble on about television. As he alights in the trap door to make his entrance on stage he bangs his head and comes round to find himself in Hell where he is greeted by the devil, played by himself:

I was angry about something,

Hollingsworth tells his alter ego.

Television, that's what it was. Television – it's an instrument of the devil.

Mr Lucifer informs Mr Hollingsworth that television is his latest mechanical device, but complains that:

It isn't working too well... It just isn't making enough people miserable enough.

Hollingsworth is dispatched to perform the devil's work and installs a television set for old Mr Pedelty (Joseph Tomelty) who has been given the set as a retirement present. Television provides companionship for the old man whose neighbors and passers-by congregate in his living room to watch television and dance along to the music programs with him. As owner of a television set, Mr Pedelty becomes host to all kinds of visitors, including a group of American sailors and a French onion seller, giving television viewing a flavor of inclusiveness and internationalism. *Meet Mr Lucifer* presents some images of television that are quite charming: the rag tag group of children dancing in the street to the tunes emanating from Pedelty's home presents a delightful picture of television's capacity to create community (see Figure 5.1). In the longer run, however, owning a television set has malign consequences: Pedelty's generous hospitality is abused to the point where lack of money obliges the old man to sell his set and his fair-weather friends abandon him. The set becomes the property of the nice young couple upstairs, Kitty and Jim (Peggy Cummins and Jack Watling), and before long their happy marriage is destroyed. Jim passes on the set to a colleague, Hector McDonald (Gordon Jackson) and this lonely bachelor begins to indulge in dangerous romantic fantasies involving television's Miss Lonely Hearts (Kay Kendall). As this particular television set is passed from one household to another, the lives of its owners are ruined and Mr Lucifer takes the credit. But the devil is a fickle trickster who soon tires of television. At the end of the film Mr Lucifer declares that he has found a new means of ruining lives. The devil's latest contraption, 3-D, is as likely to keep audiences out of the theater as television and is consequently equally as fearful to the old man of the stage. *Meet Mr Lucifer* is an attack on new media that take people away from the theater, and is equally as fearful of television as the cinema.

The BBC and the Cinema

In the UK, the license-fee-supported BBC station was the sole provider of television until the mid-1950s. Most British films made during the 1950s that address television do so in the recognition that programs are provided on the public service model. Television and the BBC are synonymous in many British films from the earlier part of the 1950s such as *The Body Said No* (Val Guest, 1950) and *Simon and Laura* (Muriel Box, 1956). Each film includes a look behind the scenes of television and thus contributes towards demystifying the processes of television (or, to be more exact, BBC) production.

Figure 5.1 An example of the community building that television can perform. Here children dance in the street to the music coming from Old Mr Pedelty's television set in *Meet Mr Lucifer* (Anthony Pélissier, 1953)

The Body Said No (1950) was written and directed by Val Guest, who also directed *The Quatermass Experiment* (discussed in Chapter 8), *Expresso Bongo* (considered in Chapter 6) and some fifty other films between 1942 and 1982. *The Body Said No* opens with an interior of a living room in which a television is transmitting *Cabaret Round Up*. Mikki (Yolande Donlan) wakes up to realize that she has dozed off in front of the television after transmissions have stopped for the night. While in the adjacent room she hears a man's voice emanating from the television set:

Now you know what to do and how to do it.

She returns to the living room and sees on the television two men talking in the studio, apparently discussing a murder. One man tells the other:

Keep the gun out of sight until the actual moment when Michael Rennie is out of sight and let him have it.

Convinced she has overheard a plot to kill the actor Michael Rennie (playing himself), Mikki attempts to alert the police and to warn Rennie of the death threat. The young woman is not taken seriously and her warnings go unheeded.

A cabaret singer by profession, Mikki has occasion to go to Alexandra Palace to perform her number, a typically homely British song, '(I Have my Feller, he's got) The Coldest Feet in the World'. When her dance is over, she recognizes Michael Rennie in the audience with John Sutherland, one of the 'plotters' she had earlier seen discussing the murder. After much ado, all is finally revealed when Sutherland shows Mikki and Rennie his *Television Demonstration Film* which includes a rehearsal of *Backstage Alibi* – a television film in which Rennie's character is shot. Of course, it was this demonstration film that Mikki had mistaken for a live transmission. The machinations of some aspects of television are revealed through the plot of *The Body Said No* which allows us to go inside Alexandra Palace to witness the recording of a cabaret program and to learn about test broadcasts. The plot is based on the premise of a well-meaning, but rather simple minded, female not understanding modern technology. Mikki is a character who frequently gets the wrong end of lots of sticks; little wonder, then, that television should confuse her. Television is constructed as a technology that needs to be explained more fully (especially to foolish women). The BBC is portrayed as the ideal, indeed the only, institution able to do this.

Simon and Laura (Muriel Box, 1956) is based on a play by Alan Melville and brooks no alternative but that television and the BBC are one. Simon and Laura Foster (Peter Finch and Kay Kendall) are a couple of stage actors in a marriage of two enormous egos, on the verge of divorce and out of work. When they are asked to play a happily married couple in a continuous serial for the BBC, the money is sufficient to persuade them to bury the hatchet. *Simon and Laura* derives its dramatic interest from the tension between the 'television' couple's idyllically happy marriage, and the violently argumentative and casually unfaithful relationship endured by the 'real' Simon and Laura Foster.

The BBC comes in for some gentle, good-natured, ribbing in *Simon and Laura*. David Prentice (Ian Carmichael), the serial's producer, represents the well-meaning silliness of the BBC, as for example in the way he refers to people in the BBC establishment by the initials of their position: thus not only is there 'DG' (Director General) but also 'CT' (Controller of Television) and 'DTD' (Director of Television Drama). Despite his pompous demeanour, the CT (Richard Wattis) does not take television terribly seriously. When he introduces the idea of a continuous serial to some fellow producers he tells them:

> Those of us who have been in television since the beginning realize that nothing succeeds like a series or a serial. I almost said, 'nothing succeeds like excess'. It's rather like advertising. Repeat a thing often enough and everybody has to buy it, whether they really like it or not. In fact, the D.G. sometimes says, jokingly, of course, that if one televises a few pages of the London telephone directory regularly for five or six weeks, one would gain an average audience of over ten million.

The recitation of the DG's 'joking' comments affirms the low regard in which television is held by the higher echelons of the BBC for whom radio remained the favored medium.

When his agent first proposes the idea of taking 'a wonderful job' at the BBC, Simon does not disguise his contempt:

> Television? And you call that a wonderful job? Ha! ha! ha! Three weeks rehearsal; hardly enough money for your fare to the studio; a technical breakdown in the middle of your big scene and no repeat performance! No thank you!

Before they embark on their new careers, Simon and Laura seek the advice of a couple of renowned television personalities. Gilbert Harding, 'Britain's first major television personality' (Medhurst, 1991: 60), renowned for his wit and expertise in television parlor games, is in his club when Simon approaches for advice. Harding tells him:

> My poor friend, my poor Simon. Do you know what happens to you when you allow yourself to be regularly exhibited in that glass rectangle? Well, I'll tell you. You become public property. Your face, electronically distorted, is huddled round and gawped at by three quarters of the population of the United Kingdom. And within a month, every wrinkle, every wart and pustule, has become part of our British way of life...

Laura is at the hairdresser's when she seeks advice from an equally famous television personality, Isobel Barnett. The woman's advice is considerably more pithy:

> My dear, for a woman on television, only three things *really* matter: hair, jewellery, clothes.

Perhaps this is meant ironically, but it is played straight enough. Gilbert Harding and Isobel Barnett are both television personalities from the pre-commercial era who excelled at the kind of parlor game antics that now only exist on Radio 4 in programs such as *Just a Minute*. They appear in cameo roles as the known face of British television and their presence adds a topical authenticity to the film's portrayal of television.

Simon and Laura displays an ambivalence towards the audience for television. The Fosters do not possess a television set and when David asks why not, Simon replies that, since he can't watch his own show (which is broadcast live), what's the point? Watching television is evidently not for people like the Fosters. A single working-class family stands in for those who do watch television, comprising mother, father, grandmother and two children. Their reactions serve as a barometer of *Simon and Laura*'s success: at first the family are indifferent to the new serial (grandma, for one, is more interested in the boxing); later they become engrossed before becoming bored. But our central characters have no contact with the class of people who actually watch television, and there is a world of difference between those who make television programs and those for whom they are intended. This is especially evident when Laura appears on *In Town Tonight* with her namesake, the winner of a competition. This 'ordinary' viewer is risible for her nervousness and awe struck attitude towards the television star.

Simon and Laura becomes a rather twee sex comedy as misunderstandings grow about the relationships between the central couple and a secondary romantic pair, David and the show's writer Janet Honeyman (Muriel Pavlow). Finally, the men and women of these two central couples are estranged from one another and it is television technology that provides the means by which the couples can be reunited once again. The mischievous boy actor, Timmy (Clive Parritt), in alliance with the Foster's butler, Wilson (Maurice Denham), arrange for cameras and sound to be turned on when Simon and David are having a heart-to-heart on the studio floor during a break in rehearsals (see Figure 5.2). The scene is relayed to a viewing room to which the women are summoned by the two Pucks so that Laura and Janet see and hear the men declaring their love for them and rush down for a closing embrace. This final scene is played in a terribly self-conscious manner and its awkward slow motion betrays a curiously English hesitancy about happy endings and physical contact. *Simon and Laura* shows the institution of television (the BBC) as benignly ridiculous. The technology of television can be used positively, though, providing the opportunity for the expression of genuine emotions and ultimately allowing the protagonists to recognize their true loves.

Figure 5.2 Laura and Janet find out the truth about Simon and David's feelings as the men's conversation on the studio floor is relayed to them in *Simon and Laura* (Muriel Box, 1955)

The Other Side and Jobs for the Boys

With the introduction of Independent Television to the broadcasting scene, the BBC could no longer stand in for television in its entirety. Commercial television came to signal fun and prosperity in British popular culture, and films of the late 1950s and early 1960s delighted in showing television advertising as a mildly amusing symbol of modernity.

The Arthur Askey vehicle *Make Mine a Million* (Lance Comfort, 1959) draws playfully on the contrasts between the stuffiness of 'NTV' (National TeleVision – a thinly disguised BBC) and the more relaxed manner of the entertainment orientated 'TAA' (a cipher for the Independent Television Association). The divisive British class system is represented in the conflict of style between the two different systems. The BBC is depicted as the same over-bureaucratic, pompous and elitist organization that it was in *Band Waggon* (discussed in Chapter 3), which, like *Make Mine A Million*, starred Arthur Askey and was produced by Jack Hylton. As in the earlier film, *Make Mine a Million* lambastes the BBC for its neglect of popular taste. This time, though, it is a lack of *advertisements* for which the BBC is ridiculed, rather than band music. In his autobiography Arthur Askey explains that, 'The country was fascinated by the commercials shown on ITV at this time, so it was quite a novelty' (Askey, 1975: 167). Askey plays Arthur Ashton whose old variety act has been made obsolete by television, compelling him to work as a humble make-up artist at NTV. Arthur asks his landlady:

> *Arthur*: Do you know what's wrong with Television?
> *Landlady*: You're not in it.
> *Arthur*: How did you guess?
> *Landlady*: You told me.

The weariness in the landlady's voice indicates that this exchange is well rehearsed. Sid Gibson (Sid James) is an entrepreneur trying to make an honest living by marketing Bonko, 'The Wonder Detergent'. Prospective customers in the street market where Sid peddles his wares are uninterested in the product:

It can't be much good – it hasn't been advertised on the telly,

one shopper tells him. When Arthur, the frustrated broadcaster, is introduced to Sid, putative advertiser, they hatch a plot to interrupt a 'national' variety programme with a placard declaring:

> It's Magic
> BONKO!
> The Wonder Detergent

In the Directors' Viewing Room, a few moments prior to this interception, the gathered executives had been commenting on the quality of their broadcast as:

> A triumph of good taste... unmarred by unsavoury interruptions.

When the Bonko advertisement appears they are enraged:

> Heads shall roll for this!

declares the Director General (Clive Morton). The rebellious insurrection causes a terrific stir: the newspapers declare it a:

> 'TELEVISION SENSATION'

and claim:

> 'Pirate TV Battle Delights Viewers'

The NTV switchboard is inundated with telephone calls from viewers wanting to know if they stock Bonko. The newspapers and the public delight in the audacious scam pulled off by Bonko's marketers.

Nowhere are people more pleased than at the rival station, TAA, which is a rich contrast to NTV. The lobby of the executive suite is plushly decorated with pot plants, drapes, even a statue of a naked goddess; three women, apparently also for decorative purposes, mill around; cool organ music sets the

Figure 5.3   Arthur Askey and his chums broadcast illegal advertising on the BBC, but here the BBC gets the last laugh at Askey's expense in *Make Mine a Million* (Lance Comfort, 1959)

scene of a relaxed, hip, and feminized environment. The Chief
Executive (Martin Benson) sits behind an ornate desk smoking
a cigar. When his secretary brings him the morning papers he
asks her: 'Be a sweetie, get me a brandy, will you?' A second
executive is eyeing up a woman who is posing for him in a
tight dress:

> That's very nice, darling, very nice indeed. Now, be a good
> girl, leave your telephone number and send the next one in,
> will you?

And he pats her on the bottom as he escorts her out of the office.
A third executive speaks with an American accent and has
money as his primary concern; his advice on learning about the
fiasco at NTV is to recommend the purchase of shares in Bonko.
Booze, sex and money are the three things that drive the TAA
station in this caricature of commercial television – even the
acronym TAA (Tits And Ass) exploits American slang. All three
of the executives at the commercial station find the Bonko scam
very amusing: 'haven't had such a good laugh for years',
exclaims one.

Over at NTV, the *other* channel, they are slower to appreciate
the humor, but quicker to identify the culprit: they trace the
caper to Arthur by the next morning. On arrival at work, Arthur
is hauled before the Board of Directors and subjected to a veri-
table interrogation by the Director General and his acolytes.
Presiding over the occasion from a raised chair, flanked on either
side by stony faced executives, the Director General looks down
on Arthur.

Director General:	Don't you realize what you've done to the pattern of National Television?
Arthur:	Dropped a stitch, I suppose.
Director General:	And it'll take at least three poetry readings and a visit to Glyndebourne to fix it up again.

This ridicule of National Television is especially effective in
contrast with the preceding scene discussed above. There is an
easy atmosphere in the 'commercial' board room and even an

American speaker: they use slang freely, drink from exaggerat-
edly large brandy glasses and have attractive women hanging
around for no particular reason. In the NTV boardroom the drab
bureaucrats speak in the clipped tones of BBC received pronun-
ciation; they look as if they could use a good drink and although
there is a woman on the Board, she is a plain looking 'doctor'
conforming to the stereotype of the spinster and hardly an object
of sexual attraction.

When the sabotage is discovered Arthur is dismissed from
National Television. Now he and his chums turn to intercepting
the outside broadcasts for which the BBC was so renowned with
sponsored messages. They build a successful business disrupting broadcasts of major sporting events. They interrupt BBC
coverage of Ascot with an announcement at the end of the race:

And here's another winner – Bonko.
You can bet on Bonko.

During a broadcast of *Swan Lake* from the highbrow Edinburgh
festival, the gang manages to insert an advertisement for their
new client, Slap Happy Cake Mix; Askey sneaks backstage and
does a turn, right in the middle of the ballet. The comedy
derives from disrupting the straight-laced formality of the
cultural form favored by the stuffy NTV with popular jokes and
performances. In the process of undermining the power of
public television, our rebels also help ordinary small businessmen like Sid to sell their products. *Make Mine a Million*
condones piracy as a legitimate response to inequality of access
to the airwaves.

In *Band Waggon*, released while all television services were
suspended for the war, the rebels are finally incorporated into
the television industry and given employment (see Chapter 3
for further discussion of this film). The same trope gives closure
to *Make Mine a Million*. Arthur apprehends a dangerous criminal, on air, during one of his illegal broadcasts, and is immediately declared a 'public hero'. NTV is honor bound to reward
Arthur with his own television show. Sid, too, becomes
poacher-turned-gamekeeper when he is made a Director at
TAA, in acknowledgment of his excellent sales acumen. The
happy resolution of *Make Mine a Million* centers around the

success of the protagonists in acquiring secure employment in the television industry.

There are many examples of British films depicting advertising as amusing and entertaining. *Dentist on the Job* (C.M. Pennington-Richard, 1961), for example, is a British comedy in the mold of the early *Carry On* or *Doctor* films. (This film was apparently released in Germany under the title *Carry on Television*.) *Dentist on the Job* was produced by Bertram Ostrer at Shepperton, where television work was keeping the film studio busy. David Cookson (Bob Monkhouse) and Ronnie Stevens (Brian Dexter) play two lackluster student dentists who are tricked into giving up dentistry to work in the promotional department of Proudfoot Industries endorsing toothpaste in television advertisements. When their jobs are threatened, David and Ronnie join forces with ex-con Sam Field (Kenneth Connors) to pull off an audacious promotional stunt. The gang successfully scheme to have their jingle for New Dreem toothpaste switched with an address by the President of the United States of America and launched on a space satellite. They exploit the latest communications technology to get their advertisement transmitted across the globe for the next seven years. Despite the illegality of their actions, the gang are lauded for having created 'the greatest commercial in history', and are duly rewarded with secure jobs at Proudfoot Industries. Commercial television is fun, but it is not maligned in these popular British movies.

The introduction of commercial television brought attention to the already bifurcated class system of Britain by introducing a popular alternative to the rather elitist BBC. Two films released at the end of the decade parody the political and social divide in Britain in the 1950s through reference to television: *Left, Right and Centre* and *I'm All Right Jack*. *Left, Right and Centre* tells the tale of a local election campaign fought between Stella Stoker (Patricia Bredin), the left-wing daughter of an ardent trades unionist, and the staunch Conservative, Bob Wilcott (Ian Carmichael), nephew of the local Lord of the Manor and, coincidentally, a renowned television personality. The two main political parties are delightfully caricatured through the campaign managers, Bert Glimmer (Eric Barker) for the Labour Party, and Harding-Pratt (Richard Wattis) for the Conservatives.

Early in the film Wilcott appears on a television panel game show, *What On Earth Was That*, a parody of the long-running television program, *Animal, Vegetable, Mineral*, with Gilbert Harding in a cameo role as himself. When Wilcott announces his candidature for parliament, Harding inquires about Wilcott's opponent.

Harding: Miss Stoker? Has she ever appeared on Television?
Wilcott: Not that I know of.
Harding: Well, that fixes her, doesn't it, ay? You'll win at a canter. I always say that the party that wins the next election is the one that raises its flag to the television mast.

Stella Stoker does not watch television, 'not since Dad threw the set out of the window', and is unimpressed by Wilcott's television fame. When Wilcott shows off about his television appearances, telling Stella, 'My name is familiar in every house', she is quite scathing: 'You could say the same for almost any detergent.' Television is dismissed as an irrelevant frippery by the staid Miss Stoker. Of course, the two protagonists become romantically involved, despite the intervention of their campaign managers.

Media coverage of the election is a recurring theme of *Left, Right and Centre*, with television taking the bill as the 'Centre' of the title. The apathetic electorate take little interest in the campaign, or its pundits, and the television crews have a struggle to summon any enthusiasm from the constituents: the television journalists are the only people who seem to care about the outcome of the election.

I'm All Right Jack also satirizes the divisive British class system, portraying the trades union movement as stubborn defenders of idleness and intransigence and British industrialists as unscrupulous and corrupt. Peter Sellers plays Fred Kite, the stubborn union man, to Ian Carmichael's upper-class twit, Stanley Windrush. Here television also takes up the center ground, providing the forum for a showdown between the two parties in a television studio. Television provides the location for a free-for-all which gives some closure to the otherwise irreconcilable class differences the film draws out.

It has often been assumed that British films of the post-war era are singular in attacking television. In fact this is far from the case. *Meet Mr Lucifer* is more of an assault on fads and on the way people are manipulated by the new – it ends on the devil moving on to the new pastures provided by 3-D cinema. *Simon and Laura* does little more than make ribaldry out of the antics of the BBC. Even when television advertising is the subject of a film, as in *Dentist on the Job*, it is treated as an excuse for high frolics. British films of the 1950s and early 1960s show commercial television as a lively alternative to the stuffy BBC. In the British popular imagination at this time advertising symbolized economic well-being and liberation from the specter of poverty which hung over most Britons until the 1960s. Commercial television marked the beginning of truly popular television in Britain. The hegemony of the BBC over broadcasting was ended, and the cinema industry, so long excluded from broadcasting, were frequently owners of the new television channels. The British cinema industry had every reason to be positive about the expansion of British television in the late 1950s and early 1960s.

The idea of advertising as harmless fun caught the public imagination and contributed to the cultural revolution of the 1960s. The pop movie – with its promotional undercurrents – was a manifestation of the next stage in the complex relationship between British cinema and commercialism and is the subject of the next chapter.

6

POP AND THE BOX:
YOUTH, TELEVISION, MUSIC
AND MOVIES IN THE 1950s
AND 1960s

The post-war boom brought technological and social changes that had enormous impacts on cultural industries, their products and consumers. A major component in these changes was the expansion in the youth market and the identification of young people as 'teenagers': a demographic category with unique social and cultural desires and resources. If the film and television industries were to survive this revolution they would have to cater to this new audience. Hollywood developed the 'teen exploitation' movie in an attempt to woo a younger crowd. The British cinema also strove to cater to an audience which was at once 'juvenile' and 'adult'. Thus, although the 1950s and 60s are typically described by film scholars as the heyday of Social Realism, the British films that were most successful at the box office were the puerile Carry On films, which began with *Carry On Sergeant* (Gerald Thomas, 1958), Hammer horror films and the rock 'n' roll influenced movies. The music industry was able to cash in on the teenage revolution most successfully: the cinema in Britain and the US responded with a new kind of product: the pop movie.

Popular Music in Britain

The 1960s were a time of increasing interest in working-class tastes and pleasures in Britain. The Cultural Revolution of that decade overthrew the old order in all areas of the arts. Pop Art declared its assault on old-fashioned gallery art; the theater was radicalized by kitchen sink dramas and the world of music publishing and recording was being swamped by rock 'n' roll. The new cultural world was young, brash and iconoclastic.

Music publishing and performance had a close, although periodically fraught, relationship with film since the coming of sound. Musical performances were a key part of television output from the earliest experimental days, as we saw in Chapter 3. There was a huge expansion of the popular music industry in the late 1950s and 1960s; Simon Frith estimates that between 1955 and 1975 the output of the British record industry tripled (Frith, 1983). The enormous expansion of the music industry demanded the reconfiguration of many relationships in the cultural arena. The relationships among cinema, music and television were dramatically altered in the 1960s.

Music was a central part of television programming from the very first transmissions and during the 1950s the variety show became a mainstay of popular television output in Britain and the United States. The popular shows Val Parnell's *Saturday Night at the London Palladium* and *Toast of the Town* (later *The Ed Sullivan Show*) became national institutions in Britain and the US respectively. During the rock 'n' roll revolution of the late 1950s and early 1960s, pop music shows like *Six-Five Special, Oh Boy!* and *Ready, Steady, Go* in Britain helped to focus public taste and became invaluable auxiliaries to popular music promotion and advertising.

The British Pop Movie

The BBC's *Six-Five Special*, which ran from 1957 to 1958, pioneered popular music television for young people. The general interest program was presented by Pete Murray and Josephine Douglas, and featured performances by popular entertainers as part of its magazine format. In the 1958 film, *Six-*

Five Special (Alfred Shaughnessy), an element of 'adult' entertainment is added in the opening scene by showing Ann (Diane
Todd) singing in the bath before going to bed. This allows for
a level of nudity which would not be permitted on television,
especially on the early evening slot occupied by *Six-Five Special*.
We are treated to lingering shots of Ann's legs when she gets
out of the bath and of her room-mate, Judy (Avril Leslie), in a
black bra. The girls discuss their determination to 'get out of a
rut and into the groove'; they decide to leave their home in the
North and take the 6.05pm train for London. The story, such as
it is, chronicles their journey to the Smoke aboard a train coincidentally packed with popular artists including teen idol Jim
Dale, the comedy duo Mike and Bernie Winters and jazz artists
Johnny Dankworth and Cleo Laine. As the two girls walk
through the train they come upon various people apparently
rehearsing for their forthcoming television performances. Of the
many performers featured most are passengers, only two have
jobs on the train – these are two black singers, Victor Soverall
and Jimmy Lloyd, who play chefs on the train. Ann and Judy
watch through the serving hatch, as if they have caught a spontaneous non-professional performance, as the two sing while
they go about their work preparing food. The performer who
is offered as a role model to Ann is not Victor Soverall or Jimmy
Lloyd, but Jim Dale. The girls are listening to their hero on the
radio when Judy asks Ann:

> Know how he got his break? That young man walked into an
> agent's office, said: 'Hello, I sing'; sang, there and then; went
> on TV and there he is – a star.

Ann finds that her opportunity to break into the big time is not
much more difficult to come by than Jim Dale's (see Figure 6.1).
When she finally plucks up the courage to sing for Pete Murray
and Jo Douglas, who also happen to be aboard the train, Ann
is immediately given the chance to appear on the television
show. The second half of the film shows the television program,
Six-Five Special, being recorded and comprises a string of addi-
tional popular performers.

Six-Five Special has much in common with the early revue
pictures such as *Elstree Calling* (discussed in Chapter 3). It

Figure 6.1   Judy and Ann (Avril Leslie and Diane Todd) dream about getting an appearance on television to make it big in pop music while their idol, Jim Dale, looks on in *Six-Five Special* (Alfred Shaughnessy, 1958)

features a wide range of acts, including *jazz* (Desmond Lane, Johnny Dankworth, Cleo Laine and the John Barry Seven); *pop* (Petula Clark and Lonnie Donegan); and *spirituals*, such as the King Brothers' spiritual number, 'Hand Me Down My Walking Cane'. For the finale, Dickie Valentine – 'The King of Dixieland' – performs with a female choir including our young hopeful. One of the most interesting things about this film is the sheer diversity of acts included. Such a film would be inconceivable a few years later, when the music market and its audience would become much fragmented. *Six-Five Special* serves as an extended promotion for the television series and for the many stars included. Its only concession to narrative is in its use of the Hollywood musical device of the naif's quest for success.

Although the television series *Six-Five Special* was a successful mix of music, entertainment and more educational items, the BBC considered the music content too high and allowed its producer, Jack Good, to leave and make a rival program for the British commercial station ABC in 1958 (Hill, 1991). Cliff Richard began his television career on *Oh Boy!* and soon became a regular featured artist. Already an established pop star following his hit, 'Living Doll', and with a film role as a troubled teenager in *Serious Charge* under his belt, Richard was cast as the star in *Expresso Bongo* (Val Guest, 1959). Richard's vehicle presents a considerably more complex view of the British pop scene of the 1950s than *Six-Five Special*. Sir Cliff Richard may cut a very wholesome image today, not least for being one of Britain's most famous Christians, but in *Expresso Bongo* he plays a rebellious young man who hates his mother and doesn't blanche at sleeping with the much older recording artist, Dixie Collins (Yolande Donlan) in order to advance his career. Christian songs seem to have been a more central part of the pop music industry in the 1950s and 60s (we have already noted that they feature in *Six-Five Special*), but it is surprising when the hip and streetwise 'Bongo' Herbert declares himself a Christian and sings 'The Shrine on the Second Floor' in *Expresso Bongo*.

The cultural diversity of London's Soho is a key theme of *Expresso Bongo*. Bongo Herbert's Christianity is unequivocally stated and several other characters are clearly identified as Jewish. The film's central protagonist, Johnny Jackson (Laurence Harvey), has a stereotypical – if intermittent – Jewish accent which he uses to cajole and flatter favors from the Soho community among whom he lives and plies his trade as a talent agent. Several of the peripheral players also speak with heavy middle European accents including the music publisher Mayer (Meirer Tzelniker), Leon (Eric Pohlman) the manager of the delicatessen and Kakky (Martin Miller) the old film producer. When Kakky tells Johnny:

Personally, I would never compromise myself by making pictures for television,

we sense that even he doesn't believe his own words. In *Expresso Bongo* everyone has to compromise themselves; most are whores of one kind or another and all are quite unabashed about it. The prostitutes and erotic dancers live and work alongside the musicians, impresarios and film-makers: the sex industry and the cultural industries entwined in a backbiting lock hold. Soho offers a whole panoply of cultural technologies: popular and classical music; television; the cinema; variety; strip shows. Kakky, always hustling for money for his latest film idea, even brags: 'I was the man who introduced the bubble bath into show business!'

Expresso Bongo distances itself from television, for example, by showing how everyone is obliged to clean up their act when the television cameras appear. When a BBC documentary team comes to film the erotic dance show at the InTime Theatre where Maisie works, the women are obliged to cover themselves up because, as the owner of the club tells them:

You didn't expect to go on television in the buff, did ya? This is a decent, respectable country.

In *Expresso Bongo* television seeks out the salacious and then sanitizes it for the viewers at home. Gilbert Harding, once again, personifies the respectable face of British broadcasting as the director and presenter of the documentary program *Cosmorama* (Harding also appears in *Simon and Laura* and *Left, Right and Centre* discussed in Chapter 5). Johnny introduces himself to Harding, hoping to get some exposure for Maisie (Sylvia Syms) his girlfriend and a stripper at the club (see Figure 6.2). The streetwise agent tells 'Mr Television':

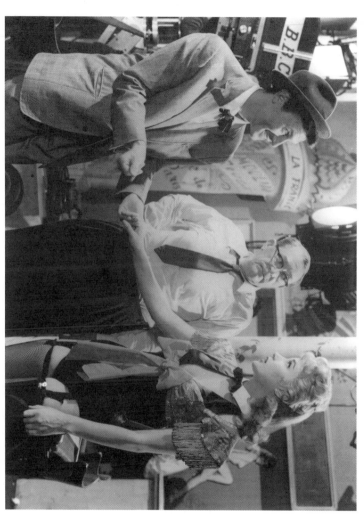

Figure 6.2 Gilbert Harding plays a BBC documentary presenter taking an anthropological trip to Soho to check out the kids in *Expresso Bongo* (Val Guest, 1959). Here he is introduced to Maisie (Sylvia Sims), an erotic dancer, by her agent and boyfriend Johnny Jackson

I just wanted to say what a great idea it was for a serious documentary mob like yourselves to take a look at the way these wonderful teenage kids live.

Harding displays polite interest in Maisie's work and even compliments her:

Well, Miss King, that was most interesting. It had an authentic quality of gay delinquency.

When Harding follows the young people down to the Tom Tom Club, the venerable gentleman looks like a fish out of water: a bespectacled, portly chap in white shirt and black tie, his clothing and deportment are at odds with the cool cats he finds there. Harding introduces the scene for the viewers at home:

Well, here we are in a typical expresso coffee bar. In this rather synthetically exotic decor, the teenagers relax after their working day. That is, if you can call it relaxation. Because you and I might prefer the quiet atmosphere of an old English pub. But the youngsters get their 'kicks', as they put it, under plastic palm trees where they sit and plot their teenage rebellion. Let's see what they think about it. You, Sir, what do you think about it?

But the young rebel refuses to play along: 'Why Me?' the yob retorts in a nasal snarl and Harding wanders off with a polite, 'Oh, Thank You'. Gilbert Harding is quite out of place and his mode of investigation fruitlessly old-fashioned. British television is risibly out of touch with the younger generation, despite its attempts to find out what makes them tick. *Expresso Bongo* portrays television as unable to fire the interests of the young people who frequent coffee bars. It shows the audience for contemporary music to have little in common with the television audience, and makes a bid for the cinema as the more youth orientated medium by comparison.

Expresso Bongo charts the painful climb up the ladder of success undertaken by 'Bongo' Herbert. His manager, Johnny, is less help to Bongo than Dixie Collins (Yolande Donlan), an older star facing a career crisis. When Bongo and Dixie have an affair the publicity this generates gives a boost to both their careers. Dixie takes Bongo under her wing, and initiates him in the world of show business. By the time Bongo graduates to a regular television contract in New York, the Soho world of Johnny and his associates looks decidedly tawdry.

Expresso Bongo, filmed in black and white, was released at the end of the 1950s and has the gritty social realism of an urban drama. The pop music film of the next decade was powerfully infused with bright colours and lively playfulness. A new attitude towards popular music performance can be found in the films of the decade after *Six-Five Special* and *Expresso Bongo*. Young people are no longer depicted as rebellious and troubled, as Bongo is, but as decadent and fun loving. In the British pop film's metamorphasis television played a critical role as an icon of youthful celebration.

Richard Lester's films bear the hallmarks of being influenced by both Pop Art and advertising:

> His was the quintessential visual style of the second half of the decade, a daring and dynamic form of montage gleefully embracing parody, pastiche and pop art (Richards, 1992: 230).

Lester directed three films during this period, *A Hard Day's Night* (1964), *The Knack... and how to get it* (1965) and *Help* (1965).

> All three films show provincial youth coming into their kingdom, conquering London and refashioning the world in their own image (Richards, 1992: 230).

A Hard Day's Night is, according to Ken Hanke, 'arguably the most influential film of the 1960s' (Hanke, 1989b: 269). This *post-musical musical* is composed of a series of performances and stunts by The Beatles, strung together on the loose premise that the lads are travelling down to London from their native Liverpool to do a televised concert. Richard Lester refutes criticisms of the film's flippancy:

> The serious structure of *Hard Day's Night* was really just the chronicling of what was a serious movement... And that was the explosion of youth as a power in this country and the sud-

den gaining of confidence of an enormous section of England. It was the chronicling of confidence in this country which hadn't happened in a long time. The Angry Young Man Syndrome was that of a sort of semi-soured cynical defeatism, whereas The Beatles told everyone you can do anything you damn well like, just go out and do it... And that seemed like a marvellous thing to examine. Although we did it in a light way, I still feel that there is a serious purpose to the film (Lester, 1995).

The Beatles were, by this time, something of a phenomenon. Their ascent to stardom was quite meteoric. Simon Frith explains that in one year, from 1963 to 1964, 'the turnover from Beatles music leapt from nothing to £6 million' (Frith, 1983: 135). They symbolized the youthful celebration of pleasure, affluence and accomplishment. Their exuberance blew away the old encumbrances of Britain's class system and boldly proclaimed the rights of a new generation to set the cultural agenda.

A Hard Day's Night is considerably more complex in its depiction of the world of pop music than *Six-Five Special*. It brings to the performance movie a pop sensibility which was much appreciated when it was released (Thompson, 1994). Richard Lester's radical direction anticipates the pop video of the television generation. *A Hard Day's Night* begins with a train journey as The Beatles travel down to London for a television broadcast and depicts the four Liverpudlians as rebellious lads whose primary goal is to have a bit of fun. In the attempt at showing The Beatles as young people generationally different from their parents, the film even infantilizes its subjects. The Fab Four frequently truant on their responsibilities just like the schoolboy, Charlie, whom Ringo meets on his foray around London – Ringo is as much a 'deserter' from work as Charlie and his mates are from school. The Beatles are frequently depicted literally on the run; often evading their fans, but just as often their minders. Norm (Norman Rossington) and Shake (John Junkin) are responsible for ensuring the young ruffians turn up to their gigs on time, which often involves chasing one or other of them around London. Norm thumbs them out of a party, mouthing *'home'* emphatically above the loud music when moments before the lads had been enjoying themselves dancing and chatting up women. Norm's action puts us in mind of a father ejecting his fifteen-year-old daughter from an orgy. The 'home' to which they are being ordered is a London hotel suite and the 'homework' which awaits them is in the form of fan letters that need to be answered. The Fab Four represent youthful insurrection and irreverent rebellion against responsible adults. The pop film is a very tongue-in-cheek take on the pop music industry.

A Hard Day's Night distances itself from television by subjecting the industry to considerable mockery. Kenneth Haigh plays the commercial television producer who is looking for the ideal teenager to talk about youth fashion on television. George is looking for the canteen when he wanders in to the executive's office, and the Beatle's famous sang-froid easily gets the better of the television man. The producer of the television show on which they are to appear (Victor Spinetti) is a harassed BBC employee who despairs of the Fab Four ever turning up on time for the show: 'It's a young man's medium', he says, wearily. 'Once you're over 30 you've had it.' The television performance comes easily to The Beatles and there are no problems when they reach the stage. *A Hard Day's Night* shows the Beatles as consummately 'natural' television performers. The band are completely at ease and have a calm confidence that is the perfect foil to the television producers' nervous anxiety.

Released just one year after *A Hard Day's Night*, *Catch Us If You Can* (John Boorman, 1965), is considerably less structured than even Richard Lester's rambling piece. Inexplicably cast as 'stunt men', the British pop group The Dave Clark Five live together in an old church. While filming a television commercial for meat, Steve (Dave Clark) decides to abscond from the meat market with Dinah (Barbara Ferris) in the company's E-type Jaguar. Where Lester presented four Liverpool lads conquering London, *Catch Us If You Can* shows five young Londoners on the lam from the big city with nowhere to go. *Catch Us If You Can* uses television to provide the initiation rather than the closure of the narrative, for it is their experience in television commercials that motivates their desertion from London. Andy Medhurst argues that:

> *Catch Us If You Can*, especially in its first startling thirty minutes, goes all out for the shiny plastic immediacy of the

moment. It is, in short, where the pop film becomes the Pop film (Medhurst, 1995: 68).

It strikes me as an extremely slight piece of film-making: a road movie with nowhere to go; a chase movie with nothing much at stake. *Catch Us If You Can* does not depict the performing skills of The Dave Clark Five; their musical talents are reduced to being part of the soundtrack. For me, it is where the Pop film becomes the pap film.

Medhurst is right to assert that: 'after the mid-60s the pop film was at best only marginal to what remained of British cinema' (1995: 61). The British film industry has since thrown up occasional pop films (*Stardust,* Michael Apted, 1974; *Tommy,* Ken Russell, 1975; *Absolute Beginners,* Julien Temple, 1986; *Spice-world: The Movie,* Bob Spiers, 1997), but by and large the genre has faded into obscurity. Television fulfills the same cultural role more successfully. Whether broadcast or satellite, television is more immediate, spontaneous and responsive than film and thus better suited to the needs of the pop music industry. Pop videos comprise the most important marketing tool of the contemporary music industry and provide a more satisfactory way than films of watching one's favorite performers.

American Pop Films

The destiny of the American pop film was to end up, like the British, killed off by the pop music promotion industry which found the pop video or televised concert more appropriate to its needs. However, the means by which the American pop film reached this demise is quite different from the British experience, not least because of the unique cultural location of the musical film in the 1950s. The Hollywood musical was one of the most successful genres and the MGM musicals produced by the Freed Unit during the 1950s mark the apogee of the genre. As we saw in Chapter 3, by the early 1960s the musical was showing signs of deteriorating and becoming out of touch with popular tastes. Television was taking over the terrain as the purveyor of popular music. According to Karal Ann Marling, a cultural historian of the period:

Rock 'n' roll and television were made for each other. In dancing blips of light, television registered the bobbing hanks of hair, the swinging jackets, the swivelling hips. Detail wasn't important: on the little living room screen, motion – new, exciting, and visually provocative in its own right – was the distilled essence of Elvishood (Marling, 1994: 179).

The musical *Bye Bye Birdie* (George Sidney, 1963) addresses television and its relationship to rock and roll celebrity head on. According to Gerald Mast, *Bye Bye Birdie* is 'one of the worst musicals of the decade (or any other)' (Mast, 1987: 317). It has many characteristics typical of a traditional musical, being based on a stage show with a fairly strong songbook, it includes conventional musical numbers alongside more 'pop' influenced pieces. It also includes animated sequences and other kinds of trick photography and a number of songs that are clearly parodic such as 'You've Got to be Sincere'. The main reason why Mast holds this musical in such low esteem is its apparent determination to appeal to all tastes:

> *Bye Bye Birdie* promised something for every one: Broadway and TV star Dick Van Dyke, Hollywood teen star Ann-Margret, teen rocker Bobby Rydell, non-singing movie star Janet Leigh in an absurd black wig, the miscast Broadway dramatic actress Maureen Stapleton, Broadway comedian Paul Lynde, Ed Sullivan himself, a deservedly unknown Jessie Pearson in the title role, and an inexhaustible supply of camera tricks (Mast, 1987: 317).

For its admirers, the multiple styles of performance and camera work are precisely what they like about George Sidney's film (Masson, 1981; Monder, 1994). Sidney had a very complex and contradictory relationship to popular culture which is evident in the way this film seems to celebrate and assault the popular in equal measure. Sidney was an iconoclast who, unlike other studio directors, seemed to genuinely welcome the opportunities offered by television (Monder, 1994). *Bye Bye Birdie* addresses the relationship between pop and television, but with an attitude that is impossible to accurately identify. Popular music is both celebrated and satirized in *Bye Bye Birdie*. This musical seems to recognise that pop heralds the end of the film musical. It marks the apogee of the classical musical before it is smashed into oblivion by the twin forces of the rock 'n' roll movie, and television variety.

The plot of *Bye Bye Birdie* is loosely based on the events surrounding the conscription of Elvis Presley, one of the most notoriously rebellious rock 'n' roll stars, with whom Sidney would make *Viva Las Vegas* the following year. *Bye Bye Birdie* has Jesse Pearson hamming it up as rock 'n' roll star Conrad Birdie, an Elvis manqué. Dick Van Dyke plays Albert Peterson, a reluctant and unsuccessful songwriter who dreams, strangely, of being a biochemist. Rosie DeLeon (Janet Leigh) is his long suffering girlfriend desperate to get married (it is hinted that she may be pregnant). Rosie introduces the idea of television by proposing that Conrad Birdie sing Albert's new song, 'One Last Kiss', on *The Ed Sullivan Show* as he 'symbolically' kisses all of his fans goodbye. This is based on Elvis Presley and his appearances on *The Ed Sullivan Show*, which occurred on three occasions during the winter of 1956–57 (he was drafted in 1958). For his television appearances, Presley's usual sexual exuberance had to be considerably curtailed. Karal Ann Marling maintains that:

> Presley's 'strip-tease behavior' was particularly repugnant to TV watchers because his performance style was, in some perverse way, ideally suited to the new medium (Marling, 1994: 176).

The ambiguity of the film in relation to Conrad Birdie is unsettling, as is its attitude towards pop music. The music the youngsters enjoy is treated extremely derisively in *Bye Bye Birdie*. Albert's latest song is called 'Mumbo Jumbo Gooey Gumbo', and Conrad's first number, 'You've Gotta Be Sincere', is an extremely cynical pastiche on the sexual appeal of the deified pop star. As women and girls faint simply at the sight of him, Conrad wreaks havoc on the small town of Sweet Apple. At the end of the song the town square is littered with the bodies of fallen fans, a visual reference to the devastation caused by the Civil War in *Gone with the Wind*. It is hard to escape the conclusion that young people and their musical tastes are the objects of more ridicule than empathy. This undermines the status of the film as a pop movie.

The visually inventive telephone number, which introduces the teenage stars, invites us to laugh at the obsessions and interests of the youngsters. The number 'What's the Matter with Kids Today', takes an adult perspective on young people, while 'I've Got a Lot of Living To Do' shows that, however much the youngsters might dress as adults, they're still kids really. The problem of the teenager is one that their parents have to face up to, not the young people themselves. In watching *Bye Bye Birdie*, we are presented with musical numbers that the director seems to be ridiculing. The film has an extremely uneasy relationship to pop music and to television.

Bye Bye Birdie is without the benefit of the influence of the British pop invasion that did so much to raise the standard of American film-making, in the estimation of one historian. Ken Hanke (1989abc and d) claims that the influence of British films in general, and of *A Hard Day's Night* in particular, was profound. Lester's film certainly had a strong influence on *Head* (Bob Rafelson, 1968) which features one of the most manufactured television pop bands of the period, The Monkees. *Head* was the first collaboration between Bob Rafelson and Jack Nicholson, who directed and produced it respectively. Rafelson had worked on The Monkees' television show and he uses *Head* to create a schism between the television personalities on which the success of the television series was based, and the extra-televisual personae of the band. Bob Rafelson says of making the film:

> It was a very carefree, strange and experimental film to make... I knew I was dismantling the careers of The Monkees: I wanted to tell the truth. I'd spent two years producing and creating their TV show, but, to do what I really wanted, I needed to make a full film. So I got Jack [Nicholson] to write it. That was really taking a step off the edge because he was crazier than I was (Rafelson, 1998: 10).

The alternative film and music worlds became mutual allies in the late 1960s. Ben Thompson maintains:

> In America, the rock 'n' roll and film industries huddled together in the fading embers of the counter culture (Thompson, 1995: 35).

Certainly *Head* demonstrates the efforts of film-makers to respond to music celebrity in relation to television. *Head* is a television spin-off, reeling in a vortex considerably far from its source. The Monkees were an enormously successful band, whose careers had been launched with a television series, but by the time they made *Head* they were beginning to distance themselves from their own television image.

The Monkees were a marketing phenomenon, designed to be an American imitation of The Beatles (although Davy Jones was famously British). The opening sequence of *Head* focuses on the fact that the film's subjects are a television-generated band. The first frame of the film contains an image of twenty television screens, in five rows and four columns. Each television screen is activated in turn, while The Monkees recite a poem. Given that they are a pop band, it is strange that no music is played at this point. The poem provides some clues to understanding the cryptic structure of the rest of the film, and at the same time expresses the cynicism of the band towards their manufactured image. The screen goes black and a voice announces:

Hey, now, wait a minute,
Now wait just a minute,
Hey, hey, we are the Monkees,
You know we love to please,
A manufactured image,
With no philosophies.

The rhyme continues this nihilistic nonsense at a frantic pace while the images on the bank of television sets rapidly change. The visual accompaniment is culled from television images. In a parody of their song *Hey, hey we're the Monkees*, they finish their rhyme with the verse:

Hey, hey we are the Monkees,
We've said it all before,
The money's in, we're made of tin,
We're here to give you more.

Images accompanying the above are of news footage, boxing, films and The Monkees' television programs. When the final television fills the grid, it shows the famous image of a North Vietnamese man being executed at close range. A girl screams, we think in response to the image, but then her scream fills the frame and she is at a concert, screaming for The Monkees to appear on stage. They run out, but her desire to see them perform is not fulfilled, as they run on to a football field and start cheering the crowd on to W.A.R. There then follows a sketch set in the war. Scene follows scene in a nonsensical parody of narrative structure.

Television is shown to be excessive in every regard. The multiplicity of images and the speed at which they are changed implies that the sheer excess of images on television make for incomprehension. The Monkees' are caught in a strange television world where at one moment they are fighting a war in the desert and the next they are flakes of dandruff in a shampoo advertisement. The film lapses in and out of reflexivity. Attention is drawn to the processes of television and film production, for example the director and producer appear on set in one of the scenes. Peter Tork discusses with Rafelson and Nicholson whether it is appropriate to hit 'a girl' for the scene. At one point Mickey Dolenz turns to the director during the shooting of a Western scene and says:

> These fake crows and this fake tree, Bob, I'm through with them.

The most direct comment on the world of television and its effect on The Monkees comes at the film's close. Our four reluctant heroes are encased in a large black box, the dimensions of a television set but the size of a trailer on the back of a truck. Behind them for no particular reason sits Victor Mature. *Head* is a strange and wayward film, which captures the confusion of the era. It shows television as the crucible of young men ensconced in things beyond their comprehension. As a pop movie it is especially troublesome; it seems bent on destroying the personae of its protagonists and ridiculing the television manufactured stars.

Figure 6.3 Teenagers dance on the pop music television program, *The Corny Collins Show* in John Waters' satire of 1960s youth television, *Hairspray* (John Waters, 1988)

Conclusion

The pop movies of the late 1950s and 1960s discussed in this chapter have an ambiguous relationship to television. They all recognize the importance of television in promoting musical performers, but do not necessarily welcome television's influence on popular music. The British *Expresso Bongo* shows television as out of touch with young people's tastes and preferences. Interestingly, Bongo eventually found success on an *American* television show – indicating that US television was considered more sympathetic to the new musical forms than their British counterparts. *A Hard Day's Night* offers a televised Beatles concert at the close of the text. While the performance is a huge success, and offers the pleasure of seeing the group perform in a live situation, this is seen to be despite the television executives. The American musical *Bye Bye Birdie* explores the relationship between television and pop music with a dispassionate cynicism; George Sidney displays disgust for the false sentimentality of the pop music industry, and the crass manipulation of television. Such downbeat themes create a dissonant cacophony in the Hollywood musical. *Head* is a meandering assault on television fame (when it stirs itself out of self-indulgence). As a piece of counter-cultural cinema, it is a harsh indictment on its central characters. It makes The Monkees appear to be, at best dupes, at worst cynical manipulators of their young fans.

The classical Hollywood musical reaches resolution when the young starlet finally finds success. In the pop film the band are already successful and the narrative concerns machinations of dealing with the problems of success. The pop movie, picking up where the musical left off, problematizes stardom.

The fans of the pop groups are constructed as problematic for the stars. The fans are depicted as frightening and herd-like in such films as *A Hard Day's Night* and *Head*, creating a difficult paradox for the audience: are we to identify with the fans in the film, or are we to identify with the stars and distance ourselves from the fans? Certainly, we must identify with the fans at one level, because we have been drawn to see the film by the lure of the performers we admire, and must therefore be fans ourselves. On the other hand, if we identify with the stars

we are obliged to recognize the fans as troublesome and disrup-
tive elements in the text. This curious paradox leaves us inclined
to feel simply alienated by the pop movie. Certainly, the spec-
tator position is considerably removed from that of the viewer
of the classical musical: there are few opportunities for escapism
here. As movies about musical performance become more of an
exegesis on the tribulations of success, the musical genre
becomes less sustainable.

The pop film about television charts the demise of its own
medium. The final collapse of the musical film came when television became the primary means of promoting musical
performers. The only role for the cinema was to satirize the days
of pop. John Waters' *Hairspray*, (see Figure 6.3) released in 1988
sends up the close relationship between television and pop
music in the 1960s. With the distance of so many years, *Hairspray* can take a light hearted approach. But the films discussed
above recognize television as a successor of technology. They
are infused with a sombre grimness that belies the cheerfulness
of popular music of the period.

7

AS MAD AS HELL: THE REEL WORLD OF TELEVISION NEWS

While some film genres have outlasted television, such as comedy and romance, and some others, such as the musical (discussed in Chapter 3) died a slow, lingering death, one genre which was completely eradicated by television was the newsreel. In the early days of the cinema newsreels were a mainstay of the program at any theater, enlarging the horizons of the audience by bringing images and sounds from at home and abroad. Newsreels brought cinema-goers views of state and ceremonial occasions, sport and entertainment events, foreign lands and peoples. The newsreel competed with newspapers and radio to bring moving pictures and later synchronous sound to news reporting. When television broadcasts permitted access to events as they happened, live to the home, the newsreel could not survive. The newsreel was completely displaced by television news in the 1960s (Barnouw, 1983; Smither and Klaue, 1996). In America newsreels were completely extinct by the 1960s; in Britain they lingered a little longer, transformed into topical factual programs (Slade Film History Register, 1984; Ballantyne, 1993). Today, the relatively small genre of the cinema documentary is the only survivor of a once robust trade in reality programming in the cinema. As we have seen in previous chapters of this book, the cinema has portrayed television workers in diverse ways, but here we examine the special opprobrium that the cinema has reserved for the television news worker.

The most sustained, and infamous, assault on television by the cinema is Sidney Lumet's *Network* (1976), whose demented news presenter rouses television audiences with his catch phrase:

I'm as mad as hell and I'm not going to take it any more!

The anti-television stance of *Network* resonated with public debate about the role of television in America in the 1970s. *Network* was made at a time when the US Government attempted to fix the blame for social problems on television, a task in which it had much assistance from researchers of various backgrounds (Surgeon General's Advisory Committee, 1972; Winn, 1977; Rowland, 1983; Gauntlett, 1995). Blaming television in general, and the networks in particular, for social problems became an easy way for governments to absolve themselves of responsibilty: attacking the networks became a matter of sport for the government. *Network* exorcised some of Hollywood's anxiety about collusion between big business and the networks. It also expressed popular anxiety about television's apparent manipulation of the political process.

More recently, newsrooms have been used as the locale for romantic dramas, as, for example, in *Broadcast News*. The pinnacle of anti-television hysteria in popular cinema seems to have passed. However, anxiety about television's 'effects' prevails in the work of Hollywood's most didactic cineaste: Oliver Stone. Stone's *Natural Born Killers* presents a ruthless news reporter, Wayne Gayle (Robert Downey Jr), as a representative of the worst excesses of television actuality reportage. A clear divide between popular and highbrow representations of television emerges in the way films represent television reporters. In the late 1990s Hollywood is confident enough to laugh off any threat from television: *Wag the Dog* (Barry Levinson, 1997) depicts the film business controlling all forms of media, including television, and having a good laugh in the process (Cheshire, 1997). *Wag the Dog* shows the manipulation of the news by Hollywood is acceptable because, after all, they are the good guys, and the end justifies the means when the Good President is reelected to office. Today, the film industry imagines television to be its hand-maiden: in the 1960s, it viewed the medium with considerably more fear and suspicion.

Television and the Counter Culture

One of the most interesting films to address television from the perspective of American 1960s counter culture is *Medium Cool* (Haskell Wexler, 1969). Wexler's background as a cinematographer is evident in this visually exciting film which incorporates a narrative of discovery with documentary footage and anti-narrative elements in a loose and open style. The cinema verité characteristics of hand-held camera work and overlapping sound eschew the polish of Hollywood film form and contribute to an impression of raw reality. The influence of French avant-garde cinema, and the work of Jean Luc Godard in particular, is evident here; Wexler uses alternative film form to signal his distance from mainstream image-making and politics.

During the preface we are introduced to camera operator John (Robert Forster) and sound recordist Gus (Peter Bonerz) as they shoot a car wreck on an empty highway; their professional identity is further signalled by the fact that their car bears the logo of Chicago television station WHJP-Channel 8 News. An ambulance is called only *after* the two men have recorded for several minutes. The film thus begins by positioning itself as inquisitor of the television workers' actions: John and Gus are damned for their dispassionate professionalism before the narrative proper is set in motion. Even the title of *Medium Cool* is a hip play on Marshall McLuhan's affirmations that 'the Medium is the Message' and that television is a 'cool' medium (McLuhan, 1964). The highly reflexive mood of *Medium Cool* is developed further in the opening scene of a discussion between several cameramen about their work. This sets the tone for a sophisticated, knowing text which reflects on media representations of the real, particularly in relation to television news. Throughout *Medium Cool*, the sophisticated cinematic style of the film contrasts with the direct simplicity of the footage required for the television news. Wexler shows how the formal characteristics of film and television allow for different takes on reality. The central characters seem to exist in a liminal space between film and television.

Medium Cool establishes the world of television within the text and the world of film, which is representing television, as two opposing entities. Through our identification with John, we are drawn into the narrative and go with him when he sets out to investigate what goes on behind the scenes of the news stories he is covering. One particularly newsworthy local story concerns an African-American cab driver who found $10,000 in the back of his taxi and handed it in to the police. The man is presented to television news audiences as a hero and his act celebrated as a gesture of civic responsibility. However, the television audiences don't see the police aggressively interrogate the cabbie, whom they suspect of playing some kind of trick. With John we witness something of the cabdriver's experience at the hands of the police and realize that the man's actions will not be taken at face value because of racist prejudice. Intrigued, John decides to pursue the story and visits the man at his home. There John finds the man's honesty has brought him under suspicion from his own community and the guy is being badgered by his friends about his motives.

The African-American people John and Gus meet at the apartment are highly critical of the white media and the two are accosted as representatives of the establishment. One African-American militant confronts them:

> We know one of the best ways of spying on black people is to impersonate TV men.

And John and Gus are accused of being from the FBI. The fears of the African-American community at first seem paranoid but later prove to be well-founded when we learn that the police and the FBI have been given access to all the footage shot by the news workers at Channel 8. As John readies to leave the apartment, the African-American people challenge the motives for John's visit and his role as lackey of the news media that misrepresent the plight of black people. There follows a scene in which African-American people talk directly to camera about the way in which the media, most especially the news media, construct them: 'You don't do it black enough' they are forcefully told. In their speeches African-American militants directly address the camera, breaking frame to tell John – and the film's audience – unequivocally: 'You are the exploiters.' Of course, none of this will make the television news. The cinecamera is able to reach a truth which the television camera will never be present to witness. Wexler interrogates the politics of film and television representation with intelligence and sensitivity.

A romantic strand to the film is offered when John befriends Eileen (Verna Bloom), a young woman newly arrived from West Virginia who is trying to raise her young son Harold (Harold Blankenship) on her own. Wexler will not permit a happy Hollywood ending for the couple, however, and John and Eileen are killed in a car crash while driving on an empty road. The soundtrack is of the car radio reporting their demise and the simultaneous civil rights riots in Chicago. A passing car slows down and the flash of the child's camera records the event. The camera pulls back and pans to reveal a scaffold on which a movie camera is mounted, and we watch the camera watching us. The camera zooms in on the frame of our camera as the soundtrack continues with reporting of the riot: 'the whole world is watching, the whole world is watching,' chant the protestors. Television shows a pale imitation of reality, which the movie camera can access, but finally, the real protest takes place outside the movie theater, beyond the confines of the frame of all images, regardless of their aspect ratio.

Medium Cool is set during the civil rights protests in Chicago and, as such, has a strong sense of time and place. It is an essay on the power of images to corrupt and of news workers' complicity – knowing or not; reluctant or not – in the presentation of one particular world view and the suppression of others. It represents a peak in 1960s paranoia about establishment politics and the suppression of protest and dissent.

Mad as Hell: Television News in the 1970s

By the 1970s anti-television sentiment was no longer the exclusive concern of the alternative sector. Television had become the official scapegoat for all manner of social ills in mainstream society, too. With film production at an all-time low – just 155 features were released in 1974 (see Table 2.1) – Hollywood jumped on the bandwagon of anti-television sentiment. A new assault on television was launched, focusing on its power of persuasion and its cult of celebrity in Sidney Lumet's vicious diatribe, *Network* (1976). Unlike *Medium Cool*, *Network* is an unashamedly Hollywood production, using many of the standard conventions including famous stars, a driving narrative structure and even a romantic angle. *Network* attacks television from a position of moral superiority but, as David Thomson argues:

> The film bristles with articulate curses against TV. It is an onslaught on trite sensation corrupting consequences. But its methods and devices are those of TV: the moving image; abrupt transitions; cheap laughs; hollow characters; activity concealing no point of view; movement as a distraction from meaning. The film is as vicious and feeble as a wasp trapped in the jam it craves... It is a satire without detachment, roots or hope of remedy (Thomson, 1977: 123).

It may seem odd, given that Paddy Chayevsky made his career in television, that he should write a script seething with such loathing and contempt. But by the 1970s he was one of many who were struggling to slough their television garments and to make a success of it in film. No doubt Chayevsky saw something of himself in the character of the benign elder statesman of television, Max Schumacher, played in world-weary style by William Holden. Perhaps he also saw his career in television as akin to Max's affair with Diana Christianson, Faye Dunaway's monstrous television executive of the new school. Their relationship symbolizes that between the 'old' school of Ed Murrow-type journalism and the 'new' one of news as entertainment. When trying to seduce Max, Diana tells him:

> Sooner or later, with or without you, I'm going to take over your network news.

It seems to be an effective chat up line; they sleep together that night. Diana will screw anyone to advance her career in television and directs all her energies to her ambition. As she informs Max:

> I seem to be inept at everything. Except my work. I'm good at my work. So I confine myself to that. All I want out of life is a 30 share and a 20 rating.

Diana is a 1970s version of Marcia from Kazan's *A Face in The Crowd* (discussed in Chapter 4). Like Marcia, Diana's drive to suceed in broadcasting dominates her life and ruins her relationships. When Max's long-suffering and sympathetically portrayed wife asks Max whether Diana loves him, he answers:

> I'm not sure she's capable of any real feelings... She's television generation; She's learned life from Bugs Bunny.

After their relationship has fizzled out like a spent cathode ray tube, Max tells his jumpy, self-absorbed ex-lover:

> You're television incarnate... you're madness, Diana,... everything you touch dies with you...

The dread in which television is held by *Network* and by *A Face in the Crowd* is a male dread of a strong career woman. Diana is 'television incarnate' and Lumet portrays both television and Diana as dangerous, castrating harridans.

Although Diana successfully uses Max to advance her career, she manages to 'hit the motherlode' when she exploits the mental instability of Max's best friend Howard Beale (Peter Finch). Diana is looking for someone 'to articulate the rage' of the American people when news anchor Beale has a nervous breakdown during his nightly broadcast. Diana sets about transforming Beale into 'an angry prophet denouncing the hypocrisies of our times'. When her boss Frank Hackett (Robert Duvall) tells her:

> For God's sakes, Diana, we're talking about putting a manifestly irresponsible man on national television,

she nods heartily, even gleefully, in agreement. Diana pulls the strings and Beale becomes her puppet. *The Howard Beale Show* becomes a smash hit, its host conducting events with televangelical zeal. Beale is further manipulated into being a lackey for big business (just as Lonesome was in *A Face in the Crowd*) by charismatic Chairman of the Board Arthur Jensen (Ned Beatty). When Beale's insanity takes him beyond the control of the network executives, however, they can see no alternative: Beale has to be killed. The crazed television presenter is executed, live, on air, during one of his shows. His demise is related in voice-over by his best buddy, and sober newsman of the old guard, Max Schumacher and his voice of reason provides the film's closure.

Faye Dunaway's viciously ambitious television executive brings a bitchy quality to broadcasting reprising the 1950s feminization of television (discussed in Chapter 4). Jane Fonda is another strong Hollywood woman, cast as a television news reporter in *The Electric Horseman* (Sydney Pollack, 1979). Like *Network*'s Diana Christianson, Hallie Martin is tough, determined and always gets her story. Hallie meets her match in Robert Redford's macho Sonny Steele; a rodeo star turned Ranch Cowboy Cereal sponsor. As the eponymous hero of the film, Sonny travels the country appearing at State fairs dressed in an illuminated cowboy suit performing tricks on horseback. The tragedy of the 'cowboy-become-commercial-image' is a heavy-handed metaphor for the demise of the mythical status of the American West and the death of the Western movie genre. The metaphor is not lost on Sonny who runs out on his sponsorship deal taking his horse with him to release into the wild. In a classic Western trope his journey to unite Rising Star with a herd of wild steers becomes a journey of self-discovery. Hallie follows Sonny into the wilderness to capture the story for television. The reporter and the fading rodeo star manage to recapture the spirit of the West on their journey through the dramatic Western landscape, turning their backs on the demands of commercialism and of television – except that Hallie is secretly recording their journey for broadcast on the evening news. *The Electric Horseman* posits television as a corrupting force against the genuine, down to earth values represented by nature. Jane Fonda also plays a spunky news reporter, Kimberly Wells, in *The China Syndrome* (James Bridges, 1978), where news workers are on the side of good uncovering the dangers posed by an unstable nuclear power station. In *The Electric Horseman* her role is considerably more ambiguous – her job as reporter conflicting with her feelings for Sonny. Although she betrays Sonny by disclosing their destination, he has second-guessed her and given her false leads. The wily old cowboy has no problems outwitting the modern female news reporter.

Manipulation of the media could not be further from the mind of Chance (Peter Sellers) in *Being There* (Hal Ashby), a film released the same year as *The Electric Horseman*. A lonely simpleton, Chance has spent all his life in the company of television and the medium is the source of all his ideas and opinions about the world. *Being There* owes something to both *Network* and *A Face in the Crowd* in that it is about a man out of his depth in the world of television. The difference is that, rather than drowning in the mire, in the end Chance can walk on water. We never know if Chance is his real name; Jerzy Kozinski apparently named his central character for John Wayne's John T. Chance in *Rio Bravo*, and no one seems sure of his real identity. Chance evidently has learning difficulties and has spent his entire life until middle age watching television and tending the garden in the house of the 'Old Man'. When his benefactor dies, Chance has to leave and in fairy-tale manner is taken home by Eve Rand (Shirley MacLaine). Eve is a wealthy socialite who introduces Chance to her ailing husband, Ben, and the couple befriend him. Both Eve and Ben are struck by Chance's demeanor which they take to be indicative of a quiet intelligence.

He's different, isn't he... he's very intense,

says Eve. Chance's platitudes are taken for aphorisms and his banal descriptions of growth and gardens are interpreted as metaphors. For example, when the President asks about the economy, Chance proffers:

As long as the roots are not severed all is well and will be well in the garden... There will be growth in the Spring.

The words of the fool are taken for gems of wisdom repeated by the President that night on television, and the simple man becomes fêted by the news media. The only person who shares our insight into Chance's character is the African-American maid who used to care for him and the 'Old Man'. When she sees Chance on television she is irate:

It's for sure a white man's world in America... Never learned to read or write... dumb as a jackass... shortchanged by the

Lord! Yessir, all you gotta be is white in America to get whatever you want.

Chance delights television news reporters when he seems to be asserting television's superiority over the press when he tells them:

I don't read papers. I watch TV.

Being There is clearly making a scathing jibe at the gullibility and self-importance of television news reporters. The gentle humor of this satire provides a quiet contrast to the bombast of *Network*.

The 1980s and a New Climate for Television

When Sidney Lumet revisited many of the themes of *Network* in *Power* (1986) the endeavor fell rather flat. *Power*'s anti-hero is a political agent, Pete St John (Richard Gere), who is expert at manipulating the media into providing the best coverage of his candidates. The critique of the media seems outdated and whiny in *Power* which does not muster the same anger that infused *Network*. It is hardly news that political agents exist to massage the media, and the rambling structure of the narrative does not give us any fresh insight on the point. *Power* simply reprises an old song without updating it for a new audience.

More centrally, we find the antagonism towards television dwindles in the 1980s and the television newsroom becomes the setting for romantic comedy in *Broadcast News* (James L. Brooks, 1987) (Figure 7.1). Tom Grunick (William Hurt) is the handsome but dim-witted golden boy of the network who finds getting laid and getting promoted both as easy as crossing the road. Jane Craig (Holly Hunter) and Aaron Altman (Albert Brooks) are sympathetic characters; dedicated and hard working they have earned their place in the newsroom. Near the beginning of the film Jane makes a desperate plea for old-fashioned news values at a broadcasting conference. Jane shows footage of a domino demonstration which she says was carried by all the network news programs. She rails against the dumbing down of contemporary news which the footage represents to her. But her colleagues cannot understand her point – they think the dominos are entertaining.

> I know it's good film. I know it's fun. I like fun. It's just not news,

she insists. But hers is a lone voice in the wilderness – the moral imperative behind news production has gone and the entertainment values of the television world have won out.

All the women warm to Tom when he does a very sensitive interview with a victim of date rape during which he cries. He loses considerable credibility with Jane when Aaron points out to her that, as there was only one camera on the shoot, Tom must have done the crying in a 'noddy' shot inserted after the interview. The revelation that he is a manipulative trickster creates the narrative justification for him being the natural successor to the network anchor, Bill (Jack Nicholson). This shady character only appears in the flesh, like the grim reaper, when the network decides to shed 27 workers from the station. *Broadcast News* attempts to mesh morality tale with romantic comedy, but the romantic element is the most dominant and the abiding image of the newsroom is as backdrop to a story about relationships (see Figure 7.1).

The Newsroom and the Modern Romance

In the later film, *He Said; She Said* (Marisa Silver and Ken Kwapis, 1991), the television newsroom is a glamorous setting for a story about a couple divided on almost every issue. *Switching Channels* (Ted Kotcheff, 1988) is a retelling of *The Front Page* located in a television newsroom with Burt Reynolds trying to woo ex-wife Kathleen Turner. The idea of the television newsroom as a good place to set a romance is taken up by *Up Close and Personal* (1996). This is a sentimentalized rendition of the life of a real television reporter, Jessica Savitch. The story was also told in a made-for-television film, *Almost Golden: The Jessica Savitch Story* (Paul Wener, 1995 TVM), with rather more honesty, depicting the alcohol and drug problems that

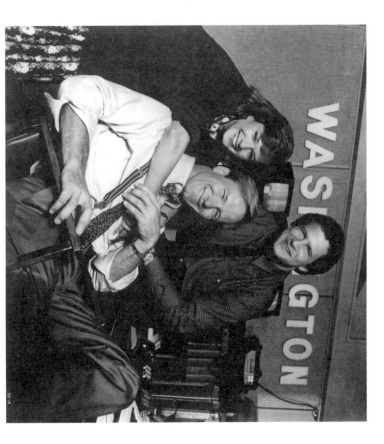

Figure 7.1 Tom Grunick (William Hurt), Aaron Altman (Albert Brooks) and Jane Craig (Holly Hunter) make news reporting romantic in *Broadcast News* (James L. Brooks, 1987)

made Savitch notorious. *Up Close and Personal* ignores the serious personal difficulties Jessica Savitch experienced and instead concentrates on Tally's (the Jessica Savitch character) affair with Warren (Robert Redford). Both the affair and television news are made to look glamorous and attractive. The only battles Tally faces here are ones of petty misogyny. The popular romantic film of the 1990s shows television news as a glamorous place to work, much as *Pretty Woman* made prostitution seem a viable career option.

Up Close and Personal may sentimentalize Jessica Savitch's sad life, but it does take itself very seriously. Other films about the news from the 1990s are more frivolous. *Dead Men Don't Die* (Malcolm Marmorstein, 1990) is a farcical comedy which sends up television news while also telling a story of ridiculous zombies and crazed voodoo queens. *Dead Men Don't Die* stars Elliot Gould as World Wide News anchorman Barry Barron who is turned into a zombie by Mabel King's Voodoo practising cleaning lady, Chafuka. *Dead Men Don't Die* uses the television studio as a backdrop for a Saturnalian tale in which the cleaning lady finally ends up running the studio, the former studio boss becomes her butler and his bimbo girlfriend is made the weather and traffic reporter.

The news worker is the butt of much of the sick humor in Oliver Stone's malicious but slight morality tale, *Natural Born Killers*. Robert Downey Jr adopts an atrocious Australian accent to play Wayne Gale, a Robin Leach-like television reporter compiling a special for *American Maniacs*, a television series focusing on the film's outlaw killers Mickey and Mallory Knox (Woody Harrelson and Juliette Lewis). Gale pursues the killers to get the perfect television moment. His naive determination to interview Mickey on death row is a catalyst for a riot and a jailbreak. While Mickey and Mallory finally walk off into the sunset, Gale is compelled to film his own death. *Natural Born Killers* includes a clumsy assault on television news from the perspective of a pretentious film-maker.

Hollywood affirms its supremacy over television news in a more humorous and lighthearted way in *Wag the Dog* (Barry Levinson, 1997). Barry Levinson, a popular director, is as comfortable with television production as film and shows television as inferior and less significant than the movies (Cheshire,

1997). *Wag the Dog* depicts television's tricks as small beer compared to what the movies are capable of. Here film producer Stanley Motts (Dustin Hoffman) manipulates the news by stage managing a war against Albania to deflect attention away from the President's sexual peccadilloes. The news is stage managed by a bunch of Hollywood insiders who run circles around the news establishment. Perhaps *Wag the Dog* shows just how confident the Hollywood film industry feels relative to television. Or perhaps it is sheer bravado.

The history of American cinema's representation of television news has seen many changes: the anti-establishment work of *Medium Cool* and the didactic aggression of *Network* showed television workers as manipulative and manipulated by forces beyond their comprehension. The representation of television news in recent popular Hollywood offerings shows being a television news reporter as fun and a good way to make a career: the television newsroom is a topical location for romantic comedies. On the other hand, films by more serious film-makers, those we are more likely to label 'auteurs', such as Oliver Stone, continue to subscribe to a negative view of television in general and television news in particular. The old-fashioned cineaste is likely to still view television as a threat and to depict it in a negative light, while the popular director is more inclined to see television as a lively and interesting hook to a story. The differences in the way popular and elitist film-makers represent television is wide, but it broadens further still in the images of television news. In the next chapter we consider how film-makers have treated television from within two of the most escapist genres – the horror and the science fiction film.

8

A FEARFUL REGARD: TELEVISION IN HORROR AND SCIENCE FICTION FILMS

From *Murder by Television* (Clifford Sanforth, 1935) to *Natural Born Killers* (Oliver Stone, 1994) the image of the television set has provided the cinema with a frightening and dangerous alterity against which to define itself. This chapter examines how television is constructed in Hollywood science fiction and horror films, investigating how television is constructed as something to be held in fearful regard.

Early Images of Television in Science Fiction

From the earliest days of television the medium has provided science fiction films with material for their fantastic projections. Maurice Elvey's *High Treason* (1929) is, according to Charles Barr (1986), the first British film to represent television. *High Treason* shows television as a futuristic technology and was made just a few years after the first public demonstrations of television in 1926. During the 1930s, television was heavily hyped and popular interest in the new medium was piqued by newspaper and magazine reports (Jowett, 1994). This interest was tinged with anxiety about television's potential applications, which finds expression in films such as *Murder by Television* and *Television Spy* (Edward Dmytryk, 1939).

Unlike Dmytryk's *Television Spy*, which seems to have disappeared, Cameo Pictures' *Murder by Television* (aka *The Houghland*

Murder Case) has survived. At the time of its release one reviewer described the actors in this murder mystery as 'stiff and ill at ease with their parts' (*Monthly Film Bulletin*, 1935: 148). They have not loosened up in the intervening years and the plot trudges along slowly and often incoherently. The identity of television is clear to Professor Houghland, one of the scientists working on the nascent medium. Houghland fervently claims that television:

> Will make of this earth a paradise we've all envisioned but have never seen.

His belief is that of the modern scientist: he has unquestioning faith that his work will help to build a better tomorrow. Professor Houghland demonstrates his jealously guarded advance in television broadcasting to a gathering of family, friends, professional allies and rivals at his home. The television display begins with a transmission of a piano performance aptly entitled, 'I Had the Right Idea'. The recital is reminiscent of parlor room entertainment, especially since the singer, Miss Florence, is accompanied on the piano by the inventor's daughter, June (June Collyer), lending the occasion a family flavor which is enhanced as the song is watched by a mixed gathering (including the peeking servants) in the drawing room. After the successful broadcast of the song, Professor Houghland introduces a number of live scenes from around the world including Paris, London and China. This magnificent feat of video technology was quite impossible at the time of the film's release and contributes to the rather fanciful regard in which television is held in this film. It is while he is promising to show a scene from Africa that the exhibition goes terribly awry and Professor Houghland suddenly collapses and dies, to the great consternation of the gathered assembly. Arthur Perry (Bela Lugosi) investigates, and eventually reveals the sinister explanation behind the Professor's murder. Dr Scofield, Houghland's rival, has apparently used sound to kill his enemy, as Perry explains:

> Dr. Scofield's equipment... radiated waves direct to Professor Houghland's laboratory. When these waves came in contact

with those the Professor's equipment was radiating, they created an interstellar frequency which is the death ray.

Television is cast as a malevolent and threatening 'radiating' machine, one of several such devices that captured the popular imagination in the early part of this century. Professor Houghland is killed during (and by) one of his own television broadcasts. The theme of the mad scientist hoist on the petard of his own invention, recurrent in horror and science fiction films, is a feature of films about television, too. Overall, *Murder by Television* is a rather dull country house murder mystery which uses television to add a touch of novelty and an excuse for scientistic gobbledygook.

Television is not always displayed as an ominous device in the science fiction film. Val Guest was 'the first of the true Hammer directors' (Cumbow, 1992); a reputation earned with *The Quatermass Experiment* (1955, aka *The Quatermass Xperiment* or *The Creeping Unknown*). The *Quatermass* stories were a successful BBC series which pioneered science fiction on British television (Leman, 1991). *The Quatermass Experiment* was a spin-off from the television series based on a BBC television play written by Nigel Keane (see Figure 8.1). Professor Quatermass is an American scientist working in Britain who has secretly launched a manned rocket into space. There are potentially catastrophic consequences when his vessel is used by an alien species that threatens to destroy all terrestrial life. The denouement occurs in the hallowed environs of Westminster Abbey where the BBC mobile television unit happens to be reporting on the restoration of the Abbey. When the scientists arrive at the scene in pursuit of the monster, filming is in process with Sir Lionel Dean as 'Your Guide'. All eyes are on the television monitors in the Mobile Broadcasting truck as the BBC cameras pan to show the alien creature atop the scaffolding, preparing to spawn and eradicate the earth's species. The electric current from the mobile generator is wired up to the scaffold, and the creature electrocuted. We see the burning alien from the point of view of the television camera through the monitor in the Outside Broadcasting Unit van. Television is a live medium, which captures the drama of the final conflict, and television boffins are just the chaps to help defeat an alien force when

Figure 8.1   BBC television cameras are on hand at Westminster Abbey when the alien strikes in *The Quatermass Experiment* (Val Guest, 1955)

scientists alone are unequal to the task. Television technology provides the narrative resolution for *The Quatermass Experiment*: this time through having sufficient electricity at hand to be able to incinerate the alien. In *The Quatermass Experiment*, television, specifically the BBC Outside Broadcast Unit, plays a vital role in destroying an alien life form that threatens to destroy the planet. It is rare for television to be depicted in such a positive light in a science fiction film of this period. No doubt the origin of *Quatermass* on television and the close relationship between the film and television industries in Britain in the 1950s influenced the fairly upbeat depiction of television, and the BBC, in this film.

Television Surveillance

In the US, such benign depictions of television are rarely found. A recurrent trope of American science fiction films is the use of the icon of television as a means of surveillance. As early as 1939 this application is evident in Charlie Chaplin's *Modern Times* where Chaplin portrays a factory worker who is literally and metaphorically attacked by modern means of mass production. A video screen that can transmit and receive sound and images is used by the President of Electro Steel Corporation to oversee his workers on the factory floor. When Chaplin steals away from the production line to take an unofficial cigarette break in the bathroom, the President sees him on the screen and looks down on him from above: 'Hey, quit stalling and get back to work! he hollers at Chaplin, who duly toddles off. Television may have presented itself as a symbol of the modern, but Chaplin's critique in *Modern Times* does not shy from including television as among the devices used to keep the working man in his place.

Video surveillance as a tool of social and political control is a theme of George Orwell's novel, *Nineteen-Eighty-Four* and, of course, of the films which have been made of the book (*1984*, Michael Anderson, 1956; *Nineteen-Eighty-Four*, Michael Radford, 1984). Orwell's potent image of 'big brother' watching everyone through ubiquitous 'telescreens' has contributed a great deal to the cultural construction of television. Television surveillance was an especially popular theme in the paranoid science fiction films of the 1970s, for example *Colossus: The Forbin Project* (Joseph Sargent, 1969), *THX 1138* (George Lucas, 1971) and *The Anderson Tapes* (Sidney Lumet, 1972). These build on the social anomie of the post-Vietnam era in America, portraying television as one more device in the armory of the state and the powers-that-be to control the lives of individuals.

The Horror of Television in the 1980s: *Videodrome,* and *Poltergeist*

While science fiction films project current trends into an unknown future, the horror film tends to present unknown phenomena in a familiar world. *Poltergeist* (Tobe Hooper) and *Videodrome* (David Cronenberg) were both released in 1982 and are set in the present day (see Figures 8.2 and 8.3). They are powerfully strong horror films, classics of the genre, bearing the hallmarks of strong auteurs. David Cronenberg is a distinctive director who had already made a powerful impression with films including *Rabid* (1976) and *Scanners* (1980). Cronenberg continues to challenge audiences with complex and powerful work such as *Naked Lunch* (1991) and *Crash* (1996). The prevailing obsessions of Cronenberg's work with the melding of body and technology – with inner torments made externally manifest – are plainly evident in *Videodrome*. Although *Poltergeist* is nominally directed by Tobe Hooper, it bears all the authorial marks more commonly associated with its producer Steven Spielberg, who also wrote the screenplay. *Poltergeist* shares a location and some of its themes with *E.T. The Extra-Terrestrial* (Steven Spielberg, 1982) which was in production at the same time. In *E.T.* we also find television depicted, although here as a way for the cute little alien to learn about life on earth in one of the film's funniest scenes. A number of commentators attest to the strong influence of Spielberg on *Poltergeist*, and he has admitted that his contribution was significantly greater than one would expect of a producer (McCarthy, 1982; Van Hise, 1982). In *Jaws* (1975), *Close Encounters of the Third Kind* (1977) and *Raiders of the Lost Ark* (1981), Spielberg reinvented the classic Hollywood adventure film and proved himself master of the genre. Spielberg's gift in the horror film is to bring out the sinister side of suburban life, and to highlight the menace in the ordinary. Steven Spielberg claims *Poltergeist* is a 'modern ghost story set smack in the middle of suburbia' (McCarthy, 1982: 53).

Poltergeist and *Videodrome* both begin by emphasizing the difference between the quality of the television image and the film image as they use a full close up of the television screen to fill the film frame. The prologues of *Poltergeist* and *Videodrome* thus draw attention to the electronic nature of television. *Poltergeist* opens with 'The Star Spangled Banner' over black titles announcing the director and title of the movie. The sound muffles slightly and the black fades to a grid of flickering cells making up an indecipherable image which changes with the rhythm every couple of seconds. The film camera holds steady on the television image as it settles and one can briefly identify the statue, Raising the Flag at Iwo Jima, while the soundtrack continues to play the national anthem which is muffled now with electronic interference. The television transmission closes, the image turns to dancing static dots and the soundtrack is overtaken by static. This typically patriotic closing sequence of the night's television broadcasting announces the beginning of the film narrative with ominous foreboding.

Videodrome also opens with a black 'television' image which fades to reveal the titles of the film. The soundtrack carries television static which pulses in anticipation of the theme of machine and human body merging into 'the new flesh' with some gravitas. The title sequence closes as the logo of Civic TV scrolls on the screen followed by the corporate slogan, 'CIVIC TV The one you take to bed with you'. The logo shows a cartoon man sitting up in bed alone watching television with his hand under the covers, probably not operating the remote control. Channel 83 is presented as a masturbation aid and thus perhaps has more claims than many to being, in Marshall McLuhan's words, one of the 'extensions of man'.

The film camera probes the very material of the television picture in these opening sequences. Television employs an electronic light which is almost too bright to look at directly. By focusing on the image at the level of the pixel and the sound as static, both films proclaim an intention to investigate the matter of television. In *Poltergeist*, the prologue also establishes the investigation of mythical American values as a theme, which is summarized by the patriotic music and images. *Videodrome* presents for our ironic appreciation the image of the masturbatory hero – and the extent to which we are invited to identify with this is an early indicator of the way Cronenberg will play with our identification throughout.

They're Here!

In *Poltergeist*, the camera pulls out from the close up of the television static. It reveals the edge of the electronic frame: a Sony television set located in an ordinary family living room and then, somnambulant, a male figure, filmed from the side, slumped in an armchair. This is the father of the family, Steve Freeling (Craig T. Nelson) asleep in front of the television after an evening's viewing. The camera pans and focuses on a dog and follows him in a tracking shot as he goes up the stairs where the rest of the family are sleeping. Inexplicably, the family's youngest daughter, Carol Anne, gets out of bed and comes downstairs, then walks towards the television set, which is now startlingly light. The child begins to talk to the television:

Hello, what do you look like?... Talk louder, I can't hear you...

Then she seems to be answering questions:

Yes... yes... I don't know... I don't know.

The menace of television is established in this opening sequence. It is the means by which a strange power can communicate with the youngest, and most innocent of the family members (see Figure 8.2).

The television set is one of the most persistently recurring images of *Poltergeist*. In the early part of the film, television is a constant in the Freeling household, an ordinary part of any suburban American home. Characters watch television socially, as when the assembly of the guys for the football game sets the tenor of the friendly middle-class neighborhood. Steve and Diane Freeling watch television in bed at night, unwinding with

Figure 8.2 The American family finds itself under threat from within when the youngest daughter is abducted by the 'tv people' – spirits wreaking revenge in the suspenseful *Poltergeist* (Tobe Hooper, 1982)

a joint after the children have gone to bed. The image of the television set is used to build suspense and humor in the film. For example, when Carol Anne sits close to the television in the kitchen watching the static, Diane gently reprimands her daughter:

> Oh, honey, you're going to ruin your eyes, this is not good for you.

She changes the channel to a station showing a violent war film.

When Carol Anne is abducted by the 'television people' the set becomes more threatening. The family sit around the television in vigil waiting for their child to return, and we are presented with an inversion of the normal family viewing situation. Diane and her young son Robbie are cuddling on the sofa of the family room in what may appear at first sight to be a parent and child enjoying a quite evening at home watching television. In fact, they have their backs to the set and are not watching, but quietly *listening* to it. Diane is straining to hear, not the broadcast programs, but the static, in the hope that they might be able to communicate through this channel with Carol Anne. The television set has been inverted from disseminator of family entertainment to stealer of small children. It makes manifest the fear that television will rob the children of their minds by being the conduit by which spirits from 'the other side' abduct the Freelings' youngest child.

Light, especially electric light, is a dominating theme in *Poltergeist*: electrical storms, electric lights, the spiritual light – the child is exhorted to 'move towards the light *or 'stay away from the light' at different times. Poltergeist* exploits natural and artificial light to create atmosphere and suspense: early in the film, the darkening sky looms over the suburb as a storm approaches. Later, the living room of the Freeling family gradually darkens as they await the return of the child. A spiritualist, called in to help retrieve the abducted girl, explains why the spirits have taken the child. Like the film-makers interest with television:

> They're attracted to the one thing about her that's different from themselves. Her life force. It's very strong. It gives off it's own light.

In *Poltergeist*, as in many Spielberg films, the happy surface reality disguises a hidden malaise. The model tract home in which the Freeling family live is part of a burgeoning suburban development where children can play safely in the streets and the neighbors all know one another. Beneath this surface, though, is a tale of corporate greed – for the homes are built on the site of an old graveyard, a fact that the developer, Steve's employer Mr Teague, has conveniently covered up. The horror literally emerges from the mud in the form of corpses seeping through the freshly dug swimming pool in the back yard.

Poltergeist ends on a comic coda: the family are intact, having survived an assault by a whole army of disturbed souls. The family home has finally been completely destroyed; sucked into a vortex of subterranean rage. Exhausted from their ordeal, the Freeling family struggle up the stairs of the Holiday Inn to the refuge of a motel room. The camera lingers and, seeming too tired to follow the weary band into the room, remains focused on the motel landing as the door of the room closes behind them. A few seconds later the door opens and Steve pushes the television set out onto the walkway. It is a humorous moment, and one that implies, very ironically, that the American family is only safe when the television is absent. The opening shot of the film showed us the television set dominating the home; by the end, the family no longer have a home and the television set is ejected from their temporary abode. But the real villain of the piece is not television, but the property developers who cynically built homes on an old graveyard without moving the corpses first. *Poltergeist* uses television as the conduit for evil, but it does so self-consciously, with humor.

Long Live the New Flesh

Humor and horror are both abundant in *Videodrome*, but are made manifest in very different ways than in *Poltergeist*. The credits sequence of *Videodrome* ends as a video tape clicks on and Bridey (Julie Khaner) delivers an early morning call to Max Renn (James Woods), head of Channel 83, who lies asleep on the sofa. *Videodrome* presents Max Renn as the perfect character for a pornography movie – the masturbatory hero – procurer of pornography

for his own cable channel, with unlimited access to all the sex
he can get, albeit on videotape. In Cronenberg's hands this
premise becomes an invitation to explore the boundaries of the
permissible; Max tells his partners at Channel 83 that he is,

> Looking for something that'll break through. You know –
> something *tough*.

And his wish is certainly fulfilled when the satellite pirate,
Harlan (Peter Dvorsky), first shows him Videodrome. The
illegal transmission Harlan picks up shows scenes of torture
and degradation, but it transpires that what Max sees is something considerably more sinister. The Videodrome transmission
is part of a megalomaniac plot for world domination; it induces
hallucinations, which in turn bring about deadly tumors, but
not before compelling complete obeisance to Videodrome's
masters. After viewing Videodrome, Max begins to have hallucinations, and as the narrative meanders in and out of the first
person, it is difficult to tell the dreams from the reality. Before
long the real world becomes so nightmarish that the difference
seems not to matter. Max is sucked into a terrifying world
where he is a pawn in a game beyond his comprehension.
Instructed by Videodrome to kill his partners, Max obeys, but
then turns his killing machine body against those who would
control him. He kills Harlan and Barry Convex before finally
killing himself.

   In *Videodrome*, images of television are as carefully constructed
as the rest of the movie. The images we see on the television
screens were all shot by Cronenberg's regular cinematographer,
Mark Irwin, and then reshot on film (Lucas, 1983–4). As a first-
person narrative, *Videodrome* presents us with only those television images that Max sees, and there are only a limited range
of television programs that fall under his gaze. Channel 83 is
concerned mostly with sex, and has a minor side line interest
in violence. In the course of his work Max is obliged to watch
various kinds of soft pornography: *Samurai Dreams*, presented
to him by the representative of Hiroshima Video, or Masha's
old-fashioned *Apollo and Dionysus*. As Max comes under the
spell of the Videodrome signal his television viewing becomes
more strange and removed from the realms of erotic fantasy,

which now begin to look cosy and comforting in contrast. Max's contacts in the pornography business are not the nubile nymphomaniacs of the movies, but seedy Japanese businessmen like those from Hiroshima Video and elderly Madams like Masha (Lynne Gorman) whose sexuality revolts Max when she comes on to a young waiter in a restaurant. If Max were a conventional hero in a pornography movie the beautiful actors in the television program would be seducing Max and he would be having sex with them. Here the process is reversed as Max's lover gets taken away from him by television. At first Max dates Nicki Brand (Deborah Harry) for real, and they make love on the floor of his apartment while watching Videodrome. After a while Nicki goes to audition for Videodrome, against Max's advice, and he never sees her in the flesh again. Nicki never reappears except in Max's fantasies – she has moved from the real to the video world.

The world of television has been carefully constructed to look more like the world of B-movie horror and pornography than the everyday medium we are familiar with. The television set is a ubiquitous presence in *Videodrome*. Max Renn's apartment is lit throughout the film largely from the glow of the television set, which adds an electronic ambience whether daylight is present or not. Careful lighting and set design ensure that television has a strong visual presence. The normal location of television is disturbed from the opening sequences when Max uses his VCR as a slightly futuristic alarm clock. In *Videodrome* the uses of television grow increasingly more bizarre. Nicki browses through Max's video collection much as anyone might do on a first visit to a new friend's apartment. Her question, 'have you got any porno?' is perhaps not too strange, especially given that she is established as a highly sexed person. Nor is it odd that they should make love on the floor of the living room. However, things get increasingly bizarre when Nicki asks Max to:

Take out your Swiss army knife and cut me here, just, just a little.

He squirms in revulsion but when she suggests they: 'try a few things', he overcomes his squeamishness enough to pierce her ears while they make love. Max's entry into the world of sadomasochism at Nicki's initiation is tentative, but irrevocable. It is done in the light of the television set; in the glow of the Video-drome, and as they make love the location of the scene is trans-formed into the Videodrome; the boundary between fantasy and reality has been completely violated.

During one of his hallucinations Nicki appears on television: 'Come to Nicki', she exhorts. Max moves closer; the image on the television becomes a fuller close up, until Nicki's lips completely fill the screen. Max moves further forward and caresses the television, which is now pulsating like a living organism. The screen of the television set becomes engorged and Max buries his head in the balloon-like surface as if penetrating the screen. He literally gives the television head (see Figure 8.3). In a later scene Nicki is on television and Max is in the bare torture room of Videodrome armed with a whip. Max beats the television set with his whip and with every stroke he adminis-ters, Nicki's image on the television set screams. Television has become the parody of what its detractors feared: a purveyor of sex and violence and a corruptor of minds and morals. Video-drome is an extreme form of television, which will kill Max, but not before he has killed many others.

Max Renn is very much David Cronenberg's alter ego: Woods was chosen to play the role in part because of his physical resemblance to Cronenberg. Like Cronenberg, Max is obliged to defend his work; also like Cronenberg, he does not really know why. When the presenter of the chat show *The Rena King Show* asks Max:

Don't you feel that such shows contribute to a social climate of violence and sexual malaise? And do you care?

Max has his answer ready:

Certainly I care. I care enough in fact to give my viewers a harmless outlet for their fantasies and their frustrations, and as far as I'm concerned that's a socially positive act.

If you take Max's words at face value, this is a plausible enough response to Rena King's enquiry. But, if you believe the words, you do so at the neglect of the performance which clearly

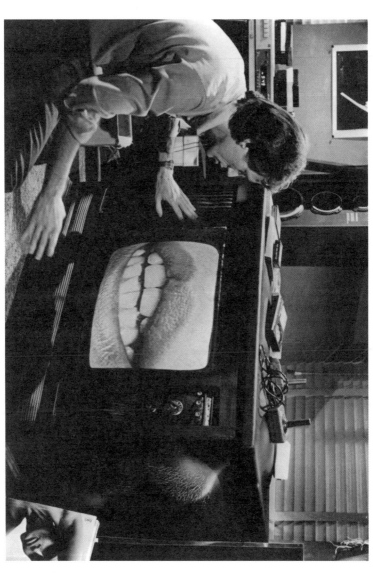

Figure 8.3 Max Renn (James Woods) is seduced into entering the realm of Videodrome by the television set which comes alive. Max penetrates the screen and becomes embroiled in an hallucinatory world in *Videodrome* (David Cronenberg, 1983)

signals dissemblance. Max is evidently accustomed to being asked such questions, and he has a stock answer ready, but as he wriggles with uncomfortable self-consciousness, he is evidently bewildered by such interrogations. Max's defences are learned, not felt, and the lingering impression is that Max does not know the answer, and isn't sure why he should care. As Bianca O'Blivion sardonically characterizes his statement afterwards:

> You said some very superficial things: violence, sex, imagi-nation, catharsis...

Max replies: 'My exact words.' The ironic distance is clear. Max has no opinion of television, no moral position to his work, any more than does Cronenberg. It is their lack of an ethical approach to their work that makes Cronenberg and Max vulner-able to abuse by those who do take a moral position. Masha warns Max against getting involved in Videodrome:

> It has got something that you don't have, Max. It has a philos-ophy and that's what makes it dangerous.

Indeed, all the dangerous characters in *Videodrome* have philosophies that they freely espouse. Masha is correct, Max is the only protagonist who does not espouse a credo of televi-sion. Brian O'Blivion (Jack Creley), the crazed inheritor of McLuhan-speak, argues that television is: 'the retina of the mind's eye', and that: 'there is nothing real outside our percep-tion of reality'. O'Blivion survives only in the library of video-tapes he has left behind, with his daughter, Bianca, as guardian of the treasure. She, too, has some unconventional, but firmly held, ideas about television. At the Cathode Ray Mission, screened booths provide the city's 'derelicts' with a chance to watch television. Bianca provides this service out of a spirit of evangelism:

> Watching TV will help patch them back into life's mixing board,

she earnestly tells Max. Meanwhile, Barry Convex, head of Spectacular Optical and controller of Videodrome plans to use the
Videodrome signal to launch an assault on the moral decrepi-
tude of the country. As his side-kick Harlan tells Max: 'North
America's getting soft, Patrón.' When Convex addresses his
crowd of agents for Spectacular Optical, it is in the manner of
a televangelist: he is a cross between Jim Baker and L. Ron
Hubbard. A demagogue of huge ambition, but who, when Max
shoots him, is totally corrupt inside: he explodes in a mess of
writhing tumor-filled flesh. In *Videodrome*, all the secondary
characters have insane views about television, which they try
to impose on Max with horrifc consequences. Max remains
uncommitted to any position until the Videodrome signal finally
denies him any thought.

Cronenberg's affinity with Max is evident when he tells Chris
Rodley:

> Part of the pressure to be creative is pressure to be medita-
> tive and philosophical. Everybody has it. It's a cliché in
> movies: you get a minor character, like a cab driver, who tells
> you his philosophy of life in thirty-eight seconds. Even if its
> bitter and negative and nihilistic, at least it's a philosophy.
> Masha tells Max Renn that Videodrome is dangerous because
> it has something he doesn't: a philosophy. Someone without
> a philosophy is weak, confused and fumbling by comparison.
> So there is a pressure to have that. Then it doesn't matter
> what your discourse is on: male/female relationships; life and
> death (Rodley, 1992: 19).

Max is Cronenberg's alter ego to the extent that he, too, is
required to have a philosophy, but, in all honesty, does not
have a clue about how to acquire one. If Cronenberg is a post-
modernist, it is not of the Baudrillard school, with an almost
mystical belief in the power of images to deny all power
(Baudrillard, 1983, 1987). Rather, his is closer to Lyotard's
brand of postmodernism: sceptical of metanarratives and most
touchy about the great modernist myth of the scientist-hero
(Lyotard, 1984). Science no longer fulfills its modernist mission:
it cannot answer questions, or solve problems, but we persist

in believing that it could, or should. Cronenberg looks coldly
at the evidence and determines that cynicism towards metanarratives is the best approach. This is unpolitical in the eyes
of Robin Wood (1983) and many others who seem to have an
unreconstructed belief in the image. Cronenberg merely tells it
like it is, with all the different positions warring with one
another. I cannot agree with Julian Petley when he argues that:

> *Videodrome*'s bizarre imagery and its apparently contemporary,
> modish sensibility express... an extremely traditional... view
> of television and video – one that has its roots deeply
> embedded in a particularly (although not peculiarly) North
> American tradition of pessimism about 'mass culture' (Petley,
> 1984: 35).

I also have trouble agreeing with Petley's assertion that:

> *Videodrome* also fits in very neatly with a certain, hardly
> surprising, 'Hollywood' tradition of negative representations
> of television, long regarded as cinema's bitterest enemy
> (Petley, 1984: 35–6).

On first appearance this does seem to be the case, but all the
expressions of a politics of television are bathed in irony or
distanced by undermining the credibility of their crazed sources.
In *Videodrome* Cronenberg has made a film that earnestly tries
to take on the issues of violence and sex in television by taking
the 'mass culture' argument at face value and running with it.
Videodrome seems to be saying, 'what if this nonsense about television being the extension of man were true?' Steven Shapiro
puts it well when he says that in *Videodrome*:

> The brutally hilarious strategy of *Videodrome* is to take media
> theorists such as Marshall McLuhan and Jean Baudrillard
> completely at their word, to overliteralize their claims for the
> ubiquitous mediatization of the real (Shapiro, 1993: 138).

Taking the theme to its logical conclusion creates a very illog-
ical world and an incredible *denouement*.

Videodrome ends with the suicidal gunshot to the head after Max Renn, his psyche now totally engulfed in the Videodrome hallucinations, has seen the act he is about to perform carried out on television. The narrative has worked itself into a frenzy of referentiality and introspection through Max's hallucinations. Max has, indeed, become video flesh, but we are unsure of what that actually means. His body has been transformed into a VCR and has produced a fleshy hand grenade, a huge slit opened in his abdomen – his physical metamorphosis has forged the body and the self with the machine.

Poltergeist and *Videodrome* both exploit all the cinematic tricks of the horror genre to construct strong images of the power of television. *Poltergeist* may be more visually restrained, but it uses the cinematic device of suspense to much greater impact. *Videodrome* is more visceral and disturbing, but it is also ironic and witty, and less involving as a consequence. Both films display a fear of television which is accompanied by fascination; a fascination for something so compellingly similar that it threatens the core identity of the medium depicting it. These representations of television seem to emanate from a fear of threat of absorption or eradication or both. The films construct television as possessing enormous power, as a symbolic regime and as a medium. In *Poltergeist* the strength of the family is powerful enough to finally resist; in *Videodrome* Max succumbs and commits suicide. In *Poltergeist* the television is ejected from the family; in *Videodrome* the set explodes and unleashes a pile of bloody viscera. Television is a compact visual icon in both films: for Cronenberg, it is a way of talking about images of sex and violence and of unraveling, or re-raveling, some of the discourses about television subscribed to by academics (many of which are in absolute need of ridicule). Spielberg uses television as a medium by which the world of spirits is able to enter the quotidian domesticity of suburban American. In Spielberg's universe no amount of technology can fully suppress the spiritual realm.

Cronenberg and Spielberg are two directors whose names are rarely mentioned in the same sentence. Cronenberg has acquired a devout art house following and is notoriously uncommercial, while Spielberg is an unabashed popular filmmaker. Julian Petley poses them as diametrically opposed, but equally reactionary (Petley, 1984: 36). Petley argues that they are both, for different reasons, perfect directors for the 1980s and he hates them both. I agree that Cronenberg and Spielberg are archetypical 1980s directors and I enjoy their work immensely: they have each forged an identity for themselves as acknowledged auteurs through profoundly filmic work which exploits the cinema to its fullest. Both directors are concerned to exploit the fantastic possibilities of film and in the works under consideration employ the special effects lab to exquisite effect, as, for example, in the depiction of the spirits wafting down the stairs in *Poltergeist* or the stomach-become-video-cassette-player in *Videodrome*. However, it is not their skill as film-makers that ensures them a place in this book. *Poltergeist* and *Videodrome* are considered here because they are powerfully important contributions to the construction of television, by two people who are most resolutely concerned to influence the meaning of the cinema. Both films address television from the point of view of the cinema and exhibit a rival's suspicion about television.

The Postmodern Turn and Television

Horror and science fiction films superficially construct television as something to be feared: but in recent years both genres have become increasingly ironic. The horror film has become self-reflexive in its representation of television as fearful. Perhaps the most extreme examples of horror pastiche have come from Wes Craven. *Shocker* (Wes Craven, 1989) takes the idea of television as corrupting to its ultimate, ironic, extreme. A television repair man, Horace Pinker (Mitch Pileggi), turns mass murderer and is executed for his crimes. At the moment of execution, however, he is able to meld with the electric current and lives on to inhabit the power supply. Pinker is able to emanate from the television sets and torment his victims further. Popular anxieties about television are ridiculed as Craven makes a risibly excessive monster out of the dread in which television is regarded. At one point Pinker jumps out of television and our hero, Jonathan, has the wit to freeze the frame: 'You bought into TV, Pinker', he tells the bad guy: 'Play by its rules.' Craven is master of the reflexive horror film, sending up the genre with glee. In *Scream* (1996) Craven has a group of potential murder victims watching and commenting on a slasher video, while unbeknownst to them a killer stands behind them. Other comical films about the putative horror of television include *TerrorVision* (Ted Nicolaou, 1986), which concerns the repercussions for an earth family when the inhabitants of the planet Pluton do not properly dispose of a mutating monster life form, the Hungry Monster pet. While the Putterman parents go out for the evening, the grandfather and son stay at home to watch television via the massive satellite dish the father has erected in the back yard. The horror film has become too parodic and television has become neutered by its domesticity.

Science fiction turned its attention to television with parodic self-referentiality in Paul Michael Glaser's *The Running Man* (1987). This extended chase movie is set in the twenty-first century when censorship has outlawed all forms of entertainment and art except for television. *The Running Man*, like the other films from the 1980s discussed above, is ironic about fears about television and makes special fun out of caricaturing the collusion between the network and the government. The film opens with all the marks of a classic action adventure, with Ben Richards (Arnold Schwarzenegger) as an officer of the law flying in a police helicopter. When required to fire on a crowd demonstrating about the price of food, Richards strenuously objects, but he is overpowered by colleagues and subsequently imprisoned for his insubordination. Later, broadcasts of these events distort the 'reality' the film cameras have shown us and the television news constructs Richards as responsible for the slaughter of that day, even dubbing him 'the Butcher of Bakersfield'. When Amber (Maria Conchita Alonso) first meets Richards she recognizes him from the television coverage and is afraid of him. Only when subsequent events at which she is present are similarly misrepresented does her faith in the media decline and her trust in Richards increase.

In *The Running Man*, television executives are as powerful as ministers of state, and their roles overlap. The host of the television game show, *The Running Man*, is played by Richard Dawson, an actor familiar to American television viewers as the host of *Family Feud*. *The Running Man* is sanctioned by the Department of Justice to broadcast the pursuit and murder of convicted criminals by a team of latter-day gladiators. Each state-sanctioned thug in 'The Stalkers' has his own preferred method of killing the luckless miscreants sentenced to death on live television. The story is told largely tongue-in-cheek, not least because of the self-parodic image of masculinity which Arnold Schwarzenegger represents at this stage in his career. As he is about to be fired down a cannon into an unknown future, Schwarzenegger delivers his famous line from *The Terminator* (James Cameron, 1984): 'I'll be back!' To which his tormentor replies, 'Only in a re-run.'

The Running Man targets the differences of television from film to create a grotesque parody of the rival medium. It is television's 'live' quality and video technology's capacity for the swift manipulation of images that are seen as especially malignant here. Television's 'liveness' has always been represented as a mark of its alterity in all manner of films about television. The VCR with its capacity for replaying and pausing images was widely adopted in the 1980s and changed the perception of television. *The Running Man* closes with a classic Hollywood trope: Richards and Amber walk off into the sunset to applause from onlookers. The superiority of the film narrative over television is affirmed in this heavy-handed closing shot. The attacks on television here are remarkably unsubtle and finally, the satire falls flat. As Julian Petley says:

> The film ends up facing both ways at once by providing exactly the kind of violent spectacle that it criticizes Killian (the villain) for manufacturing and twenty-first century audiences for watching (Petley, 1988: 312).

RoboCop (Paul Verhoeven, 1987), released the same year as *The Running Man*, presents a more subtle critique of television as part of the backdrop to a considerably more sophisticated chase story. The films from the 1980s we have discussed send television up, but hardly construct the medium as a serious threat for the dread is always tinged with knowing irony.

In this chapter we have seen that the fearful regard in which television is held has long been a fecund source of imagery for film-makers. In the films of the 1980s, however, we find that the fantastic genres have reached a high point of reflexivity about their own image-making and indulge freely in ironic represen- tation. These films use the icon of television to represent some- thing that we should find frightening, but that is also comical. Television no longer has the power to terrify; but the mythology of television as harmful persists to be ridiculed by film-makers like Cronenberg and Craven. Only the most naive can believe that television can still terrify.

9

SEEING THE FUNNY SIDE: TELEVISION AS A FIGURE OF FUN IN POPULAR COMEDY

In the previous chapter we saw how television is no longer regarded as fearful by Hollywood cinema. The horror and science fiction genres have become so parodic and self-referential that they are not able to take anything seriously. Hollywood comedies have frequently approached television and they often represent cinema's rival as a good source of humor. Television is figured in all manner of comedies, including screwball comedies such as *The Gazebo* (George Marshall, 1959) or *The Thrill of it All* (Norman Jewison, 1962); it is present in the drug influenced humor of *The Groove Tube* (Ken Shapiro, 1974) or *TerrorVision* (Ted Nicoloau, 1986) and can also be found in more 'serious' comedies. Films such as *Being There* (Hal Ashby, 1979), *The King of Comedy* (Martin Scorcese, 1983) and *The Cable Guy* (Ben Stiller, 1996) stretch the boundaries of the comedic and venture into the realm of the tragic in their exploration of characters who have been affected in one way or another by television. The comedies provide us with a valuable counter to claims that the cinema represents television exclusively as a dangerous medium. In this chapter we examine how the Hollywood comedies have found plenty to laugh at in television.

Television and the Comedienne

In Chapter 4 we saw how, during the 1950s, the mass media debate resonated with fears about female empowerment to contribute to an image of television as frighteningly feminine. The Hollywood melodrama contributed to this image, by constructing television as a suspect feminine industry in which gender roles are frequently unstable. Doris Day is the epitome of Hollywood femininity, and when she gets a job in television we see the medium depicted as ridiculous in the extreme.

The Thrill of it All stars Doris Day as Beverly Boyer, wife of Dr Gerald Boyer (James Garner) and mother of two children. Quite serendipitously, Beverly meets the paterfamilias of a family business, which produces Happy Soap, and becomes their television sponsor. Beverly is an ordinary housewife plucked almost at random to appear on television. Her first assignment proves a complete embarrassment: she looks at the wrong camera, fluffs her lines and even gets the name of the product wrong. Nonetheless, 1200 people called in to say she was:

> The most refreshing, sincere person that ever sold a bar of soap.

The Old Man declares:

> Beverly's my new Happy Girl.

Beverly's naivety and lack of professionalism is evidently responsible for her success. Norman Jewison's film shows how television and Beverly are ideally suited to one another: both are silly and ingenuous. Beverly is guileless enough to speak up when she notices the formulaic narrative of Happy Playhouse:

> Say, isn't that scene like the one last week, with the Nazi and the, you know, woman...?

She is assured by the television executive that:

> The public doesn't notice things like that.

Jewison sets up the knowing professionals against the public they claim to know by juxtaposing this scene with one of Beverly's children watching television at home with the housekeeper. Young Andrew observes:

They did that play last week except they wore different costumes.

Even his little sister concurs:

Yeah, it's the same story.

Meanwhile, back in the studio viewing room another television executive insists:

It's much too subtle a variation for the public to detect,

while the gathered assembly sagely nod their agreement. Clearly, the film audience know better and the joke is at the expense of the urbane television professionals, not the television audience.

Although run by male executives, television is constructed as a very feminine medium. Beverly's 'natural' ability at television stems from her stereotypical female traits of naivety, lack of dissimulation and old-fashioned straight talking. Working in television causes a crisis in gender identity for Beverly, though, for she is torn between her responsibility to be a good housewife and being a successful television performer. A huge strain is placed on her marriage as a consequence. For example, when the Old Man decides to build his favorite sponsor a swimming pool, Beverly is so busy she simply forgets to inform Gerald about it. More importantly, she omits to tell her husband that the pool has been built in front of the family garage. The predictable consequence is that Gerald accidentally drives his car straight into the swimming pool when he comes home after dark. A heated argument ensues that touches upon the issue of women's work. 'What ever happened to my rights as a woman?' Beverly asks him. 'I'll tell you what happened to them,' Gerald replies,

They grew and they grew until they suffocated my rights as a man. Whoever said all men are created equal didn't anticipate a woman making a hundred thousand dollars a year and spending it on swimming pools.

He begins to pack his things to leave and she asks him to stop.

> I'm going to continue to do it until you give up this asinine career and go back to being a wife,

he says and he leaves her, but not before kicking several boxes of Happy Soap detergent into the pool. Gerald is resentful of his wife's career, not least because the work seems so 'asinine' to him. Gerald has to eat his words if he wants to return home, however, and says:

> Forgive me for acting like a Victorian fool and refusing to accept the fact that you have a career.

Ultimately, Beverly resists the opportunity of striking a blow for women's liberation, and decides instead to return to being 'a Doctor's wife again'. The idea of having another child becomes much more fulfilling than having a career of her own after she helps Gerald to deliver a baby in an emergency.

The Thrill of it All finally affirms that a woman's place is in the home and ridicules the notion that a woman should have a career. The only possibility of employment for women is as a television 'sponsor'; a job requiring no evident skill or training. This film perpetuates the idea of television as a mendacious, feminine medium. In Chapter 4 we saw how films such as *My Blue Heaven* established motherhood as antithetic to having a career in television. *The Thrill of it All* goes further and shows television employment as undermining the structure of the American family; work in the medium gives Beverly lucrative employment that disrupts familial gender roles and power relations. When she is in employment, Beverly's children and husband are neglected. Working in television allows Beverly no time to do the kinds of domestic tasks she used to do, such as making her own tomato ketchup.

Part of the humor of this reactionary comedy comes from the nature of television success as symbolized by the very feminine star persona of Doris Day. The irony is that Doris Day was one of the top paid actresses of the time, no doubt earning considerably more than Beverly Boyer and many other television performers. *The Thrill of it All* affirms film as superior to television, by showing how its rival medium insults the intelligence of the viewer. This film dismisses television as a threat by representing executives as removed from their public and performers as silly female amateurs. The image of cinema is enhanced and the ego of the cinema-goer massaged in *The Thrill of it All*.

The rather old-fashioned comedy of manners and marriage, which *The Thrill of it All* typifies, was a dying genre in the 1960s. The female audience was abandoning the cinema and found television suited their domestic routine more appropriately. The light romantic comedy genre was failing to attract cinema audiences while the television sitcom was building a strong following. Television's most successful genre, the situation comedy, put the romantic comedy through a crisis of confidence in the 1960s.

A Juvenile Take on Television

The comedy film shifted significantly in the 1960s to appeal to the increasingly young audience for the cinema. The 'family film' became a euphemism for the children's film and some comedies aimed at this age group play upon the youngsters knowledge of television. *Never a Dull Moment* (Jerry Paris, 1968) is a Walt Disney production which stars Dick Van Dyke as Jack Albany, a struggling television actor. When Jack is mistaken for a hit man, Ace Williams, by a criminal gang run by Edward G. Robinson, he reckons that his best chances of survival rest with acting out the part. All he knows about gangsters is what he learned from television, but it stands him in good stead as he bluffs his way with the criminal fraternity. Disney further lampooned the television industry in the children's movie *The Barefoot Executive* (Robert Butler, 1971) which features a monkey who is more adept than any human programmer at predicting the success or failure of television shows.

The teenage and young adult audience of the 1960s and 70s were the first generation to have grown up with television. Films addressing a youth audience at this time could rely on a fairly high degree of knowledge about television. Indeed, there were many films produced to exploit successful television comedy series during this time, including British offerings: *On the Buses* (Harry Booth, 1971), *Bless This House* (Gerald Thomas, 1972), *Steptoe and Son* (Cliff Owen, 1972), and in the US such films as *McHale's Navy* (Edward J. Montagne, 1964) and *Munster, Go Home* (Earl Bellamy, 1966).

In the 1960s and 70s television grew to be very unhip, associated as it was with suburban domesticity. Young people found their entertainment outside of the home and television broadcasters had a hard time attracting them. Cinema audiences grew younger and the movies began to cash in on the image television had for youngsters of being a medium aimed at the older generation. The cinema was able to define itself as a rebellious medium in contrast. Hollywood film production companies, often staffed by people who had learned their trade in television, turned their attention to satirizing television. The less regulated world of films allowed for a broader, more vulgar humor than was acceptable on television at the time, permitting parodies of television to flourish.

The Groove Tube (Ken Shapiro, 1974) stars comedian Chevy Chase and is little more than a series of sketches sending up television programs, advertisements and other areas of popular culture. For example, the film opens with a television set being discovered by a group of primitive men, in a direct reference to Kubrick's *2001: A Space Odyssey* (1968). The subject matter is substantially more risqué and liberal than would have been permitted on American (or British) television at the time as, for example, in the International Sex Games sketch. As a satire, *The Groove Tube* fails because it bears too many similarities to its subject and thus fails to have much of a critical edge. The absence of any continuity in this series of largely unconnected sketches is reminiscent of an evening watching television but is also typical of the drug-infused counter cultural offerings of the time. Other films in the same groove include those of the Kentucky Fried Theater, *The Kentucky Fried Movie* (John Landis, 1977) and *Amazon Women on the Moon* (Joe Dante, 1987). The relationship between film and television comedy has always been close: there have been films of television programs and television programs based on films since the very earliest days of broadcasting. But one American television program has proven a particularly rich source of films. The late night comedy and variety show *Saturday Night Live* has spawned innumerable films, including *Caddyshack* (Harold Ramis, 1980), *Coneheads* (Steve Barron, 1993) and *It's Pat* (Adam Bernstein, 1994), many of which build on the characters who first appeared on the television show. The divide between television and film has narrowed in the subgenre of alternative and zany comedy.

Television Nostalgia

Film-makers who came of age in the television age are able to look back on the early days of television with a degree of nostalgia. Billy Crystal's *Mr Saturday Night* (1992) recounts the eponymous hero's life working in entertainment and television. Comedies about television have found nostalgia a useful shield against any residual animosity between film and television. *My Favorite Year* (Richard Benjamin, 1982) tells of the conflict between the very different worlds of silent cinema and television variety as embodied in the two heroes: Alan Swann (Peter O'Toole), swashbuckling hero of the days before sound, and King Kaiser (Joseph Bologna), fast talking and vulgar pioneer (based on the real television comedy pioneer Sid Caesar). The story is told through the first-person narration of Benji Stone (Mark Linn-Baker) who is a youngster with his first job in television assigned to look after Swann. The film is set in 1954 when:

Television was live and comedy was King.

Alan Swann is attempting to rejuvenate his acting career which was decimated by the coming of sound. Terrified at the prospect of appearing on live television, Swann asks his young minder:

You mean it all goes into the camera lens and just spills out into people's houses?

When Swann learns that the show is performed before a live audience he is even more stunned, 'I am not an actor,' he declares, 'I am a movie star,' as he begins to remove his costume. The world of television is completely alien to Swann, and the world of silent cinema is exotic to Benji. Finally, the two worlds are brought together when Swann swings from the lighting cables above the studio enchanting the studio audience as he does so. Swann's act is captured on the multiple monitors around the studio and seems to unify the disparate worlds of television and film in harmonic counterposition.

My Favorite Year is a gentle satire on television's early days and looks at its subject through rose tinted spectacles. By contrast, *Quiz Show* (Robert Redford, 1994), also about television in the 1950s, presents a significantly less romantic picture than *My Favorite Year*. While Richard Benjamin's film projects a vision of television as a lively and exciting place to work, *Quiz Show* shows much darker forces in play. Based on the true events of American television's most ignoble hour – the quiz show scandals which came to light in 1959 – *Quiz Show* tells how the producers of a popular television program, *Twenty One*, groomed contestants and fixed the outcome of their shows. It portrays television as a deceitful, manipulative industry.

Quiz Show sets up cinema as the more honest medium by undermining the credibility of television performance. The producers of *Twenty One* deceive their viewers into believing that the contestants on the show are *not* acting. The television show presents itself as a genuine contest of wits between unstaged competitors. Film narrative has the capacity to reveal a truth that is hidden from television audiences, however. Redford affirms the greater credibility of cinema technology over television by using the film projector at a crucial stage in the narrative. The denouement of the film comes when a kinetoscope recording of *Twenty One* is brought into court and played in slow motion: the film projector plainly reveals the cheating which television audiences were unable to discern. *Quiz Show* is made by a dedicated cineaste: Redford's intellectual investment in cinema cannot be doubted – his attitude towards television is that of a competitor. Richard Benjamin, by contrast, began his career in television and has no problem in depicting the medium with respect. The director who believes that film is a unique art form technogenetically constructs television as different from cinema. The director who has worked in television and film has a different relationship to both media – Benjamin is able to portray television as a medium of entertainment; Robert Redford can only depict it as a mass medium with dangerously ominous implications.

Television as a Saturnalia

There are many other examples of films with a nostalgic approach to television which lack the critical edge of *Quiz Show*. *Grief* (Richard Glatzer, 1993) is a camp tale about people working for a low budget television production company which makes a soap opera of alarming awfulness, *The Love Judge*. Comedy films are frequently set in the world of television entertainment, for example, *SoapDish* (Michael Hoffman, 1990) and *Delirious* (Tom Mankiewicz, 1991). These films use television as an everyday setting for their comedy. Other films, however, use television as a location far removed from the real world. Indeed, television often provides a liminal space where Saturnalia rules; a fantasy locale where satirists can experiment with, and comment upon, the prevailing power structures. In *Being There* (Hal Ashby, 1979) Peter Sellers plays a dim-witted man who becomes a television guru when his asinine sayings are taken for profound aphorisms. The ordinary Joe becomes counselor to the President of the United States on the basis of knowledge acquired from a lifetime of watching television. Social class is turned topsy turvy in Ashby's satire on fame and celebrity politics (*Being There* is discussed further in Chapter 7). Sydney Pollack investigates gender prejudice and stereotypes in *Tootsie* (1982) through the eyes of Michael Dorsey (Dustin Hoffman), a struggling stage actor. Noticing that women stand a better chance of being cast in the lucrative daytime television soap operas, Michael dons the apparel of a woman to become Dorothy Michaels and is cast in a daytime hospital drama (see Figure 9.1). His borrowed gender leads him to discover how the other half live and teaches him to be a more sensitive human being. Television performance provides the committed stage actor with a greater insight into the human (especially female) condition.

   Perhaps the most painfully embarrassing satire on television celebrity is Martin Scorcese's *The King of Comedy* (1983). The television world itself is turned upside down when a fan, Rupert

Figure 9.1 Michael Dorsey (Dustin Hoffman) cross-dresses and assumes the persona of Dorothy Michaels in order to secure a lead role in a hit day-time soap opera in *Tootsie* (Sydney Pollack, 1982)

Pupkin (Robert De Niro), decides to abduct his hero, television host Jerry Langford (Jerry Lewis). 'Jerry' is modelled very closely on Johnny Carson, whose nighttime show became a venerable institution on American television with many latter-day imitations. Pupkin is one of Scorcese and De Niro's most frightening characters who rehearses for his dream television appearance on Jerry's show with cardboard cutout figures and a prerecorded laughter track. Where other devotees might daydream about being on the show, Rupert acts on his fantasies and concocts an elaborate plan to take Jerry hostage and appear on the show in his stead (see Figure 9.2). Rupert succeeds in his plan but is arrested and sent to prison. However, the most terrifying feature of *The King of Comedy* is that ultimately all Rupert's wishes seem to come true and Rupert becomes a famous television personality. Society indulges Rupert in a fantasy which the film constructs as being deranged. Television fans are under attack here and our sympathy is with Jerry throughout his harrowing abduction. Scorcese vindicates the television obsessive in the end; television is depicted as a fickle industry in which success is based on determination and manipulation. Film-making seems a much more gentle art in comparison.

The 1990s Romantic Comedy and Television

In contrast with *The King of Comedy*, which shows television success as bordering on the pathological, two 1990s romantic comedies feature central male characters who become successful and sane television workers. *Mrs Doubtfire* (Chris Columbus, 1993) and *Groundhog Day* (Harold Ramis, 1993) both utilize television as a plot element through which the central male character renegotiates his personal relationships. In each case the protagonists are disgruntled television performers with unhappy private lives when the film opens: both have to reconfigure their relationship with television before they can overcome obstacles to private fulfilment.

The male leads in both *Mrs Doubtfire* and *Groundhog Day* (Robin Williams and Bill Murray respectively) were established television performers before they came to work in the cinema.

Figure 9.2 Rupert Pupkin (Robert De Niro) succeeds in presenting the Jerry Langford Show after abducting Jerry (Jerry Lewis) in *The King of Comedy* (Martin Scorsese, 1983)

Robin Williams and Bill Murray both began their show business careers as stand-up comedians, following a path into film via television. Williams' television career was founded on his character Mork, originally appearing in *Happy Days* and subsequently featuring in the spin-off series *Mork and Mindy*; while Murray is most celebrated for his distinguished stint on *Saturday Night Live*. Williams and Murray clearly bring their established television personae to their film work and in *Mrs Doubtfire* and *Groundhog Day* these are fully exploited in the development of character and plot motivation.

The directors of these films have excellent television and film credentials. Harold Ramis, director of *Groundhog Day*, co-wrote *National Lampoon's Animal House* (1978) before he directed *Caddyshack* (1980) and *Ghostbusters* (1984). Ramis first worked with Bill Murray in 1974 on a *Second City TV* special and both worked with John Belushi on various *National Lampoon* projects. Ramis says of his collaborations with Murray:

> Our five previous efforts had generated over half a billion dollars in gross box office – in fact, some of the grossest box office ever generated – and *Ghostbusters* had become a pop-culture phenomenon (Ramis, 1993: 69).

Groundhog Day is a successful, popular film, by a director with a solid track record in the genre. In *Groundhog Day*, Bill Murray plays the cynical and urbane Phil Connors, a TV weatherman covering the corny event of Groundhog Day from Punxsatawney, Philadelphia, once too often. Rita Hanson (Andie MacDowell), a new producer assigned to work with him, is quickly established as naive by her evident enchantment with the weatherman's blue-screen – a feature of television production with which most people are familiar. The studio hand likes her, and tells Phil that she is fun, but the grumpy weather man is not convinced: 'She's fun, but not my kind of fun', he avers. Phil will learn to change his idea of Rita and of fun as the film progresses.

On arriving in Punxsatawney with Rita and cameraman Larry (Chris Elliott), Phil squirms with discomfort at small town life. He is especially irritated by Rita's enthusiasm for the way the people of the town get involved in the Groundhog Day festivities. He dismisses them, 'They're hicks, Rita', he tells her. Although Rita encourages Phil to participate, advising him: 'You're missing all the fun', he is adamantly unmoved.

Part of Phil's urbanity comes from the sophistication of working in the glamorous world of television; his frustration is that he is only a weather man. Phil does an adequate job of introducing the Groundhog Day ceremony, in which the groundhog is pulled out of his cage at dawn by the elders of Punxsatawney who declare that, since he does cast a shadow, this presages another six weeks of winter. After the ceremony, Phil is expected to record a concluding piece, but his cur-mudgeonly nature prevents him from joining in the spirit of the event:

> This is one time where television really fails to capture the excitement of a large squirrel predicting the weather. I, for one, am very grateful to have been here. From Punxsatawney, this is Phil Connors. So long.

Rita asks him to rerecord his sign-off, this time 'without the sarcasm'. But Phil walks away in disgust: 'We got it. I'm outta here.' His characteristic grouchiness is embellished through his refusal to perform properly for television.

The night after the broadcast a snowstorm prevents the crew from leaving Punxsatawney and Phil grows increasingly annoyed at being compelled to stay an extra night in this parochial community. Phil's frustration is compounded when he wakes the next day to find that it is Groundhog Day all over again. As Harold Ramis puts it, Phil is:

> Stuck in Punxsatawney and *every* day is Groundhog Day until he learns how to be a decent human being and finds true love (Ramis, 1993: 68).

Caught in a time loop; destined to relive the same day over and over again, Phil is trapped in a place he finds bogus on an occasion he finds sentimental. He becomes angry, frustrated and overcome with despair. He addresses the camera on his umpteenth Groundhog Day, as follows:

This is pitiful. A thousand people freezing their butts off waiting to worship a *rat*. What a hype! Groundhog Day used to mean something in this town. They used to pull the hog out and they used to *eat* it. You're hypocrites, all of you... I'll give you a winter prediction. It's gonna be cold. It's gonna be grey. And it's gonna last you for the rest of your life.

The camera closes in on Phil's haggard face and his performance garners a perplexed response from Rita and Larry. Phil's fate seems to be interminable now: looking drawn and exhausted, this spiritual low point is followed by numerous attempts at self-destruction, all of which end with him waking at six in the morning on Groundhog Day.

Numerous recordings are made of Phil's Groundhog Day item, but the final recording initiates the film's resolution, and breaks the spell. Phil has tried repeatedly and unsuccessfully, to save the life of an old homeless man whose time has come and the man's passing becomes Phil's epiphany. The next day Phil is surrounded by smiling well-wishers when he makes the following recording:

When Chekhov saw the long winter, he saw a winter bleak and dark and bereft of hope. Yet we know that winter is just another step in the cycle of life. But standing here among the people of Punxsatawney, and basking in the warmth of their hearths and hearts, I couldn't imagine a better fate than a long and lustrous winter. From Punxsatawney, it's Phil Connors. So long.

A single cutaway during Phil's speech shows Rita looking at him as if she suddenly sees something impressive in him that she has not previously recognized. Following the speech, the crowd of people gathered around him break out into spontaneous applause and congratulate Phil on his performance. Even Larry, the usually taciturn technician, shakes his hand in congratulation: 'man, you touched me', he says, stifling a tear. Phil has learned some Capra-esque lessons: to love small town life and to appreciate the people he had formerly dismissed as 'hicks'. On his last day trapped in Groundhog Day, Phil makes friends among the community: he catches a boy falling from a tree, changes the burst tire of some elderly women and saves a diner from choking to death in a restaurant. He stays on at the Groundhog Day dance he had eschewed the first time round and is the life and soul of the party, playing boogie woogie piano to rapturous applause. Finally, he is auctioned off to Rita, who buys him for $339.88 – all the money she has in her purse.

Groundhog Day is the story of an education and its moral is that even a hardened cynic like Phil can be redeemed. Phil has learned three interconnected things: to appreciate small town American life; to woo Andie MacDowell, *and* to make the perfect television broadcast. Learning to abandon his cynicism towards television is symbolic of Phil's reformation, enabling him to advance psychologically so that he can form a relationship with Rita. *Groundhog Day* is a delightful romantic comedy about the reformation of a television-hardened cynic.

The credits sequence of *Mrs Doubtfire* establishes that Daniel Hillard (Robin Williams), like Phil Connors at the beginning of *Groundhog Day*, has an unhappy relationship with television. Daniel makes his living 'doing voices' and in the opening credits sequence he is dubbing the voice of a cartoon character, Pugsie the Parrot, singing *Figaro* before being captured for a cat's 'afternoon snack'. But when the bird's captor offers him 'a nice, soothing cigarette' as his final luxury before being executed, Daniel begins to break from the script and improvise. While the images show the bird apparently enjoying his last smoke, Daniel puts contradictory words into the character's mouth:

> I will not do this. I cannot. Oh, what a foul way for a bird to die. I don't want to get beak cancer! No! My lungs are blackened!

Daniel improvises the bird coughing and spluttering and subsequently argues that it is immoral to show a cartoon character enjoying a cigarette. Reprimanded by the smoking, pragmatic, studio manager, Daniel walks out on the job, telling the manager to 'piss off' rather than compromise his belief that children should not be set a poor example.

Later he is ejected from his family home by his earnest wife, Miranda (Sally Field), partly for losing his job, but also because of a history of irresponsibility, not least in allowing a 'mobile petting zoo' to wreck the home on the occasion of their son's twelfth birthday. Excluded from employment and from his home, Daniel decides to fill both absences at once by working as housekeeper to his own family. He still keeps one foot in the door of television by working in the shipping department of television station KTVU, but at 2.30 each afternoon he clocks off and dons the apparel of an elderly English woman (although, bizarrely, her accent is Scottish) to pass himself off as Mrs Doubtfire, housekeeper and child minder to the Hillard children. Daniel thus has the peculiar honor of being one of the few characters in the history of film to wear drag in order to be reunited with his family. He gets no special *frisson* from cross-dressing, and there is none of the sexual energy of classic gender-bending movies like *Some Like it Hot* (Billy Wilder, 1959), nor the faux feminism of *Tootsie* (Sydney Pollack, 1982). He insists throughout that he must be able to *see* his children and the cross-dressing strategy allows him to do this, albeit through an unreciprocated gaze, since they do not (at first) recognize him. The tension of having the erstwhile father of the family dressed as an elderly foreign lady is finally diffused when Daniel is hired to play Mrs Doubtfire as a character on children's television at KTVU. Daniel does not have to give up on the cross-dressing character in order to be reunited with his children, merely to find a different place for her to exist. Mrs Doubtfire continues to be the responsible breadwinner through the agency of television. *She* (Mrs Doubtfire) continues to earn money that *he* (Daniel) needs to redeem himself as a good father in the eyes of his ex-wife and children.

Towards the end of the film, the family (minus Daniel) are preparing a meal in the kitchen and talking about how they miss Mrs Doubtfire. They are interrupted by Mrs Doubtfire's familiar voice calling 'hello, my dears' from the television set in the adjacent family room. The fractured family is momentarily reunited around the image of their father, in drag, contained within the frame of the family television set. The mother and children find his performance both very funny (they laugh) and very moving (tears well up in their eyes). The modern American family, it seems, can survive quite well without a father, but like to be able to see him on television from time to time – if only to be assured that he is still working.

Both *Groundhog Day* and *Mrs Doubtfire* tell tales of self-discovery. The more mature relationship with television these characters forge enables them to advance personally and form a new domestic or romantic relationship. Daniel is reinstalled in the family, albeit in grotesque; Phil is sufficiently reformed to enter a new romance. In *Groundhog Day* and *Mrs Doubtfire* the male television worker must abandon cynicism about television by giving an exemplary on screen performance, on television's terms. Giving a great television performance has become, in the 1990s popular film, a signal of one's social acceptance and success. At an earlier time, in *A Face in the Crowd*, for example, good television performers are always mendacious manipulators.

The shifts in the cinematic representation of television are, in part, the consequences of the changes in the relationship between the film and television industries. The popular 1990s films discussed above show television as an integral part of everyday life, and television workers as people with whom we can identify. The increasingly close relationship between the television and film industries, economically, technologically and socially, creates an environment where television can no longer be seen as alien to film. *Groundhog Day* and *Mrs Doubtfire* show television work as a curative rather than a corrosive agent, more capable of contributing to a happy resolution than a tragic end. Television is something that Hollywood has evidently learned to love.

There are notable exceptions to the above. *The Cable Guy* (Ben Stiller, 1996) stars one of today's biggest box-office comedians, Jim Carrey, as the eponymous anti-hero in an anti-television tract. *The Cable Guy* is the brooding tale of a pathologically clingy cable installation worker who latches on to Steven Kovacks (Matthew Broderick) and begins to meddle with his life. Jim Carrey's character is a chameleon figure with no fixed identity who goes by various names – all of them belonging to sitcom characters. His only recollection of childhood is of being left alone to watch television while his mother went out to work in the evenings. The Cable Guy represents the television generation of the mass media nightmare: all grown up but emotionally stunted; physically ready for adult relationships but psychologically unprepared. The central thrust of the mass media rhetoric that television is necessarily bad for you under-pins the film.

The Cable Guy failed at the box office because of its dark mood. The more typical image of television in contemporary comedy is not malign. Today's film-makers readily use televi-sion properties as the basis for comedies. Characters from old television shows have become the subject of many films in recent years such as *The Brady Bunch Movie* (Betty Thomas, 1995). This film is based on the premise that the Brady Bunch of the successful and long-running television series still exist in today's California, unchanged since the 1960s. *The Brady Bunch Movie* succeeds in ridiculing young people of the 1960s and 90s in equal measure. As film studios and television companies have found themselves part of the same conglomerates (see Chapter 2), television properties have been readily exploited as subjects for films such as *The Flintstones* (Brian Levant, 1994) and *The Addams Family* (Barry Sonnenfeld, 1990).

In the 1990s, television has become part of the experience of cinema audiences and film-makers alike. Broadcast images are familiar to everyone and television is a medium that provides many film-makers with work. The divide between television and film is no longer as wide as it once was. Directors of popular films, in particular, are able to work in both media without feeling that one is necessarily better than the other. Most of the more recent comedy films discussed eschew the image of tele-vision as a harmful mass medium; instead, television is often depicted as fun and pleasurable. The cultural technology of tele-vision is no longer seen as a challenge to film workers, but is just one in the armature of popular media in which today's film-makers can work.

10

SO, WHAT'S THE IDEA OF TELEVISION?

At the beginning of this book I posed the question: 'What does television mean?' In attempting to answer this question, I have focused on the images of television presented by the cinema, a technology that has long been television's close contender. The overall project of *On Screen Rivals* has been to chart the genealogy of television's alterity as seen through the cinema's projections. At the same time, *On Screen Rivals* has aimed to present a new way of understanding how all cultural technologies come to mean what they do. This book has charted the *technogenesis* of one cultural technology by another, showing how the image of television has changed according to the relationship between the cinema and television industries.

Cinema's representation of television has not remained fixed across the three-quarters of a century that this book has covered, not least because the broader meaning of television has varied. Our study began with the first public demonstrations in the 1920s, when television was hailed as a wonderful, modern invention. During the 1930s and 40s, media companies around the globe attempted to capitalize on the new audiovisual medium, which continued to be a novelty in the public imagination. After the end of World War II, television was relaunched in Britain and the United States as a mature medium which changed little for the next thirty years. The idea of television mutated in the post-war era as the medium reached larger audiences and became more central to our culture. Television became a powerful entertainment and information tool; dominated in America by big business and in Britain by a state-funded corporation, the BBC. In the US, the three major networks formed an oligopoly which carved up the market between them competing for advertising revenues and audiences by offering very similar fare. In Britain, the system admitted of no competition to the BBC until the mid-1950s when the single commercial network was introduced. The introduction of Independent Television (ITV) resulted in a revolution in the meaning of television in Britain. More recently, deregulation in the 1980s saw television businesses expanding while new means of television delivery provided the potential for unprecedented growth. In an increasingly global economic environment television became a multinational business dominated by the balance book. At the same time, the new forms of television – video, cable, satellite, digital – generated a more varied and fragmented market for television programs (see Chapter 2 for further discussion). Today, television is an everyday technology: no longer marveled at; it is a central medium in our expanding multimedia homes. As essential as a refrigerator, more common than a telephone, televisions are part of contemporary interior decor.

The cinema has also been through many changes in the years this book covers. When television began, the cinema was the leading entertainment medium, dominating British and American popular culture in the 1920s and 30s. The cinema industry had to struggle to retain audiences through the 1950s and 60s when other distractions, including television, provided a wide range of alternatives to the movie house. The 1970s and 80s saw the American industry gradually recover following new investment and a major restructuring of the industry. Today, the film business is more fully integrated into the entertainment industry as a whole, largely because of deregulation in the US and Europe. The British cinema industry, always overshadowed by Hollywood, has had a tumultuous history, with the prospect of a romantic renaissance always just over the horizon. The television and cinema industries, so long separated by legislative, technological and cultural divisions, have become increasingly entwined in recent years. Today, we can rent movies at the store to watch on television at home; we can see leading television performers such as George Clooney headlining in films; subscription television channels compete for audiences on the basis of their film programming. It seems that the improved fortunes of the cinema industry are the product of its closer relationship with television. The electronic medium now provides more lucrative outlets for cinema than the theaters while video and transmission sales drive movie production. In the rivalry between the film and television industries there is plenty of evidence to suggest that television is the victor.

Cinema and Television: Two Popular Media

Both cultural technologies under consideration in this book are popular media. The introduction of first cinema and later television brought entertainment to a more extensive range of people and contributed to a general democratizing of culture in Britain and the United States. However, precisely because they have historically appealed to more working-class audiences than more high culture technologies, cinema and television have been subject to criticism for being *mass media*.

Since at least the 1930s and the Payne Fund Studies, the cinema has been criticised for offering unsuitable entertainment to children (Charters, 1933). The movies were damned along with television by many of the mass media critics of the 1950s who saw both as creating a dumbing down of cultural mores and standards. The mass media critique always carries an anti-democratic impetus as it typically serves to vindicate the tastes of the elite and vilify those of the working classes. Such criticisms continue to be made by cultural guardians who assault the preferences and tastes of working-class people in their attacks on the media (for a contemporary mass media assault see Stallabrass, 1996).

Each new technology defines the previous one as an art form, according to McLuhan (1964) but it is also true that each old technology takes the opportunity of defining itself as art against ascending technologies. Thus, cinema workers were at pains to take the opportunity of making the established medium seem more highbrow with the introduction of television. When television was first perceived as a serious threat to cinema in Hollywood in the mid-1950s, the studios joined in with the anti-mass media invective, affirming the villainy of television while claiming the status of art for their own products. The imperative to identify films as art has driven a lot of critical writing in cinema studies, most particularly auteur theory. Film-makers today may be divided into 'popular' and 'art' directors, depending on their aspirations for their work. This study has shown that one of the key differences between the 'popular' and the 'art' movie is in the representation of television.

Television in Popular and Art Cinema

As already discussed in Chapter 9, 1990s comedy movies such as *Groundhog Day* and *Mrs Doubtfire* show an acceptance of television by the Hollywood system, as workers in television are depicted as people with whom we can identify. The popular directors of these films have no difficulty in sympathetically portraying television workers. If we look at the work of an avowedly non-popular, auteurist director, Oliver Stone, we can see that his work displays a considerably more negative attitude towards television.

Natural Born Killers (Oliver Stone, 1994) is a 1990s assault on television in which the incorporation of the electronic medium into the psyche has progressed to grotesque proportions. Here, the principal characters, Mickey and Mallory even remember the past as a vulgar inversion of a family situation comedy with the pro-social mores of that gentle genre transformed into a tale of systematic abuse and butchery. Television has become so absorbed into the psyches of the central protagonists that it has merged with their own memories. Stone casts television as the universal villain, recognized as such by the sagacious Native American who sees the words 'too much t.v.' illuminated on the chests of hell-bent protagonists Mickey and Mallory. Mickey is played by Woody Harrelson, best known for his character Woody, the guileless barman of *Cheers*. Harrelson wears his television persona like the shrunken head trophy of his slaughtered alter ego with magnificent awkwardness to create a powerfully villainous character. But Mickey stands alone as an heroic piece of cinematic creativity among the detritus of a shambolic film. *Natural Born Killers* is a pretentiously portentous movie and bears all the hallmarks of Oliver Stone's most unrelenting didacticism. Stone is a director with an avowed determination to distance himself from the Hollywood mainstream, in spite of a willingness to accept Hollywood finance (Oliver Stone's three most recent films were backed by Warners: *JFK*, 1991; *Heaven and Earth*, 1993 and *Natural Born Killers*, 1994). Larry Gross claims that *Natural Born Killers* represents a duplicitous attack on the Hollywood industry, arguing that Stone received $40 million from Warner Brothers only to use the money to insult the industry (Gross, 1995). If the film constitutes an assault on cinema, as Gross argues, its attack on television is considerably more sustained and oozes with a more pungent vitriol. Primarily, though, *Natural Born Killers* is an assault on the contemporary economy of images, with television and cinema two faces of the same Janus-like icon of false representations.

In order to generalize about the representation of television in American cinema, it is necessary to focus on popular genres: films that are representative of the Hollywood mainstream and thus more likely to reflect the opinions and attitudes of the majority of people working in the industry. The idea of television for the cinema industry is most likely to be apparent in films made by industry insiders with an eye to maximum audiences. In contemporary film studies, this work is frequently ignored: all too often scholars concentrate on the more highbrow offerings from producers marginal to the Hollywood mainstream. *On Screen Rivals* has attempted to challenge the canon of texts studied by film scholars through an examination of films that share a common *subject*.

On Screen Rivals has shown that the meaning of television is socially constructed, not innate, and is the product of multiple constructions. The technogenetic construction of television by the cinema posits a meaning of television that serves the interest of cinema. We have seen that movies about television have been very active contributors to the idea of television, but it is an idea that has been constantly changing. Television is at times constructed as a despised Other (*A Face in the Crowd*); at other times, it is debased by ridicule (*The Thrill of it All*); while sometimes television is used simply as a dramatic device to link scenes neatly, as in *Short Cuts*, or to introduce information necessary to advancing the narrative, as in *Libel*. In each case, the different depictions can be explained by the unique relationship between film and television at that point in time for the film's producers.

In the earliest days of television the new medium was very different from film and the early works depicted this difference without any special malice, showing broadcasting in a neutral way. We saw how the cinema viewed television as an extension of itself: a chance to put on a show in the musical, for example (discussed in Chapter 3). Indeed, throughout the history of cinema's technogenesis of television many films have shown the depicted medium as no special threat. We saw in Chapter 9 that many comedies use television a location in which to set their action. In Chapter 7, when we considered the treatment of news in the movies, we found that the newsroom has become, especially in more recent years, a novel place in which to set a romance. Even the horror film treats the idea that television might be frightening with a heavy pinch of salt: most of the films in this genre that address television distance themselves from the more heavy-handed mass media critiques by being very ironic.

However, we have also seen that some films construct television as a malevolent medium. Historically, these films did not appear until the Hollywood majors were excluded from television ownership. In the 1950s, anxiety about television grew and was focused on its difference from film: television was dangerous because it was live; because it was advertiser supported; because it was cheap; or because it was more obviously a 'mass' medium.

The presentation of this book has been roughly chronological, but we can now draw out some themes that run throughout the history of television's technogenesis in cinema. The main themes relate to the way television is shown to intervene in the assignation of gender roles in society; the status of television as both deception and confessional; and television as an icon of the contemporary.

Television: A Gender Bender

One theme that recurs in a number of chapters is the way television contributes to transforming gender relations. This was evident even in the earliest film we have discussed, *Vagabond Queen* from 1927: Sally (Betty Balfour) is permitted to assume 'masculine' attributes eschewed by her boyfriend because he is preoccupied with inventing television. Television provides the justification for the exploration of gender identities in a number of films that feature women working in television, for example Jackie Leighton (Cyd Charisse) in *It's Always Fair Weather* or Diana Christianson (Faye Dunaway) in *Network* (discussed in Chapters 3 and 7 respectively). Men who work in television are often emasculated, like Henry in *The Glass Web* (see Chapter 4) or are obliged to adopt a female persona, as Michael Dorsey does in *Tootsie* and Daniel Hillard in *Mrs Doubtfire* (see Chapter 9). New technologies provide an opportunity to challenge prevailing gender relations, as women find employment in nascent industries. Television is seen as a female technology in many of the films discussed in this book; the film industry having constructed television as 'feminine' in order to affirm its otherness. The discourse of gender in films about television serves to affirm the importance of film as masculine. As part of the drive to affirm that television is more abhorrently mass than film, movies have frequently constructed the medium as feminine.

Television: Deception or Confessional

The mass media critique of television also constructs the medium as deceptive and illusory, and films have often contributed to this image. However, in *On Screen Rivals* we have also often found that television is the means by which hidden truths are revealed. In films as diverse as *Simon and Laura*, *Broadcast News* or *The Glass Web*, television is a vehicle for false images at first. However, in each of these films the technology is finally used to reveal how things really are. A recurring theme in many films about television is the dramatic tension around the identity of television as both deception and confessional. When they become television personalities, Simon and Laura have to deceive the world into believing that they are happily married, and the institution of the BBC is complicit in this deception. Finally, though, television is the means by which declarations of love are extracted from the men in *Simon and Laura* and some kind of closure offered. The admission on television is all the more credible for being caught unawares and television is thus ultimately a conduit of honesty. In *The Glass Web*, Henry's dying confession occurs in a television studio when he is unaware that the cameras are rolling. *A Face in the Crowd* uses television to crucify Lonesome Rhodes when his insults to the audience are relayed against his knowledge. Television created the beast, but ultimately reveals his demagogic duplicity. We have seen in a number of films how the imagery of the television screen provides a useful device to convey narrative information, and ultimately the technological qualities of television are valued, although the institution of television may be condemned.

In a similar vein, we have seen that the television studio is frequently figured as a kind of limbo: a place separate from the real world but where insights can be made. Here grievances can be aired and arguments thrashed out. Out of the saturnalian chaos of the studio fight, in *I'm All Right Jack*, or *It's Always Fair Weather*, comes resolution. These films use the television studio as a location for a finale or denouement bringing several characters together in a relatively neutral setting. The film industry betrays an ambivalence towards television which it depicts as both deceptive and revelatory.

Television: An Icon of the Contemporary

Although the status of television *vis-à-vis* cinema has shifted considerably over the last fifty years, the television set remains an icon of enormous power in the contemporary symbolic world. *On Screen Rivals* has shown a wide range of uses to which the icon of television is put in film. Because the television set is so much a part of our social history, the use of an identifiably old set can immediately define the period of a film; just as an ultra modern or expensive one can add nuance to a location.

The 1996 *William Shakespeare's Romeo & Juliet* (Baz Luhrmann) updates the romantic tragedy by replacing swords and daggers with guns; the Prince wears the costume of a police chief. The Montagues and Capulets are engaged in a vicious struggle which is as much indebted to the Hollywood movie gangsters of *The Godfather* (Francis Ford Coppola, 1972) and *GoodFellas* (Martin Scorsese, 1990) as to Shakespeare's original play. Television reportage serves the narrative function of introducing the drama of the modern *Romeo and Juliet*. An African-American female news reader delivers the lines of the opening chorus allowing the audience to engage with the action. In this contemporary rendering of the tale, it is fitting that the part of the chorus should be played by television.

Television also figures the contemporary in Robert Altman's *Short Cuts* (1993) where it provides a structuring motif linking diverse Los Angeles households. The social uses of television in modern America is a theme of Ron Howard's *Ransom* (1996). Here television is part of the everyday world of the (working-class) bad guys, but is noticeably absent from the home of the child they kidnap (Brawley Nolte) and his millionaire father Tom Mullen (Mel Gibson). The head of the gang, Jimmy Shaker (Gary Sinese), describes contemporary society as being composed of the 'aboves' and 'belows' and class hatred is a powerful motivation for his criminality. Ron Howard uses what we know about television audiences (that working-class people watch television more than others) to underline the differences in socioeconomic status between the perpetrators and the victims of the ransom. Shaker's gang are defined as 'belows' by the way they while away the hours *watching* television: Mullen is able to *appear* on television. A man in his position has no difficulty in pulling a few strings and arranging to display the ransom money on the evening news. Mullen offers the two million dollars in cash as a bounty on the head of the kidnapper, raising the stakes in a complex and dangerous battle of wills. Finally, of course, the hero-victim wins and Shaker is killed: the status quo is restored and television has played its role as the medium by which the 'aboves' can address and manipulate the 'belows'.

Television is a crucial player in the doggedly zany *Mars Attacks!* (Tim Burton, 1996). The invading Martians make known their arrival on earth by interrupting a television broadcast. As the film continues, the increasingly aggressive and adolescent behaviour of the invaders is monitored by television. Even the President of the United States (Jack Nicholson) is powerless to do anything other than watch on television as his Chief of Staff is massacred along with a multitude of gathered dignitaries, officials and soldiers. *Mars Attacks!* sends up the homely image of the family gathered round the television set to show the first family watching as their country is destroyed and every last edifice of democracy ruined. In this comic-book world television is a central part of everyone's lives; even the horrible trailer park inhabitants who insist that they will fight off the aliens with shotguns are adamant 'they're not gonna get the TV!' Television provides a valuable structuring device here, operating to create a comic distance from global destruction. It also provides one of the few signals that the film is set in the contemporary world.

The Scopic Regimes of Cinema and Television

Materially, television has identifiable similarities with, as well as differences from, the cinema (Ellis, 1982). Film is the last mechanical medium: for all its efforts to embrace electronic and digital technologies, cinema remains a chemically based medium mechanically displayed when light is shone through strips of celluloid. In the rostra of electronic and digital technologies, film is something of a dinosaur, even though in terms of quality of image it remains unparalled. However, there can be no doubt that film's aesthetic hegemony is under threat, as television seems better able to adopt computer technology. The cinema remains superior aesthetically because of the chemical quality of its image, but this will be lost when television can mimic cinema's palette.

Although film and television are both regimes of audiovisual representation, they differ considerably in the kinds of images produced. Both media are dominated by narratives, but television took over the function of factual narrativizing formerly held by newsreels and travelogues through news, current affairs and lifestyle programs. Television has also taken over the serial form, and cinema is (with the exception of sequels) dominated by the one-off, single story of one-and-a-half to two hours' duration. John Ellis is correct to state:

> Cinema is rather more on the side of innovation than broad-cast TV can be: this is one of the implications of cinema's production of prototypes rather than TV's industrial series production (Ellis, 1982: 224).

The fact that cinema offers us 'prototypes' and television 'series production' has further repercussions. Television has become the more quotidian medium, its top shows are soap operas and situation comedies. Even more enmeshed within the everyday lives of people than the cinema, television is now the archetypical *Democratic Art* (Jowett, 1976) bringing drama to everyone (Williams, 1989). The cinema's propensity for the 'prototype' has been exacerbated with the blockbuster and the megablockbuster of the 1990s (see Chapter 2). Television is an almost constant companion of many, while most people are on little more than visiting terms with the cinema, if they go at all.

The scopic regimes of television and film have always been separate and will remain so for the foreseeable future. The viewing experience of each is quite specific: one medium is typically consumed within the home and the other typically in a theater built exclusively for that purpose. Legislatively, the two are treated quite differently and the laws of Britain and the United States exercise separate controls over each. All of the above differences contribute to the fact that television and cinema are unique cultural technologies producing distinct artifacts. Although there are areas of overlap and interdependence, the scopic regimes of cinema and television are clearly demarcated.

New technologies have brought the two media closer together: the adoption of video tape, allowing for programs to be more easily recorded and edited; and later the VCR, enabling that technology to be brought into the home changed the way people watched television, engendering huge shifts in the relationship between film and television. The camcorder has also altered the relationship between the two technologies, giving people an accessible way to make their own moving pictures. Video recording skills are now shared among a broader base of the population and are no longer confined to a technocratic elite. The implications of domestic video recording for both film and television is profound, for now a formerly highly specialized art of audio-visual production is within reach of ordinary people. The industrial and technological reality of television shifts as more user access is permitted and a broadening skills base is developed. This expansion of the distribution of skills creates a more democratic idea of image making as accessible to people beyond the technocratic elite.

At the same time that video skills have become more widely distributed across the population, the industrial base of television has grown. Television is a very lucrative business with profitable companies at all levels from small independent producers to massive international companies employing many thousands of people around the world.

The idea of television advanced by the films has changed according to the economic and cultural status of television, and according to the film industry's relationship to television.

The Idea of *On Screen Rivals*

On Screen Rivals reaffirms the importance of *content* in the study of the cinema. The subject matter of films, and other art works, are too frequently overlooked by academics keen to proselytize an aesthetic or formal argument. I believe that this has led to a separation of academic film studies from the ordinary appreciation and understanding of films. It is necessary for scholars to re-engage with *the subject of the subject*.

The films I have studied in *On Screen Rivals* all figure television, but do not fall into any established category for studying cinema, such as genre or a movement. Because there have been no aesthetic criteria for including films, I have been compelled to examine the run of the mill works alongside some very exceptional films. My objective has been to understand how the meaning of one medium is partly constructed through another: this has little to do with beauty or excellence. Evidently a poor film can contribute as much to the idea of television in the public imagination as a good one. Indeed, the ordinary film is most telling about the attitude of the film industry towards television.

In eschewing the aesthetic as a primary criterion for inclusion, this book brings to light the work of the ordinary craftsmen and women of the film industry: directors like Val Guest, for example, who happens to have directed films in at least three of the genres I have studied – *The Body Said No* (1950), *The*

Quatermass Experiment (1955) and *Expresso Bongo* (1959). As Kenneth Cavander argues:

> Val Guest's talent lies in the skilful and immediate exploitation of the current fashion in popular entertainment. He can turn his hand to farce or horror with equal facility and is one of the few people who have survived a successful career in the 'thirties and followed it up with another, equally successful, in the 'fifties. If few of his films will survive as well as him, they at least stand as a memorial to an extraordinary flair for catching the public's eye (Cavender *et al.*, 1958: 295).

One of the devices Guest has used to catch the public eye is television. Bringing greater attention to the jobbing director is more beneficial to understanding the history of cinema as an industry than focusing on the accepted canon of accomplishment.

Another advantage of looking at 'ordinary' films is that it unearths texts that have not attracted serious study before, films like *Make Mine A Million*, a gem of an English comedy, which has long been ignored by academics and critics alike. Exploring films other than those that have received the official stamp of the canon of film criticism can only be a good thing. All too often film criticism and theory relies on a limited body of texts, which seems to become more restricted as the number of films produced grows. I hope that this book will contribute to the reversal of this tendency by bringing some previously unstudied films to scholarly attention.

Television has been used here as an example to explain a broader process of how the social construction of a technology works: how one cultural medium contributes to our knowledge of another. Also, this construction is a product of the relationship between two media in a broader sense. I wanted to explore the cultural construction of television because the medium is politically so potent. So many rash theories and wild beliefs are postulated about television: I wanted to understand where some of these extreme ideas came from. I found that some of the most extreme statements about television were to be found in film, as for example in *Network* and *Videodrome*. I have no doubt that these and other films contribute in part to the idea of television circulating at large.

It is possible to find people who subscribe to the views of pessimistic writers like Neil Postman (1987) and Jerry Mander (1978) who believe that television is inherently bad. Postman and Mander have both written books with academic and dema-gogic aspirations, managing to find their way on to both the bestseller lists and undergraduate reading lists. Purporting to examine whether or not television has been, on balance, good for society, these authors are predisposed to determine that it has been absolutely disastrous. In spite of the stringency of the shrill arguments offered in these texts, television continues to be a central – perhaps *the* central – entertainment and informa-tion medium in western society. What is the point of these assaults? I believe they constitute the locus of a struggle for the hegemony between cultural technologies in which television is consistently devalued. *On Screen Rivals* is an attempt to show how the meaning of television is a discursive construct of film. Television is not only technogenetically constructed by film-makers, but by novelists, playwrights, song writers and yes, academics. The idea of a technology – its cultural meaning – is the product of many different representations and discourses.

Today, the cinema and television industries are converging under the auspices of one overarching global entertainments industry which also embraces computing and telephony. The national forces of regulation, control and censorship are increas-ingly less powerful in the face of international big business and commerce as multinational conglomerates increasingly own the world's television and film companies. For multinational corpo-rations like Sony and MCA, there can be no interest in retaining separate identities for the two media; now that it is possible to exploit software across a number of different kinds of hardware, a 'television' property is not necessarily any different from the 'film' property. On the technological front, digital technologies will soon absorb the chemical and electronic images of film and television. Will future generations of audiences even recognize the difference between film and television texts?

The computer rather than the television set is the technology most likely to be presented as a fearful new medium in contem-porary discourse. In the popular imagination, parents worry more about their children sitting for hours at the computer than in front of the television set; newspaper reports of pornographic trials are as likely to refer to the number of computer discs the offender possessed as the number of videos. The demonized medium of the early twenty-first century is the fully integrated digital entertainment system. In the cinema, the image of the computer screen, not the television set, has come to represent a frightening and alien power. The film industry's response to the computer would make another book.

So, what's the idea of television? The answer to that question depends on who you ask: if you ask the film-makers of Britain and America you will find some very interesting responses.

ANNOTATED FILMOGRAPHY

1984. Michael Anderson. GB. 1956.
Edmund O'Brien stars in this adaptation of Orwell's dystopian vision of a future world where citizens are constantly subject to surveillance by Big Brother via various methods including state-operated 'telescreens'.

Absolute Beginners. Julien Temple. GB. 1986.
This musical, loosely based on Colin MacInnes' novel, stars Patsy Kensit and Eddie O'Connell in London's Soho and Notting Hill Gate in 1958. It includes parodies of *haute couture* and property development as well as the nascent pop and television industries.

All That Heaven Allows. Douglas Sirk. USA. 1955.
Carey Scott (Jane Wyman) is a middle-aged widow who finds her sexual feelings are aroused by the gardener and all-round outsider, Ron Kirby (Rock Hudson) in this classic 1950s melodrama. Carey's friend Sarah (Agnes Moorehead) is just one of the folk in her small town community who try to dissuade Carey from involvement with Ron, suggesting television as an alternative. Female sexual fulfillment is directly opposed to watching television in this exquisite women's weepy directed by the master, Douglas Sirk.

Amateur Hour. Stanford Singer. USA. 1985.
Paul and Donna (Adam Nathan and Julie Hanlon) are two rebellious teenagers who run away from small town America to work for the television company run by Paul's estranged father. The youngsters become quickly disillusioned when they are abused and exploited by their new employers. Paul and Donna seek revenge by turning first to crime and then to terrorism. This muddled and half-hearted teen exploitation movie was released on video by Troma Video under the title *I was A Teenage T.V. Terrorist*.

The American Way. Maurice Phillips. GB. 1986.
Alternative title: *Riders of the Storm*.
  Dennis Hopper heads a gang of Vietnam war veterans monitoring US television output and broadcasting their own pirate television station.

Band Waggon. Marcel Varnel. GB. 1939.
  This lively comedy, based on a BBC radio variety show of the same name, stars Arthur Askey and Richard Murdoch. We first find the chums squatting on the roof of the BBC's Broadcasting House, but before long the Director General himself comes to evict them. The two find a new home in a haunted castle which is the location of a secret television studio being used by enemy spies to transmit images of British military equipment to Germany. Askey and Murdoch team up with band leader Jack Hylton and his dance orchestra to take over the illegal television station. The 'chums' interrupt stuffy BBC broadcasts with popular performances and songs which the elitist mandarins of the Corporation prefer not to air. *Band Waggon* is a cheerful jibe at the expense of BBC radio and television programming policy made at the very start of World War II. It was made at Gainsborough studios from a script by Marriott Edgar and Val Guest.

The Barefoot Executive. Robert Butler. USA. 1970.
Alternative title: *The Rating Game*.
  This children's live action picture from Disney sends up the television scheduling game when Raffles the chimpanzee proves expert at predicting television hits.

Being There. Hal Ashby. USA. 1979.
  Chance (or Chauncey) (Peter Sellers) is a naif with an uncanny gift for television communication in this film based on Jerzy Kosinski's novel. Chance is a simpleton who has lived a comfortable and sheltered existence, cared for by servants and entertained by television in the house of the 'Old Man'. When his benefactor dies, Chance confronts the real world for the first time, a world that he only knows through television. Befriended by wealthy socialite Eve Rand (Shirley MacLaine) and her husband Ben (Melvyn Douglas), Chance finds himself mixing with the US power elite. Before long the simple man's random platitudes are taken for wise aphorisms and Chance becomes a media celebrity tipped to be the next president.

The Body Said No. Val Guest. GB. 1950.
  Alone in her flat one evening, cabaret singer Mikki (Yolande Donlan) sees something on television after transmissions have finished for

the night. In the belief that she has witnessed two men plotting to kill Michael Rennie (playing himself), Mikki resolves to warn the actor. Her anxieties are not taken seriously and finally the mysteries of television test transmissions are explained to her (and the audience). The denouement of the film is shot at Alexandra Palace following Mikki's own televised performance.

The Brady Bunch Movie. Betty Thomas. USA. 1995.
The Brady Bunch Movie reprises the 1970s sitcom about a large and lively family and replaces them in contemporary American suburbia. The comedy revolves around the anachronism of a 1970s television perfect family living in modern day Los Angeles.

Broadcast News. James L. Brooks. USA. 1987.
Tom Grunick (William Hurt), Aaron Altman (Albert Brooks) and Jane Craig (Holly Hunter) make up a romantic triangle of co-workers in television. Broadcast News chronicles the conflicts and confusion of their various ambitions: moral, sexual, romantic, and career.

Bye Bye Birdie. George Sidney. USA. 1963.
Originally a Broadway show, this messy musical is based loosely on the phenomenon of Elvis Presley and his enlistment in the US Army, with Jesse Pearson as the teen idol Conrad Birdie. Song writer Albert Peterson (Dick Van Dyke) needs a big break to advance his stagnant career. His ambitious business (and erstwhile romantic) partner, Rosie DeLeon (Janet Leigh), hits on the idea of having Conrad Birdie perform one of Albert's compositions on *The Ed Sullivan Show* on the eve of his enlistment. Moreover, Birdie should sing to one of his many fans chosen at random. Kim McAfee (Ann-Margret) is the lucky teenager; Paul Lynde plays her disapproving father and Bobby Rydell the jealous boyfriend, Hugo. The pop music world is subject to serious ridicule here, with Ed Sullivan offering a fleeting center of sanity in an otherwise incoherent movie.

The Cable Guy. Ben Stiller. USA. 1996.
Jim Carrey stars as the eponymous anti-hero, who befriends Steven Kovacks (Matthew Broderick) in this anti-television film. The Cable Guy gives his name as various television sitcom characters, first going by the name of Ernie or 'Chip' Douglas (*My Three Sons*) then Darren Stevens (*Bewitched*) and later Larry Tate (Darren's boss in *Bewitched*). The Cable Guy is an obsessive who desperately wants to be loved, and attributes his pathologically poor social skills to the fact that his mother worked at night and left him watching television alone. Contemporary television trials are satirized in a subplot about the trial of a former television child star for the murder of his

twin brother and co-star. This black comedy misses its mark by having Jim Carrey play such an extremely unsympathetic character while making his counterpart, Steven, so insipid.

Catch Us If You Can. John Boorman. GB. 1965.
British 1960s pop group The Dave Clark Five star in this early John Boorman film about the difficulties of escaping from fame. The band are reluctant stars in a meat advertising campaign and the film takes a few stabs at the advertising industry. However, the extremely loose structure of *Catch Us If You Can* does not allow for any sustained assault on anything much.

Caught by Television see *Trapped by Television*.

The China Syndrome. James Bridges. USA. 1978.
An earnest attack on the politics of the nuclear power industry. With Jane Fonda and Michael Douglas as television reporters Kimberly Wells and Richard Adams investigating safety scandals at a nuclear power station run by Jack Goddell (Jack Lemmon).

The Comedy Man. Alvin Rakoff. GB. 1963.
Chick Byrd (Kenneth More) is an out of work stage actor who finds success more readily when he takes work in television commercials. Based on the novel by Douglas Hayes.

The Creeping Unknown see *The Quatermass Experiment*.

Dead Men Don't Die. Malcolm Marmorstein. USA. 1990.
Barry Barron (Elliott Gould) is an egomaniacal television news presenter at World Wide News who is shot dead by some thugs in the station parking lot. His body is revived by the voodoo princess Chafuka (Mabel King) who works as a maid at World Wide News. There follow several more murders and the zombies gradually take over the television station. Finally, the hierarchy of the television bureaucracy has been completely reversed.

Delirious. Tom Mankiewicz. USA. 1991.
A comedy spoof on television soap operas with John Candy and Mariel Hemingway.

Dentist on the Job. C. M. Pennington-Richards. GB. 1961.
David Cookson (Bob Monkhouse) and Brian Dexter (Ronnie Stevens) are two newly qualified dentists who graduate to jobs promoting Dreem toothpaste. Aided by ex-con Sam Field (Kenneth Connor) and actor Jill Venner (Shirley Eaton), our heroes create a new toothpaste

formula. They also pull off a great advertising heist by smuggling an advertisement for the new product onto a satellite rocket. *Dentist on the Job* relates how our cheeky heroes create 'the first commercial in space'.

Desk Set. Walter Lang. USA. 1957.
Alternative title: *His Other Woman*.
An amusing comedy of manners starring Spencer Tracy as 'Methods Engineer' Richard Sumner, contracted to introduce a time saving computer into a television company. Katharine Hepburn stars as Bunny Watson, the head of the station's all-female research department. Based on a 1955 Broadway play.

Dreamboat. Claude Binyon. USA. 1952.
Thornton Sayre (Clifton Webb) is proud of his vocation as Professor of English Literature at Underhill College. The fuddy duddy and his college-age daughter Carol (Anne Francis) find their tranquil existence in academia shattered by the revelation of Sayre's former career as 'Bruce Blair' – swashbuckling hero of silent movies. Now that television has given the old movies a new outlet, Sayre's former partner Gloria (Ginger Rogers) wants to reprise their early hits. Television itself is put in the dock when Sayre takes court action to prevent the films from being broadcast.

The Electric Horseman. Sydney Pollack. USA. 1979.
Sonny Steele (Robert Redford) is a washed-up rodeo star forced to make a living touring county shows promoting cereal as the Ranch Breakfast Cowboy. In a sad parody of the Western hero, Sonny enacts the role of rodeo rider dressed in a neon suit astride doped horses. Sonny breaks free and resolves to unite his steed, Rising Star, with a herd of wild horses. Television reporter Hallie Martin (Jane Fonda) follows Sonny into the wilderness for the news.

Elstree Calling. Adrian Brunel. GB. 1930.
A gloriously wide-ranging revue including performances by English and American acts such as Lily Morris, Teddy Brown, Anna May Wong, Cicely Courtneidge and Jack Hulbert. Some of the sketches are directed by Alfred Hitchcock, and the compère is the great comedian Tommy Handley. *Elstree Calling* uses television as a narrative device to link the many disparate acts and to present the idea of theater television to cinema audiences.

Everybody's Dancin'. Will Jason. USA. 1950.
A musical comedy set in a rodeo starring Spade Cooley as himself.

Expresso Bongo. Val Guest. GB. 1959.

Soho talent promoter and wide boy Johnny Jackson (Laurence Harvey) discovers young Herbert Rudge (Cliff Richard) playing bongos in a hip coffee bar. Johnny develops 'Bongo' Herbert's career quite successfully until the lad realizes he is being exploited. With the help of older performer Dixie Collins (Yolande Donlan), Bongo leaves Johnny and Soho for a run on New York television. *Expresso Bongo* features a cameo appearance by Gilbert Harding as presenter of a BBC television documentary program which films the Soho subculture.

Eyewitness. Peter Yates. USA. 1981.

Alternative title: *The Janitor*.

William Hurt plays Daryll Deever, a humble janitor enamored of Tony Sokolow (Sigourney Weaver), a television news reporter. Has Daryll really witnessed a murder or is he stringing Tony along to develop a relationship with her?

A Face in the Crowd. Elia Kazan. USA. 1957.

Elia Kazan told Ciment that he made this intense melodrama: 'to warn the public: look out for television'. Andy Griffith plays Lonesome Rhodes, the Face in the Crowd discovered by small town radio presenter Marcia Jeffries (Patricia Neal). The meteoric rise to fame of Lonesome and his crashing descent is watched over by the jaundiced eye of news reporter Mel Miller (Walter Matthau), who dubs the anti-hero 'Demagogue in Denim'. There are many worthy speeches in this overlong film which is a didactic assault on television celebrity and manipulation.

The Front. Martin Ritt. USA. 1976.

Woody Allen plays Howard Prince, a small-time bookie who is hired to act as a 'Front' for a group of black-listed writers in the 1950s.

The Gazebo. George Marshall. USA. 1959.

Eliot Nash (Glenn Ford) is an uptight television producer who is told by his doctor: 'You have televisionitis, also known as the Madison Avenue heebie jeebies, induced by an over application and an under-application of common horse sense.' He and his zany wife Nell (Debbie Reynolds) become embroiled in farcical antics when Nash believes he has buried the corpse of a blackmailer under the gazebo in the garden.

The Glass Web. Jack Arnold. USA. 1953.

A dark tale of betrayal and ruthless ambition set among the community at a television station. *The Glass Web* stars Edward G. Robinson as Henry Hayes, a humble writer for television who will do anything to advance his career. Television is shown as a world of vicious self-advancement and low morality.

The Great Man. José Ferrer. USA. 1956.
José Ferrer directs himself as Joe Harris, a radio reporter for Amalgamated Broadcasting System. Harris gets the opportunity to 'make like a real journalist' when assigned to write an obituary for Herb Fuller – a much respected Ed Murrow-type figure. As he delves into the life of The Great Man, Harris finds that Fuller's private dealings with family, friends and colleagues are deplorable. Unsure of whether or not to perpetuate the myth of Fuller's almost saintly public persona, Harris finally goes on air with the real story.

Gremlins 2. The New Batch. Joe Dante. USA. 1990.
In this sequel to the hit children's film *Gremlins*, the cute Mogwai run once again run amok; now their target is corporate rather than suburban America. Young Billy Peltzer (Zach Galligan) and his friend Kate Beringer (Phoebe Cates) have moved to New York where Billy works as a draftsman at the Clamp Center. The building is headquarters of the Clamp Corporation (headed by an amalgam of Ted Turner and Donald Trump), and home to the Clamp Cable television station.

Grief. Richard Glatzer. USA. 1993.
A camp, low budget story about a group of writers working on a low grade television series, *The Love Judge*, set in a Californian divorce court.

The Groove Tube. Ken Shapiro. USA. 1974.
This comedy comprises inexorable spoofs on television programming and advertising, and stars Chevy Chase and Ken Shapiro.

Groundhog Day. Harold Ramis. USA. 1993.
Phil Connors (Bill Murray) is a worn-out weather man with a cynical snarl and a spiteful disposition. Caught in a bizarre time loop he is condemned to relive reporting on the corny ritual of Groundhog Day from the small town of Punxsatawney day after day. Not until he learns the value of true humanity is he liberated from his cynicism and able to begin a relationship with television newcomer Rita Hanson (Andie MacDowell). The gentle tone of this successful romantic comedy owes much to Frank Capra's *It's a Wonderful Life*.

Hairspray. John Waters. USA. 1988.
Tracy Turnblad (Ricki Lake) is a Baltimore teenager in the early 1960s whose dreams come true when she wins a dance competition and becomes a regular dancer on *The Corny Collins Show*. Tracy and her friends are appalled at the segregation that occurs on the teenage dance scene. Finally they triumph when Corny Collins (Shawn Thompson) rebels against the station's bosses to declare *The Corny Collins Show* integrated.

Happy Anniversary. David Miller. USA. 1959.
A farce about the damage television can cause to married life, starring David Niven as Chris Walters and Mitzi Gaynor as Alice.

A Hard Day's Night. Richard Lester. GB. 1964.
The Beatles play themselves, a pop group down in London from the North determined to have a good time. Their minders, Norm and Shake (Norman Rossington and John Junkin), struggle to keep the crazy quartet on the straight and narrow in time for a television performance which marks the film's climax. *A Hard Day's Night* is a pop musical rich in commentary on the ephemeral quality of celebrity.

He Said; She Said. Marisa Silver and Ken Kwapis. USA. 1991.
Two television presenters become romantically entangled and end up with their personal lives sparking up their public performances. Starring Kevin Bacon as 'he' and Elizabeth Perkins as 'she' with Sharon Stone as the other woman.

Head. Bob Rafelson. USA. 1968.
High jinx with The Monkees and some zany film-making from Bob Rafelson and Jack Nicholson including many swipes at television and commercialism.

High Treason. Maurice Elvey. GB. 1929.
One of the earliest films to show television, *High Treason* forecasts what life will be like in 1940.

His Other Woman see *Desk Set*.

The Houghland Murder Case see *Murder by Television*.

I Was a Teenage T.V. Terrorist see *Amateur Hour*.

I'm All Right Jack. Jack Boulting. GB. 1959.
   This tale of England's social divide stars Peter Sellers as the Luddite
   trades union representative, Fred Kite, and Ian Carmichael as Stanley
   Windrush, the well-meaning upper-class twit who naively becomes
   an accomplice in his wicked Uncle Bertram's (Dennis Price) plot to
   engineer industrial unrest. A climax is reached when a television
   debate on the program *Argument*, chaired by Malcolm Muggeridge,
   brings all parties together. Stanley realizes he has been duped while
   on air and confronts his uncle with his misdeeds. There follows
   pandemonium as the television studio becomes the location of free-
   for-all fisticuffs.

International House. A. Edward Sutherland. USA. 1933.
   Musical comedy starring W.C. Fields set in the International House
   Hotel in Wu Hu, China where Dr Wong (Edmund Breese) is
   exhibiting his new television device. Dr Wong's 'radioscope' is the
   means by which musical performances by the likes of Rudy Vallee,
   Cab Calloway and Baby Rose Marie are shown to the gathered
   ensemble. This entertaining variety picture also features George
   Burns and Gracie Allen as the hotel doctor and nurse.

It's Always Fair Weather. Gene Kelly and Stanley Donen. USA. 1955.
   This musical from the masters at MGM's Freed unit shows the fate
   of three soldiers reunited ten years after leaving the armed forces.
   The relationships among Ted (Gene Kelly), Doug (Dan Dailey) and
   Angie (Michael Kidd) have weakened over the years and they are
   little more than strangers. However, they become comrades in arms
   once again when they are tricked into appearing on a television show
   by wily television producer Jackie Leighton (Cyd Charisse) and
   presenter/performer Madeline Bradville (Dolores Gray).

Just For Fun! Gordon Flemyng. GB. 1963.
   A loose story links a range of musical performances when teenagers
   are given the vote and rebel against reductions in television pop
   shows. They stand for election, and win, organizing a television
   extravaganza.

The Kentucky Fried Movie. John Landis. USA. 1977.
   An unstructured compilation of sketches ridiculing many aspects of
   popular culture, including television commercials and courtroom
   dramas.

The Killing of Sister George. Robert Aldrich. USA. 1968.
   A character actress in a long-running BBC soap opera, June Buck-
   ridge (Beryl Reid) finds her role as Sister George is under threat. At

the same time she begins to have doubts about the fidelity of her lover, Alice 'Childie' McNaught (Susannah York). Filled with self-pity, George indulges in a self-destructive drinking spree. Coral Browne plays the disdainful Mrs Croft from the BBC in this adaptation of Frank Marcus's play.

The King of Comedy. Martin Scorcese. USA. 1983.

This is an excruciatingly embarrassing satire on television celebrity and fandom. Rupert Pupkin, one of Robert De Niro's most odious creations, joins forces with Masha (Sandra Bernhard) to abduct their hero, television presenter Jerry Langford (Jerry Lewis). Rupert blackmails the television station into allowing him to perform live on *The Jerry Lewis Show*. Pupkin is arrested and sentenced to prison where he spends his time writing his memoirs only to be released from prison a star.

L.A. Story. Mick Jackson. USA. 1991.

Briton Mick Jackson directs Steve Martin's endearing portrayal of Los Angeles stereotypes. Martin stars as Harris K. Telemacher, a sometimes sleazy weatherman with a heart of gold who falls for English visitor Sara McDowel (Victoria Tennant). L.A. is a magical backdrop against which Harris woos Sara away from her obnoxious estranged husband, Roland (Richard E. Grant).

Left, Right and Centre. Sidney Gilliat. GB. 1959.

The 'Left' and 'Right' of the film's title represent the two main British political parties, Labour and Conservative. Their candidates, Stella Stoker (Patricia Bredin) and Robert Wilcot (Ian Carmichael) respectively, are competing to represent the constituency of Earndale in a local election. The 'Centre' is represented by the television reporters struggle to elicit some enthusiasm from an indifferent electorate. Some topical piquancy is added by the fact that Robert Wilcot, the Conservative candidate, is also a television personality of some repute, appearing on game shows with the likes of Gilbert Harding, who puts in a cameo role.

Libel. Anthony Asquith. GB. 1959.

This story of mistaken identity with a powerful homoerotic undercurrent is initiated when former prisoner of war Jeffrey Buckenham (Paul Massie) sees an old comrade Sir Mark Loddon (Dirk Bogarde) on television. Loddon is showing Richard Dimbleby round his country estate, but Buckenham is determined to investigate further when he suspects that Loddon is an imposter.

Look Before You Laugh see *Make Mine a Million*.

The Love Pill. Kenneth Turner. GB. 1971.
Candy that turns women into nymphomaniacs while also claiming to prevent conception is sold using television advertising. Pregnant women seek revenge on the perpetrators.

The Love Machine. Jack Haley Jr. USA. 1971.
Based on the novel by Jacqueline Susann, about a megalomaniac television reporter, Robin Stone (John Phillip Law) and his sex life.

Make Mine a Million. Lance Comfort. GB. 1959.
Alternative title: *Look Before You Laugh*.
Produced by Jack Hylton, this Arthur Askey vehicle also stars Sid James. Our two heroes team up to produce illegal television advertising with which they interrupt the National Television service – a thinly disguised BBC.

Man of the Moment. John Paddy Carstairs. GB. 1955.
Norman Wisdom comedy which reaches its chase finale in the studios of the BBC interrupting several television rehearsals and broadcasts in the process.

The Man Who Fell To Earth. Nicholas Roeg. GB. 1976.
Alien Thomas Jerome Newton (David Bowie) crash lands his space ship on earth. Desperate to return home, he sets about creating a new generation of electronic equipment in order to earn sufficient funds to launch his space ship. Newton wiles away the hours watching a bank of televisions tuned to different stations.

The Man with the Deadly Lens see *Wrong is Right*.

Mars Attacks! Tim Burton. USA. 1996.
Television reportage provides the structure to this narrative of vicious and stupid invaders from Mars destroying earth with zealous glee.

Medium Cool. Haskell Wexler. USA. 1969.
A romantic story set against the backdrop of the Democratic Convention in 1968, this film mixes cinema verité, television reportage and conventional film-making. *Medium Cool* investigates the relationship of the media to the social problems behind the civil rights movement by following the characters of news camera operator John (Robert Forster) and sound recordist Gus (Peter Bonerz).

Meet Mr Lucifer. Anthony Pélissier. GB. 1953.

Thespian Sam Hollingsworth (Stanley Holloway) finds his stage career is washed up and he is reduced to playing the devil in a second-rate repertory company pantomime to empty houses. Mr Lucifer (also played by Stanley Holloway) tells Hollingsworth that television, his latest diabolical invention, is not working well – it is not making people miserable enough. Hollingsworth is assigned to ensure that television does more damage in future. Finally, the devil declares that he has decided to dispense with television and move on to the next thing – 3-D cinema.

Modern Times. Charlie Chaplin. USA. 1936.

Chaplin's critique of mass production and Taylorism includes the use of television as a means of surveillance over the workers.

Morons From Outer Space. Mike Hodges. GB. 1985.

Bernard (Mel Smith) is only marginally more intelligent than his traveling companions from the planet Blob, Sandra (Joanne Pearce), Julian (Paul Brown) and Desmond (Jimmy Nail). The dim-witted aliens are taken under the wing of quiet UKBC television reporter, who is transformed into a ruthless media manipulator, Graham Sweetley (Griff Rhys Jones). Starring on television chat shows, the morons develop a career as pop stars before a repossession man from Blob comes to charge them with failing to return a hired space ship.

Mr Saturday Night. Billy Crystal. USA. 1992.

A nostalgic tribute to the early stand-up comedians through the eyes of Buddy Young Jr (Billy Crystal) as he looks back on a lifetime in show business.

Mrs Doubtfire. Chris Columbus. USA. 1993.

Cross-dressing comedy in which Daniel Hillard (Robin Williams) dresses up as the redoubtable Mrs Doubtfire in order to work as a nanny to his own children. Daniel finally finds more appropriate employment playing the character on children's television. Mrs Doubtfire stars Sally Fields as the long-suffering wife, Miranda, and Pierce Brosnan as her lover.

Murder by Television. Clifford Sanforth. USA. 1935.
Alternative title: *The Houghland Murder Case*.

A plodding murder mystery starring Bela Lugosi as Detective Arthur Perry taking an inordinately long time to solve the mystery of how Professor Houghland was murdered during one of his own experimental television broadcasts.

My Blue Heaven. Henry Koster. USA. 1950.
Kitty and Jack Moran (Betty Grable and Dan Dailey) are a married couple who are also radio stars desperate to have a family. The expansion of television offers career opportunities which at first appear to provide an alternative to parenthood for Kitty. The female dilemma of work or family is set against a background of the entertainment industry in this weak musical.

My Favorite Year. Richard Benjamin. USA. 1982.
This lively comedy is set in the heyday of American comedy television. King Kaiser (Joseph Bologna) bears more than a passing resemblance to the great American comedian Sid Ceaser. We witness the halcyon days of 1950s television through the eyes of novice Benji Stone (Mark Linn-Baker). When Alan Swann (Peter O'Toole), a swashbuckling movie star, is set to appear on the show it is Benji's job to keep his hero out of mischief until the (hilarious) live broadcast.

The Naked Truth. Mario Zampi. GB. 1957.
Alternative title: *Your Past is Showing*.
A clunky British comedy starring Terry-Thomas, Peter Sellers and Peggy Mount among a group of people being blackmailed by Dennis (Dennis Price). Sellers plays Sonny McGregor, a television presenter and impersonator whose wholesome public image could be tainted if the public knew of his off-screen liaisons.

Nashville. Robert Altman. USA. 1975.
Robert Altman's labyrinthine representation of the Nashville Country and Western community loosely gathered around preparations for a television broadcast. *Nashville* was co-produced by ABC and Paramount Pictures and was originally written for television.

Natural Born Killers. Oliver Stone. USA. 1994.
Mickey and Mallory Knox (Woody Harrelson and Juliette Lewis) are latter-day Bonnie and Clyde fugitives on the run from themselves. Oliver Stone heavy-handedly condemns the mass media for its prurient interest in the murderers in this adaptation of Quentin Tarantino's script. The killers inspire a prison break and go on the run with Wayne Gayle (Robert Downey Jr) a television reporter. *Natural Born Killers* is suffused with a range of imagery culled from nature documentaries, the movies and animation.

Network. Sidney Lumet. USA. 1976.
One of the most startlingly vitriolic assaults on television the cinema industry has ever made. This vicious film shows television execu-

tives to be exclusively self-interested and ratings-led. Traditionalists like Max Schumacher (William Holden) and Howard Beale (Peter Finch) look like old-timers next to the driving Diana Christianson (Faye Dunaway) and the Machiavellian Frank Hackett (Robert Duvall). Pulling the strings at the network is the omnipotent Arthur Jensen (Ned Beatty), who exploits Howard Beale's delicate mental state. Beale is promoted by the Network as 'an angry prophet denouncing the hypocrisies of our time'. Paddy Chayevsky's script also gave us: 'I'm as mad as hell and I'm not going to take it any more!' A bit rambling in parts, *Network* rubs its point home a little too hard.

Never a Dull Moment. Jerry Paris. USA. 1967.
Jack Albany (Dick Van Dyke) is a humble bit-part actor in television who is mistaken for a gangster. He maintains the pretense out of survival instinct when members of the gang escort him to the home of criminal mastermind Leo Joseph Smooth (Edward G. Robinson).

Nineteen Eighty-Four. Michael Radford. GB. 1984.
John Hurt plays Winston Smith in the film of George Orwell's novel. A range of surveillance devices, including the famous 'telescreens', are used to subjugate the citizenry in this dark dystopia.

No More Mr. Nice Guy see *Shocker.*

Oh! For a Man see *Will Success Spoil Rock Hunter?*

Oh Say You Can Sing see *Slightly Scandalous.*

On Velvet. Widgey R. Newman. GB. 1938.
A farce about a couple of pals who start a successful television advertising company after incurring debts on the racecourse. Starring Joe Hayman and Wally Patch.

Poltergeist. Tobe Hooper. USA. 1982.
A great contemporary ghost story in which the youngest daughter of an all-American family is abducted by 'the TV people'. Starring Craig T. Nelson and JoBeth Williams, *Poltergeist* was co-written and produced by Steven Spielberg.

Power. Sidney Lumet. USA. 1986.
Sidney Lumet takes another shot at directing a film about the media, a decade after his success with *Network*. *Power* examines the complicity of the media in the manipulation of the American political system by campaign managers. This is a film that fails to shock

in a post-Watergate world and the film rather drags as a result. Richard Gere turns in a good performance as Peter St John with Julie Christie and Gene Hackman co-starring.

Public Access. Bryan J. Singer. USA. 1992.
Whiley Pricher (Ron Marquette) arrives in small town Brewster and quickly sets about establishing his own cable television show, *Our Town*. He creates havoc among the insular community by asking, 'What is wrong with Brewster?' before simply leaving town one day.

Putney Swope. Herald Productions. Robert Downey. USA. 1969.
Black militants take over a New York advertising agency in this anarchic comedy.

The Quatermass Experiment. Val Guest. GB. 1955.
Alternative titles: *The Quatermass Xperiment*; *The Creeping Unknown*.
Based on the pioneering British television science fiction series, *The Quatermass Experiment* relates the consequences of ambitious Professor Quatermass' unofficial space rocket launch. The rocket returns to earth host to an alien life form which threatens the existence of all life on the planet. The final denouement occurs in Westminster Abbey during a live television broadcast when the chaps from the BBC are able to hook up enough power from their generator to zap the creature to smithereens.

Quiz Show. Robert Redford. USA. 1994.
Robert Redford directed this drama based on the 'Twenty One scandal' of the 1950s, when television game shows were rigged by their producers to manipulate ratings. John Turturro stars as the luckless Herbie Stempel who is engineered to lose to Ivy League contestant Charles Van Doren (Ralph Fiennes). *Quiz Show* is an entertaining, albeit over-earnest, indictment of television at its worst hour.

Ransom. Ron Howard. USA. 1997.
When the bad guys hold his child for ransom, Tom Mullen (Mel Gibson) goes on television to appeal to their accomplices to give up the kidnappers by offering a reward. Gary Sinese plays Jimmy Shaker, the head of the kidnappers, whose accomplices spend an inordinate amount of time watching television.

The Rating Game see *The Barefoot Executive*.

Reality Bites. Ben Stiller. USA. 1994.
The slacker generation leave college and go their different ways – one of them as a television intern. This twenty-something drama stars Winona Ryder, Ethan Hawke, Janeane Garofalo and Ben Stiller.

Riders of the Storm see *The American Way*.

The Rise and Rise of Michael Rimmer. Kevin Billington. GB. 1970.
Peter Cook stars as Michael Rimmer, in this satire of public life. Rising through the ranks of the advertising and public opinion industries, Rimmer manipulates the electorate to become the first British President.

Robocop. Paul Verhoeven. USA. 1987.
Television is a ubiquitous presence in the future world Paul Verhoeven creates for Murphy/RoboCop (Peter Weller).

The Running Man. Paul Michael Glaser. USA. 1987.
Arnold Schwarzenegger and Maria Conchita Alonso star in this futuristic tale of the corruption at the heart of television. *The Running Man* satirizes the relationship between entertainment, justice and blood lust.

Scandalous! Rob Cohen. GB. 1984.
Lightweight comedy in which an American television reporter believes he has hit upon an important case of industrial espionage.

Scrooged. Richard Donner. USA. 1988.
Frank Cross (Bill Murray) is the irascible, mean-spirited and egomaniacal president of New York television station IBC. As the 'Jewel in the Crown' of the IBC Christmas season, Cross has scheduled a live musical version of the classic, *A Christmas Carol*. But Cross is subjected to the 'Scrooge' treatment himself when he is visited by the ghosts of Christmas past, present and future. Finally, Cross is reformed and declares good will to all during the live broadcast on Christmas Eve.

Shocker. Wes Craven. USA. 1989.
Alternative title: *No More Mr Nice Guy*.
Wes Craven wrote the script as well as directing this slightly rambling tale of a television repair man Horace Pinker (Mitch Pileggi) sentenced to the electric chair for mass murder. Through the intervention of a vague mystical force his spirit survives electrocution and lives on in the electricity supply, murdering his victims through their television sets.

Short Cuts. Robert Altman. USA. 1993.
Several of Raymond Carver's short stories are interwoven by Altman and television provides a link between the diverse strands of his Angelino characters. Local television news coverage provides typical and topical Los Angeles themes for the prologue and epilogue: Malathion spraying and an earthquake respectively.

Simon and Laura. Muriel Box. GB. 1955.
When Simon and Laura Foster (Peter Finch and Kay Kendall) are invited to feature in a BBC television family situation comedy, they are so desperate for work that they patch up their marital differences. The Fosters put on a façade of marital bliss to accommodate their new employers at the BBC, but their feuding continues unabated. They are finally reconciled, but not before the film pokes fun at television in general and the BBC in particular.

The Six-Five Special. Alfred Shaughnessy. GB. 1958.
Named for the pop television series which went on air at 6.05 pm, this film concerns two youngsters, Judy and Ann (Avril Leslie and Diane Todd), who board the 6.05 train to London determined to get 'out of a rut and into a groove'. The teenagers watch various singers and musicians rehearsing *en route* to London. Ann gets her first break to appear on the television show after auditioning for Pete Murray and Jo Douglas on the train. The film features performances by Lonnie Donegan, Dickie Valentine, Jim Dale, Cleo Laine, Petula Clark, Victor Soverall and Jimmy Lloyd among others.

Slightly Scandalous. Will Jason. USA. 1946.
Alternative title: *Oh Say You Can Sing.*
A romantic musical comedy starring Fred Brady as twin brothers, one of whom is putting on a television show.

SoapDish. Michael Hoffman. USA. 1991.
Celeste Talbert (Sally Field) is the star of daytime television series *The Sun Also Sets* and has earned the moniker America's Sweetheart as a result. Such success necessarily breeds jealousy and her rivals are many. Celeste's real past, almost as complicated as that of the character she plays on the show, catches up with her when both her daughter Lori (Elisabeth Shue) and Lori's father (Kevin Kline) come back into her life at the same time. Rose Schwartz (Whoopi Goldberg) is the soap writer who advises on what is to be done.

Spiceworld: The Movie. Bob Spiers. GB. 1997.
Star vehicle for the ubiquitous Spice Girls, British female pop band.

Static. Mark Romanek. USA. 1985.
A strange tale of a young man who tries unsuccessfully to get in touch with the spirits of his dead parents through adapting television technology.

Stay Tuned. Peter Hyams. USA. 1992.
A couple become trapped in television in this parodic exploration of television genres.

Sunny Side of the Street. Richard Quine. USA. 1951.
Musical starring Frankie Laine set in the early days of television.

The Sunshine Boys. Herbert Ross. USA. 1975.
Al Lewis (George Burns) and Willie Clark (Walter Matthau) are two old-time vaudeville performers asked to reprise their act for television in this Neil Simon screenplay.

Switching Channels. Ted Kotcheff. USA. 1988.
Kathleen Turner plays a television reporter in this remake of *His Girl Friday/The Front Page*.

Television Talent. Robert Edmunds. GB. 1937.
This British revue film chronicles the attempt of young performers to get into television.

Television Spy. Edward Dmytryk. USA. Paramount Pictures, 1939.
A tale of industrial espionage involving early television.

TerrorVision. Ted Nicolaou. USA. 1986.
A tiresome science fiction comedy in which an earth family of the future, the Puttermans, are visited by a Hungry Monster pet from the planet Pluton who arrives via the home-built satellite dish. The parents, hedonistic 'swingers' are eaten along with their guests before Medusa – a television presenter not unlike Elvira – kills the monster.

There's a Girl in My Soup. Roy Boulting. GB. 1970.
Peter Sellers plays television personality Robert Danvers, who picks up a young American, Marion (Goldie Hawn), and travels round France with her.

The Thrill of It All. Norman Jewison. USA. 1963.
Doris Day comedy with James Garner as her obstetrician husband, Dr Gerald Boyer. When Beverly Boyer is offered a job in television, her naive charm makes her such an enormous success that her

greater earning power becomes a threat to the Boyer's marriage. Finally, she decides being a wife and raising children is the most fulfilling job a woman can have and turns her back on her career in television to have another baby.

Tomorrow Never Dies. Roger Spottiswoode. GB. 1997.
Pierce Brosnan's 007 battles against crazed media mogul Elliot Carver (Jonathan Pryce), who believes starting the next war is the best way to gain global domination over broadcasting.

Tootsie. Sydney Pollack. USA. 1982.
Michael Dorsey (Dustin Hoffman) is unable to find work in his profession as a stage actor. Out of desperation he assumes the persona of Dorothy Michaels and secures a lead role in a hit daytime soap opera.

Trapped by Television. Del Lord. USA. 1936.
Alternative title: *Caught by Television*.
A tale of rivalry and industrial espionage among competing television inventors.

The Truman Show. Peter Weir. USA. 1998.
Jim Carrey plays Truman Burbank, the ultimate television soap star. Unbeknownst to Truman, his entire life has been the subject of a 24-hour a day television production. His friends and family are all played by actors and he has no knowledge of the world beyond the studio-created environment he inhabits.

Tunnelvision. Neal Israel and Brad Swirnoff. USA. 1976.
Parody of the future of television programming, featuring Chevy Chase.

Two Tickets To Broadway. James V. Kern. USA. 1951.
Young Nancy (Janet Leigh) leaves her small town heading for success on Broadway. Finally she hits the big time to sing and dance with her new friends on Bob Crosby's television show.

The Twonky. Arch Oboler. USA. 1953.
Hans Conried plays Kerry, whose television takes over his life.

UHF. Jay Levey. USA. 1989.
'Weird' Al Yankovic co-wrote *UHF* and stars as George Newman, a loser who cannot hold a job down. George and his best friend Bob (David Bowe) surprise even themselves when they are successful at managing a local television station which George's uncle won in a

card game. When Channel 62 begins to challenge the hegemony of network affiliate Channel 8, the competitor's CEO (Kevin McCarthy) resorts to nefarious practices to buy out the small station. Community television finally wins out when the FCC revokes Channel 8's license.

Up Close and Personal. Jon Avnet. USA. 1996.
Ostensibly based on the life story of NBC news reporter Jessica Savitch, this film ignores the suffering of an alcoholic drug abuser and instead constructs a sentimental love story between senior newsman Warren Justice (Robert Redford) and new girl Tally Atwater (Michelle Pfeiffer).

The Vagabond Queen. Geza von Bolvary. GB. 1929.
Betty Balfour stars as Sally, a young domestic servant hired to impersonate Princess Zonia of Bolonia. Sally needs the money to help her boyfriend, Jimmy (Glen Byam Shaw), invent television. Balfour turns in a spirited performance in the dual roles of streetwise Sally and graceful Zonia, but the shaky sets let the whole enterprise down.

Videodrome. David Cronenberg. USA. 1983.
James Woods at his seediest as cable television executive Max Renn looking for something really tough. He finds it in Nicki Brand (Debby Harry), who enters the sinister world of Videodrome. One of Cronenberg's finest films and a paranoid assault on the realm of the televisual.

Wag the Dog. Barry Levinson. USA. 1997.
The television campaign to reelect the President of the United States of America is built on the corny slogan, 'Don't change horses in midstream'. But when evidence emerges alleging that the President has had sex with an underage girl, the damage control shows just how powerful the media can be. The shady Conrad Brean (Robert De Niro) engineers a strategy to manipulate the news media by feeding it false snippets of information and bogus war footage. Assisted throughout by Hollywood producer Stanley Motss (Dustin Hoffman) and White House worker Winifred Ames (Anne Heche), a propaganda war is waged in which the elaborate manipulation of the public is made into a game.

Wake Up and Dream. Eddie Cline. USA. 1942.
Juvenile troupe get a television contract in this light musical comedy.

Wayne's World. Penelope Spheeris. USA. 1992.
Mike Myers and Dana Carvey of *Saturday Night Live* fame feature in this amusing tale of teenagers who present a no-budget cable television program.

Wayne's World 2. Stephen Surjik. USA. 1993.
Sequel to *Wayne's World* with the same crew a little older and a little sharper.

Will Success Spoil Rock Hunter? Frank Tashlin. USA. 1957.
Alternative title: *Oh! For a Man*.
Tony Randall plays television advertising executive Rockwell Hunter who tries to persuade Rita Marlow (Jayne Mansfield) to advertise Stay-Put Lipstick.

William Shakespeare's Romeo & Juliet. Baz Luhrmann. USA. 1996.
A television news crew stands in for the chorus in this frenetic updating of Shakespeare's romantic tragedy starring Leonardo Di Caprio and Claire Danes.

Wrong is Right. Richard Brooks. USA. 1982.
Alternative title: *The Man with the Deadly Lens*.
Sean Connery stars as an international television reporter who discovers a global CIA conspiracy.

Your Past is Showing see *The Naked Truth*.

REFERENCES

Abramson, Albert, 1987. *The History of Television, 1880–1941.* Jefferson, NC: McFarland and Company.

Adorno, Theodor W., 1991. How to Look at Television. *The Culture Industry. Selected Essays on Mass Culture.* London: Routledge. pp. 136–53. Originally published in *The Quarterly of Film, Radio and Television* 1954. **8**(3): 213–35.

Adorno, Theodor W. and Max Horkheimer, 1977. The Culture Industry: Enlightenment as Mass Deception. In James Curran, Michael Gurevitch and Janet Woollacott (eds) *Mass Communication and Society.* Beverly Hills/London: Sage, pp. 349–83.

Allen, Robert C., 1992. *Channels of Discourse Re-Assembled. Television and Contemporary Criticism.* London: Routledge/New York: University of North Carolina Press.

Altman, Karen Elizabeth, 1989. Advertising the American Television Set. *Journal of Popular Film and Television* **17**(2): 46–56.

Altmann, Rick (ed.), 1981. *Genre: The Musical: A Reader.* London/New York: Routledge & Kegan Paul in association with the British Film Institute.

Anderson, Christopher, 1991. Hollywood in the Home: TV and the End of the Studio System. In James Naremore and Patrick Brantlinger (eds) *Modernity and Mass Culture.* Bloomington: Indiana University Press, pp. 80–102.

Anderson, Christopher, 1994. *HollywoodTV. The Studio System in the 1950s.* Austin, Texas: University of Texas Press.

Appadurai, Arjun (ed.), 1986. *The Social Life of Things. Commodities in Cultural Perspective.* Cambridge: Cambridge University Press.

Askey, Arthur, 1975. *Before Your Very Eyes: An Autobiography.* London: Woburn Press.

Balio, Tino (ed.), 1976. *The American Film Industry.* Madison, Wisconsin: University of Wisconsin Press.

Balio, Tino (ed.), 1990. *Hollywood in the Age of Television.* Boston: Unwin Hyman.

Balio, Tino (ed.), 1993. Grand Design: Hollywood as a Modern Business Enterprise, 1930–1939. *History of the American Cinema*. Volume 5. New York: Charles Scriber's Sons.

Ballantyne, James, 1993. *Researchers' Guide to British Newreels*. London: British Universities Film and Video Council.

Banks, Leslie *et al.*, 1949. *The Elstree Story. Twenty one Years of Filmmaking*. London: Clerke and Cockeran.

Barker, David, 1991. The Emergence of Television's Repertoire of Representation, 1920–1935. *Journal of Broadcasting and Electronic Media* **35**(3): 305–18.

Barker, Martin, and Julian Petley (eds), 1997. *Ill Effects: The Media/Violence Debate*. London: Routledge.

Barnouw, Erik, 1966. *A Tower in Babel. A History of Broadcasting in the United States*. Volume I – to 1933. New York: Oxford University Press.

Barnouw, Erik, 1968. *The Golden Web. A History of Broadcasting in the United States*. Volume II – 1933 to 1953. New York: Oxford University Press.

Barnouw, Erik, 1970. *The Image Empire. A History of Broadcasting in the United States*. Volume III – from 1953. New York: Oxford University Press.

Barnouw, Erik, 1982. *Tube of Plenty. The Evolution of American Television*. New York/Oxford: Oxford University Press. Revised Edition.

Barnouw, Erik, 1983. *Documentary: A History of Non-Fiction Film*. New York/Oxford: Oxford University Press.

Barr, Charles, 1986. Broadcasting and Cinema 2: Screens Within Screens. In Charles Barr (ed.) *All Our Yesterdays. Ninety Years of British Television*. London: British Film Institute, pp. 206–24.

Baudrillard, Jean, 1983. *Simulations*. Translated by Paul Foss, Paul Patton and Philip Beitchman. New York: Semiotext(e).

Baudrillard, Jean, 1987. *The Evil Demon of Images*. Translated by Paul Patton and Paul Foss. Sydney: The Power Institute of Fine Arts, University of Sydney.

Bilby, Kenneth, 1986. *The General. David Sarnoff and the Rise of the Communications Industry*. New York: Harper Row.

Bioscope, 1930. 'Elstree Calling'. 12 February, p. 30.

Boddy, William, 1985, The Studios move into Prime Time; Hollywood and the Television Industry in the 1950s. *Cinema Journal* **24**(4): 23–37.

Boddy, William, 1990. *Fifties Television. The Industry and its Critics*. Urbana and Chicago: University of Illinois Press.

Boddy, William, 1995. The Beginnings of American Television. In Anthony Smith (ed.) *Television. An International History*. Oxford: Oxford University Press.

Bordwell, David and Kristin Thompson, 1994. *Film History: An Introduction*. New York: McGraw Hill.

Bordwell, David and Kristin Thompson, 1997. *Film Art: An Introduction* (5th edn). New York: McGraw Hill.

Bourdieu, Pierre, 1984. *Distinction. A Social Critique of the Judgement of Taste*. Translated by Richard Nice. London/New York: Routledge & Kegan Paul.

Braun, Eric, 1980. In Camera. Cicely Courtneidge: Some Personal Notes. *Film and Filming*. **26**(9): 6–7.

Brecht, Bertolt, 1964. The Modern Theatre is the Epic Theatre. *Brecht on Theatre*. Translated by John Willett. New York: Hill and Wang/London: Methuen.

Briggs, Asa, 1961. *The History of Broadcasting in the United Kingdom*. Volume I: *The Birth of Broadcasting*. London: Oxford University Press.

Briggs, Asa, 1965. *The History of Broadcasting in the United Kingdom*. Volume II: *The Golden Age of Wireless*. London: Oxford University Press.

Briggs, Asa, 1970. *The History of Broadcasting in the United Kingdom*. Volume III: *The War of Words*. London: Oxford University Press.

Briggs, Asa, 1979. *The History of Broadcasting in the United Kingdom*. Volume IV: *Sound and Vision*. London: Oxford University Press.

Briggs, Asa, 1995. *The History of Broadcasting in the United Kingdom*. Volume V: *Competition*. London: Oxford University Press.

British Broadcasting Company, 1937. *The London Television Station. Alexandra Palace*. London: BBC.

British Film Insitute, 1996. *The British Film Institute Film and Television Handbook, 1997*. London: British Film Institute.

British Film Insitute, 1997. *The British Film Institute Film and Television Handbook, 1998*. London: British Film Institute.

British Film Insitute, 1998. *The British Film Institute Film and Television Handbook, 1998*. London: British Film Institute.

Brooks, Tim, 1987. *The Complete Directory to Prime Time Stars 1946–present*. New York: Ballantine.

Brown, Geoff, 1975. 'Elstree Calling'. *Monthly Film Bulletin*. **42**(502): 246–7.

Buscombe, Ed., 1981. *Granada: The First 25 Years*. British Film Institute Dossier number 9. London: British Film Institute.

Buscombe, Ed., 1991. All Bark and No Bite: The Film Industry's Response to Television. In John Corner (ed.) *Popular Television in Britain*. London: British Film Institute.

Carver, Benedict, 1996. Marriage of Convenience. *Screen International* July 19, p. 9.

Cavander, Kenneth, *et al.*, 1958. British Feature Directors. An Index to Their Work. *Sight and Sound*. **27**(6): 295.

Chappell, Connery (undated, BFI held). *Rank's Uncelluloid Empire*.

Charters, Werrett Wallace, 1933. *Motion Pictures and Youth; A Summary*. New York: The Macmillan Company.

Cheshire, Godfrey, 1997. Wag the Dog. *Variety.* December 15–21: 58.

Ciment, Michel, 1974. *Kazan on Kazan.* New York: The Viking Press.

Corner, John (ed.), 1991. *Popular Television in Britain.* London: British Film Institute.

Cumbow, Robert C., 1992. Pictures on the Walls of the House of Hammer. *Film Comment.* **29**(3): 51–3.

Dayan, Daniel and Elihu Katz, 1992. *Media Events: The Live Broadcasting of History.* Cambridge, MA/London: Harvard University Press.

Dempsey, John, 1998. Nets Bet Bucks on Pix Appeal. *Variety* January 12–18: 79 & 84.

Dinsdale, Alfred, 1928. *Television.* London: The Television Press Ltd.

Drew, Wayne (ed.), 1984. *David Cronenberg.* British Film Institute Dossier. London: British Film Institute.

Eckersley, Roger, 1946. *The BBC and All That.* London: Sampson Low, Marston and Company.

Egan, Jack, 1983. HBO Takes on Hollywood. *New York Times.* undated press clipping, BFI Library.

Ellis, John, 1982. *Visible Fictions: Cinema: Television: Video.* London: Routledge & Kegan Paul/Boston: Henley.

Engleman, Ralph, 1996. *Public Radio and Television in America. A Political History.* Thousand Oaks, CA: Sage.

Everson, William K., 1986. Arthur Askey. *Films in Review.* **37**(3): 169–75.

Feuer, Jane, 1982. *The Hollywood Musical.* London: Macmillan.

The Film Daily, 1968. *The Film Daily Yearbook of Motion Pictures.* New York.

Forman, Denis, 1997. *Persona Granada. Some Memories of Sidney Bernstein and the Early Days of Independent Television.* André Deutsch.

Franklin, Harold B., 1929. *Sound Motion Pictures. From the Laboratory to their Presentation.* Garden City, New York: Doubleday, Doran and Company.

Frith, Simon, 1983. *Sound Effects. Youth, Leisure, and the Politics of Rock 'n' Roll.* London: Constable.

Gauntlett, David, 1995. *Moving Experiences. Understanding Television's Influences and Effects.* London: John Libbey.

Goldie, Grace Wyndham, 1977. *Facing the Nation. Television and Politics 1936–1976.* London: The Bodley Head.

Gomery, Douglas, 1984. Failed Opportunities: The Integration of the U.S. Motion Picture and Television Industries. *Quarterly Review of Film Studies.* **9**(3): 219–28.

Gorham, Maurice, 1949. *Television. Medium of the Future.* London: Percival Marshall.

Gross, Larry, 1995. Exploding Hollywood. *Sight and Sound.* **5**(3): 8–9.

Groves, Don, 1998. Local Pix Bite Into Majors' Pie. *Variety.* January 12–18: 11 & 16.

Guback, Thomas H., 1976. Hollywood's International Market. In Tino Balio (ed.) *The American Film Industry*. Madison, Wisconsin: University of Wisconsin Press, pp. 387–409.

Guider, Elizabeth and Michael Williams, 1997. Euros Create Suction for H'w'd production. *Variety*. April 21–22: 27 & 37.

Handling, Piers (ed.), 1983. *The Shape of Rage. The Films of David Cronenberg*. Ontario: Academy of Canadian Cinema.

Hanke, Ken, 1989a. The British Film Invasion of the 1960s. *Films in Review*. **40**(4): 213–19.

Hanke, Ken, 1989b. The British Film Invasion of the 1960s. Part II. *Films in Review*. **40**(5): 269–77.

Hanke, Ken, 1989c. The British Film Invasion of the 1960s. Part III. *Films in Review*. **40**(6): 348–56.

Hanke, Ken, 1989d. The British Film Invasion of the 1960s. Part IV. *Films in Review*. **40**(7): 405–13.

Hanna, Vincent, 1976. Television was Ludicrous, but it was Fascinating that it was Possible at all. *Radio Times*. **213**(2764): 74, 75 & 81.

Hill, John, 1991. Television and Pop. The Case of the 1950s. In John Corner (ed.) *Popular Television in Britain*. London: British Film Institute, pp. 90–107.

Hill, John and Martin McLoone (eds), 1996. *Big Picture, Small Screen. The Relations Between Film and Television*. London: John Libbey.

Hilliard, Robert L. and Michael C. Keith, 1997. *The Broadcast Century. A Biography of American Broadcasting*. Boston: Focal Press.

Hilmes, Michele, 1985. Film Industry Alternatives to the Networks: Subscription Television, 1949–1962. *Quarterly Review of Film Studies* **10**(3): 213–23.

Hilmes, Michele, 1990. *Hollywood and Broadcasting. From Radio to Cable*. Urbana/Chicago: University of Chicago Press.

The Hollywood Reporter, 1948. *Television... And What the Motion Picture Industry is Doing About it*. Hollywood Reporter Fact Booklet.

Hulbert, Jack, 1949. Television and Entertainment. Address to the Royal Society of Arts. 6 December 1948. *Journal of the Royal Society of Arts*. **XCVII**(4788): 203–13.

Huyssen, Andreas, 1986. *After the Great Divide. Modernism, Mass Culture and Postmodernism*. London: Macmillan.

International Motion Picture Almanac, 1998. New York: Quigley Publishing.

Jacobs, Norman (ed.), 1964. *Culture for the Millions? Mass Media in Modern Society*. Boston: Beacon Press. Originally published in 1959. Republished 1992, with a new introduction by Garth S. Jowett as *Mass Media in Modern Society* New Brunswick/London: Transaction Publishers.

Jewell, Richard B., 1984. Hollywood and Radio: Competition and Partnership in the 1930s. *Historical Journal of Film, Radio and Television.* **4**(2): 125–41.

Jowett, Garth, 1976. *Film, the Democratic Art.* Boston/London: Focal Press.

Jowett, Garth, 1994. Dangling the Dream? The Presentation of Television to the American Public, 1928–1952. *Historical Journal of Film, Radio and Television* **15**(2): 121–45.

Joyrich, Lynne, 1988. All that Television Allows: TV Melodrama, Postmodernism and Consumer Culture. *Camera Obscura* (16): 128–53.

Katz, Richard and John Dempsey, 1998. TV: The Big Uneasy. *Variety.* 19–25 Jan: 1 and 103.

Kazan, Elia, 1957. Introduction, in Budd Schulberg *A Face in the Crowd. A Play for the Screen.* New York: Random House.

Kinetograph Weekly, 1933. *International House.* Review. 1368: 11.

Klady, Leonard, 1998. H'wood's B.O. blast. *Variety.* 5–11 January: 1 & 96.

Kopytoff, Igor, 1986. The Cultural Biography of Things: Commoditization as Process. In Arjun Appadurai (ed.) *The Social Life of Things. Commodities in Cultural Perspective.* Cambridge: Cambridge University Press.

Larner, E.T., 1928. *Practical Television.* London: Ernest Benn.

Leman, Joy, 1991. Wise Scientists and Female Androids. Class and Gender in Science Fiction. In John Corner (ed.) *Popular Television in Britain.* London: British Film Institute.

Lester, Richard, 1995. Interview on *A Hard Day's Night* Video, Walter Shenson.

Levy, Mark and Barrie Gunter, 1988. *Home Video and the Changing Nature of the Television Audience.* London/Paris: John Libbey.

Logan, Pamela W., 1995. *Jack Hylton Presents.* London: British Film Institute.

Lucas, Tim, 1983/4. David Cronenberg's *Videodrome. Cinefantastique.* December/January: 32–49.

Lyotard, Jean-Francois, 1984. *The Postmodern Condition: A Report on Knowledge.* Translated by Geoff Bennington and Brian Massumi. Manchester: Manchester University Press.

MacDonald, Barrie, 1993. *Broadcasting in the United Kingdom. A Guide to Information Sources.* London: Mansell.

Macdonald, Dwight, 1957. A Theory of Mass Culture. In Bernard Rosenberg and David Manning White (eds) *Mass Culture. The Popular Arts in America.* New York: The Free Press/London: Collier-Macmillan, pp. 59–73.

Macnab, Geoffrey, 1993. *J. Arthur Rank and the British Film Industry.* London: Routledge.

Macnab, Geoffrey, 1996. British Cinema. *Sight and Sound* **6**(7): 22–5.

Mander, Jerry, 1978. *Four Arguments for the Elimination of Television*. New York: Morrow Quill Paperbacks.

Marling, Karal Ann, 1994. *As Seen on TV: The Visual Culture of Everyday Life in the 1950s*. Cambridge, MA/London: Harvard University Press.

Masson, Alain, 1981. George Sidney: Artificial Brilliance/The Brilliance of Artifice. In Rick Altman (ed.) *Genre: The Musical*. London: Routledge & Kegan Paul/The British Film Insitute, pp. 28–40.

Mast, Gerald, 1987. *Can't Help Singin'. The American Musical on Stage and Screen*. New York: Overlook Press, Woodstock.

McCarthy, Todd, 1982. Sand Castles. Interview with Steven Spielberg. *Film Comment*. May–June: 53–9.

McLuhan, Marshall, 1964. *Understanding Media: The Extensions of Man*. New York: McGraw Hill.

Medhurst, Andy, 1991. Every Wart and Pustule. Gilbert Harding and Television Stardom. In John Corner (ed.) *Popular Television in Britain*. London: British Film Institute.

Medhurst, Andy, 1995. It Sort of Happened Here: The Strange, Brief Life of the British Pop Film. In Jonathan Romney and Adrian Wootton (eds) *Celluloid Jukebox. Popular Music and the Movies Since the 50s*. London: British Film Institute, pp. 61–70.

Monder, Eric, 1994. George Sidney's Hi-tech Vaudeville Show. *Film Comment*. July-August: 50–9.

Monthly Film Bulletin, 1935. *Murder by Television*. **2**(21).

Moore-Gilbert, Bart and John Seed (eds), 1992. *Cultural Revolution? The Challenge of the Arts in the 1960s*. London/New York: Routledge.

Morgan, Simon and Tim Westcott, 1997. Global Enterprise: The T.B.I. 100. *Television Business International*. July/August: 29–33.

Moseley, Sydney A., 1952. *John Baird. The Romance and Tragedy of the Pioneer of Television*. London: Odhams Press.

Moseley, Sydney A. and Robert McKay, 1936. *Television. A Guide for the Amateur*. London: Oxford University Press.

Moseley, Sydney A. and H.J. Barton Chapple, 1930. *Television To-Day and To-Morrow*. London: Sir Isaac Pitman and Sons.

Moseley, Sydney A. and H.J. Barton Chapple, 1938. *A Simple Guide to Television*. London: Sir Isaac Pitman and Sons.

Moser, James D., Tracy Stevens, William Pay and Patricia Thompson (eds), 1998. *International Motion Picture Almanac* (69th edn). New York: Quigley Publishing.

Motion Picture Herald, 1951, *Two Tickets to Broadway*. Review. 13 October: 25.

Mulvey, Laura, 1986. Melodrama in and out of the Home. In Colin MacCabe (ed.) *High Theory/Low Culture: Analysing Popular Television and Film*. Manchester, England: Manchester University Press.

Neale, Steve and Frank Krutnik, 1990. *Film and Television Comedy*. London: Routledge.

Pedler, Garth, 1984. Betty Balfour in *The Vagabond Queen* 1929. *Classic Images*, (108) June: 29, 30 & 50.

Petley, Julian, 1984. V.D. O'Nasty. In Wayne Drew (ed.) *David Cronenberg*. British Film Institute Dossier. London: British Film Institute.

Petley, Julian, 1988. *The Running Man*. Review. *Monthly Film Bulletin*. **55**(657): 311–12.

Petroski, 1990. *The Pencil: A History of Design and Circumstance* New York: Knopf.

Picturegoer, 1933. 'International House', *Picturegoer* **3**(133): 30 & 32.

Pinch, Trevor J. and Wiebe E. Bijker, 1987. The Social Construction of Facts and Artifacts. Or How the Sociology of Science and the Sociology of Technology Might Benefit Each Other. In Wieber E. Bijker, Thomas P. Hughes and Trevor Pinch (eds) *The Social Construction of Technological Systems*. Cambridge, MA: The MIT Press.

Postman, Neil, 1987. *Amusing Ourselves to Death. Public Discourse in the Age of Show Business*. London: Methuen. First published in 1985.

Pym, John, 1992. *Film on Four. 1982/1991. A Survey*. London: British Film Institute.

Rafelson, Bob, 1998. Jack is even crazier than you'd think. *Guardian*. May 1: Section 2: 10.

Ramis, Harold, 1993. We are Stardust, we are Frozen. *Premiere*. **6**(6): 68–9.

Richards, Jeffrey, 1992. New Waves and Old Myths: British Cinema in the 1960s. In Bart Moore-Gilbert and John Seed (eds) *Cultural Revolution? The Challenge of the Arts in the 1960s*. London/New York: Routledge.

Robinson, David, 1996. *From Peepshow to Palace: The Birth of American Film*. New York: Columbia University Press.

Rodley, Chris (ed.), 1992. *Cronenberg on Cronenberg*. London: Faber.

Romney, Jonathan and Adrian Wootton (eds), 1995. *Celluloid Jukebox. Popular Music and the Movies since the 50s*. London: British Film Institute.

Rosenberg, Bernard and David Manning White, 1957. *Mass Culture. The Popular Arts in America*. New York: The Free Press.

Rowland, Willard D. Jr, 1983. *The Politics of TV Violence. The Policy Uses of Communication Research*. Beverly Hills: Sage.

Salt, Barry, 1992. *Film Style and Technology: History and Analysis* (2nd edn). London: Starword.

Scannell, Paddy and David Cardiff, 1982. Serving the Nation: Public Service Broadcasting Before the War. In Waite, Bennett and Martin (eds) *Popular Culture: Past and Present*. London: Croome Helm.

Scannell, Paddy and David Cardiff, 1991. *A Social History of British Broadcasting*. Volume 1: *1922–1933. Serving the Nation*. London: Blackwell.

Sendall, Bernard, 1982. *Independent Television in Britain.* Volume 1: *Origin and Foundation 1946–1962.* London: Macmillan.

Sendall, Bernard, 1983. *Independent Television in Britain.* Volume 2: *Expansion and Change 1958–1968.* London: Macmillan.

Seymour-Ure, Colin, 1991. *The British Press and Broadcasting Since 1945.* London: Basil Blackwell.

Shapiro, Steven, 1993. *The Cinematic Body.* Minneapolis/London: University of Minnesota Press.

Sheldon, H. Horton and Grisewood, Edgar Norman, 1929. *Television... Present Methods of Picture Transmission.* New York: D. Van Nostrand.

Sklar, Robert, 1976. *Movie-made America.* New York: Vintage Books.

Sklar, Robert, 1993. *Film: An International History of the Medium.* New York: Harry N. Abrams.

Slade Film History Register, 1984. *British Newsreels.* Bedford: Graphic Data Publishing.

Smith, Anthony, 1995a. Television as a Public Service Medium. In *Television. An International History.* Oxford: Oxford University Press.

Smith, Anthony (ed.), 1995b. *Television. An International History.* Oxford: Oxford University Press.

Smither, Roger and Wolfgang Klaue, 1996. *Newsreels in Film Archives.* Trowbridge, Wiltshire: Flick Books.

Spigel, Lynn, 1990. Television in the Family Circle. The Popular Reception of a New Medium. In Patricia Mellencamp (ed.) *Logics of Television. Essays in Cultural Criticism.* Bloomington, Indiana: Indiana University Press.

Spigel, Lynn, 1991. *Make Room For TV: Television and the Family Ideal in Postwar America.* Chicago/London: University of Chicago Press.

Spraos, John, 1962. *The Decline of the Cinema.* London: Allen & Unwin.

Stallabrass, Julian, 1996. *Gargantua. Manufactured Mass Culture.* London: Verso.

Surgeon General's Advisory Committee on Television and Social Behavior, 1972. *Television and Growing Up: The Impact of Television Violence.* Washington, D.C.: Government Printing Office.

Thomas, Howard, 1962. *The Truth About Television.* London: Weidenfeld & Nicolson.

Thomas, Howard, 1977. *With an Independent Air. Encounters During a Lifetime of Broadcasting.* London: Weidenfeld & Nicolson.

Thomson, David, 1977. Network. *Sight and Sound* **46**(2): 122–3.

Thompson, Ben, 1994. Fade into Colour. *Sight and Sound.* April: 13–14.

Thompson, Ben, 1995. Pop and film: The charisma crossover. In Jonathan Romney and Adrian Wootton (eds). *Celluloid Jukebox. Popular Music and the Movies.* London: BFI, pp. 32–41.

Thompson, Kristin, 1985. *Exporting Entertainment. America in the World Film Market 1907–1934.* London: British Film Institute.

Threadgall, Derek, 1994. *Shepperton Studios. An Independent View.* London: BFI.

Tischi, Cecelia, 1991. *The Electronic Hearth: Creating an American Television Culture.* New York/Oxford: Oxford University Press.

Tiltman, Ronald F., 1927. *Television for the Home: The Wonders of 'Seeing by Wireless'.* London: Hutchison.

Udelson, Joseph H., 1982. *The Great Television Race. A History of the American Television Industry 1925–1941.* Alabama: University of Alabama Press.

UNESCO, 1997. *UNESCO Statistical Yearbook, 1996.* Unesco Publishing and Bernan Press.

Van Hise, James, 1982. Poltergeist. The making of 'things that go bump in the night'. *Cinefantastique.* **13**(2/3): 76–87.

Vogel, 1998. *Variety.* 19–25 January.

Walker, James R., 1991. Old Media on New Media: National Popular Press Reaction to Mechanical Television. *Journal of Popular Culture* **25**(1) Summer.

Warren, Patricia, 1983. *Elstree. The British Hollywood.* London: Elm Tree Books.

White, Timothy R., 1990. Hollywood's Attempt at Appropriating Television: The Case of Paramount Pictures. In Tino Balio (ed.) *Hollywood in the Age of Television.* Boston: Unwin Hyman, pp. 145–63.

White, Timothy R., 1992. Hollywood on (re)trial: The American Broadcasting–United Paramount Merger Hearing. *Cinema Journal* **31**(3): 19–36.

Williams, Raymond, 1989. *Raymond Williams on Television* Edited by Alan O'Connor. London/New York: Routledge.

Winn, Marie, 1977. *The Plug-In Drug.* New York: Viking Press.

Wood, James, 1992. *History of International Broadcasting.* London: Peter Peregrinns.

Wood, Robin, 1983. Cronenberg: A Dissenting View. In Piers Handling (ed.) *The Shape of Rage: The Films of David Cronenberg.* New York: New York Zoetrope.

INDEX